Praise for *Deadly Powers*

"While mythological studies routinely look back to ancient Mesopotamia, Egypt, or Greece, this author pushes back to the Pleistocene. There, he suggests, as *Homo sapiens* developed and experienced their impotence before carnivorous beasts up to two tons in mass, fear was of course the primary response. As language developed, primordial storytelling flourished, and eventually myth. This is a strongly researched, insightful volume treating themes from across the world."

—William G. Doty, professor emeritus, University of Alabama
and author of *Mythography: The Study of Myths and Rituals*
and several other books in the field

"Living as many of us do in safe, modern surroundings, it's easy for us to forget how large predators have loomed over human lives during most of our species' history on earth. In *Deadly Powers*, Paul Trout brings together science and art to remind us how important predators have been in shaping our literatures, our imaginations, and even our minds. If you've ever wondered why you can't get enough of zombies, werewolves, and aliens, this is the book for you."

—Clark Barrett, associate professor of anthropology,
University of California, Los Angeles

Deadly Powers

In this Native American carving from the Northwest, a mythic bear with human traits grips in its claws a human head with a terrified grimace. The bear, while menacing, has been given an almost sardonic expression, as if the Native American artist who carved the bear somehow understood the irony that humans are gripped by the very fear that has engendered this mythic bear. No image captures more powerfully the complex relationship between animal predators and the mythic imagination. Item A7878 is in the collection of the Museum of Anthropology at the University of British Columbia, Vancouver, Canada. *Photo used with permission from the Museum of Anthropology.*

Deadly

Animal Predators and the Mythic Imagination

Powers

Paul A. Trout

FOREWORD BARBARA EHRENREICH

Prometheus Books

59 John Glenn Drive
Amherst, New York 14228–2119

Published 2011 by Prometheus Books

Cover illustration *Hercules and the Hydra of Lerne* by Gustave Moreau
used by permission of Bridgeman Art Library/SuperStock
Cover design by Nicole Sommer-Lecht

Inquiries should be addressed to
Prometheus Books
59 John Glenn Drive
Amherst, New York 14228–2119
VOICE: 716–691–0133
FAX: 716–691–0137
WWW.PROMETHEUSBOOKS.COM

15 14 13 12 11   5 4 3 2 1

Library of Congress Cataloging-in-Publication Data

Trout, Paul A., 1940–
    Deadly powers : animal predators and the mythic imagination / by Paul A. Trout.
        p. cm.
    Includes bibliographical references and index.
    ISBN 978–1–61614–501–9 (cloth : alk. paper)
    ISBN 978–1–61614–502–6 (ebook)
    1. Animals—Folklore. 2. Animals—Mythology. 3. Predatory animals—Folklore.
4. Predatory animals—Mythology I. Title.

GR705.T76—2011
398.24'5—dc23

                                                                    2011028692

Printed in the United States of America on acid-free paper

To those I love. You know who you are.

Contents

CHAPTER 5. THE EMERGENCE OF THE MYTHMAKING MIND

CHAPTER 6. IN THE BELLY OF THE BEAST: THE PREDATOR AS MYTHIC MONSTER

CHAPTER 7. FEAR AND TREMBLING IN THE PLEISTOCENE: THE PREDATOR AS A GOD

CHAPTER 8. KINDLY KILLERS: THE PREDATOR AS KIN, FRIEND, PROTECTOR, AND BENEFACTOR

CHAPTER 9. MODEL OF MENACE: THE PREDATOR AS EXEMPLAR AND OBJECT OF ENVY

CHAPTER 10. SCARING OURSELVES TO *LIFE*

Foreword

*T*his book is the most ambitious survey to date of the relationship between humans and the wild carnivores that preyed on them as long as *Homo sapiens*, or our hominid ancestors, have existed. I first started thinking about animal predation on humans while researching my 1998 book *Blood Rites: On the Origins and History of the Passions of War*, and argued in that book that, in many ways, especially those involving the use of violence, "human nature" has been shaped by our long, terrifying history as the prey of creatures far bigger, faster, and better armed in the tooth-and-claw department than our distant ancestors were. In *Deadly Powers*, Paul Trout goes over some of the same ground—with generous acknowledgments of my work, I should note—but he has far more material to work with and takes it in some novel directions.

He begins with a bracing catalog of some of the more formidable creatures our Stone Age ancestors had to contend with. There were far bigger cats than we can imagine today, such as the New World saber-tooth tiger, which sported ten-inch long tusks and weighed over 750 pounds, twice the weight of African lions today. Bears were another problem, especially the now-extinct American short-faced bear, which was eleven feet tall when it stood on two legs. Human residents of Paleolithic Egypt had to worry about snakes up to 65 feet long weighing in at about 800 pounds, and early Australians faced *Megalania*, a 30-foot-long, 2,000-pound carnivorous lizard. As for the canids that today are increasingly employed as "therapy dogs," Trout reminds us that "hunting in packs, they were as dangerous as any single big cat." He supplements this nightmare bestiary with archaeological evidence for predation on early humans—hominid skulls pierced by holes spaced at the exact distance between the teeth of Pleistocene leopards, for example—which were at first mistakenly attributed to intra-hominid homicide.

Within recent decades, there has been a certain amount of resistance to the idea of predation by carnivores as an important factor in human evolution. For one thing, it contradicts the triumphant "man-the-hunter" model of evolution, prevalent in the 1960s and '70s, in which our distant ancestors came down from the trees and strode confidently into the savanna with sharpened sticks in hand. And, of course, the idea of being preyed upon by animals, whether routinely or opportunistically, is offensive to human vanity. "Man," the eminent archaeologist Louis Leakey once blustered, "is not cat food."[1] But for all we know, early humans may have been an especially delectable carnivore snack. Trout reports that in many African myths, "humans are casually referred to as the 'meat without hair.'"

The reasons to think that early humans were preyed upon have mounted over the years. Wild primates, including our close relatives the chimpanzees, are preyed upon today, as proved by the presence of their DNA in the scat of leopards and lions. It is now widely accepted that the exigencies of predation are a major factor in making us, like most other primates, social animals, whose ultimate reason to stick together is for mutual defense. An individual is more likely to survive in a noisy, fast-moving group than as a solitary creature in the wild, which is why, for example, fish swim in schools. In addition, group living offers opportunities for more aggressive forms of collective defense: Monkeys may "mob" a predator; young baboon males sometimes sacrifice their lives in an effort to drive a predator away from the females and young.

While some scientists have, like Leakey, been queasy about predation on humans, classicists, folklorists, and the like can hardly ignore it.

If there is one central human mythological theme, from Gilgamesh to Beowulf, it is of the human-eating creature that ravages the countryside until someone—hero or god—successfully confronts it. The predator in these stories is often dismissed as a "symbol" for some entirely human fantasy or preoccupation. But as Trout argues, human storytelling, and hence literature, grew out of encounters with real animal predators and served as a means of fear management as well as a means to ready the group for future encounters. Lions, for example, were a real and widespread threat to humans into historical times. When the Achaean heroes weren't fighting Trojans, Homer tells us that they were tasked with trying to keep their kingdoms lion free. Tigers took a huge toll on humans in India well into the nineteenth century, leaving large swaths of the subcontinent uninhabitable for humans, and they still do in the Sundarbans, where every village has its "tiger widows." In Eurasia, wolves not only preyed on travelers but threatened rural villagers well into the eighteenth century.

Deadly Powers does not skimp on the horrors of being eaten alive. Sometimes predation is a silent affair, as when a giant snake swallows a victim—a child, for example—whole. But predators may emit terrifying sounds—the roars of big cats, the growls of wolves or hyenas, the "sonic shrills" of attacking raptors—for the apparent purpose of causing their prey to freeze. As for the prey, Trout tells us, "Some of them snort, some bellow, some bray, some screech, some bleat, some shriek, some scream, some squeal, and some wail, as they protest being clawed, bitten, eviscerated, and dismembered." Surviving conspecifics may find few fragments of the victim left to mourn, or they may find too many. Trout reports that "one of the most horrifying collections of stomach contents taken from an African crocodile included eleven heavy brass arm rings, three wire armlets, wire anklets, a necklace, fourteen human arm and leg bones, and three human spinal columns." And, he reminds us, the ultimate humiliation, referred to in "myth after myth," is to be eaten and then passed out as excrement.

The experiences of being stalked, of being attacked in the night, or of having one's child snatched up in broad daylight left deep marks in our species and, in many ways, Trout argues, made us what we are today. Our brains are wired for fight or flight. Our nightmares still feature devouring beasts, both imagined monsters and actual animals. Our cultures evolved out of the need for defense against creatures far mightier, and at one time far more numerous, than ourselves, and the experience of rallying to confront a dangerous intruder still provides an ecstatic high, even if the "enemy" is only another town's football team. Over the millennia, early humans had to find ways to imitate their animal enemies by, for example, sharpening stones to mimic beaks and claws, making loud noises, and donning body paint and headdresses to make themselves look more intimidating. Our proudest achievement—language— may have evolved out of the alarm calls used to signal the approach of a predator.

Religion and mythology recall the eons when nonhuman alpha predators ruled the earth. The earliest known deities were animals, mostly carnivores, like the jaguar gods of the Maya and the tiger gods worshipped in tribal India. Even the anthropomorphized Yahweh of historical times reveals his craving for blood: he "savors" the smoke from the sacrificial animals prepared for him and fatefully rejects Cain's vegetarian offerings. The imagined monsters that afflict many cultures are, Trout argues, ultimately derived from actual predators and apparently provide no survival advantage. He gives the example of the Inuit, who abandoned productive hunting and fishing areas to white colonizers rather than risk encountering the wolf-like creatures that were thought to haunt them.

Ten thousand years after our collective ascent to the status of global alpha predator, we are still obsessed with nonhuman predators and in ways that are not particularly productive or healthy. We pay money to see movies in which our conspecifics are ambushed, torn limb from limb, and often consumed right in front of us. As the old animal predators have gone extinct, we have substituted monsters of our own imagining, from medieval dragons to the extraterrestrial beast in the *Alien* series, and at this particular cultural moment, we seem to be drawn to creatures—vampires and werewolves—who are always conflating appetite with eroticism. On the far fringes of predator fixation, Trout reports that there are even a few surgically altered "were-predators," like the man who "had his teeth filed into fangs and underwent dozens of operations and tattoos to make himself look like a tiger," including the surgical implantation of a tail.

There is a potential second volume to *Deadly Powers*, not that Trout is in any way obligated to write it: on the story of how humans have used our own predatory powers *against other animals* once we ascended to the top of the food chain. In no small part because of our own terrifying prehistory as prey, humans *could not seem to stop killing*, as if we had to keep reassuring ourselves, over and over, that we had indeed evolved from prey to predator. Many explanations have been offered for the massive extinctions of large animals (megafauna) that began about twelve thousand years ago—viruses, meteor hits, climate changes—but the soundest hypothesis is summarized by the word *overkill*: humans killed what they needed to eat and then killed much more, eliminating animal populations as they spread out over the globe on foot or by sea. In the Americas, the Pacific Islands, and Australia, megafaunal extinctions follow closely upon the arrival of humans. Prehistoric hunting peoples drove herds of bison off of cliffs, often leaving the bottom layers of crushed animals to rot. White settlers and colonialists hunted for fun or at most for trophies like tiger skins. Today, the whaling industries in Japan and Iceland persist in their exterminatory mission despite a near-complete absence of demand for whale meat.

Any full accounting of human evolution has to include our ancestors' violent interactions with the other animals with which we share the planet. If nature is "red in tooth and claw," our species and its evolutionary predecessors provided much of the coloration, both as predators and as prey. We began as prey and then evolved, over tens of thousands of years, into mighty predators—although always, Trout reminds us, haunted by the ghosts of the deadly carnivores that ate our kind. The only way to wake up from this nightmare is to reconstruct, as best we can, what actually happened in the killing fields of the Pleistocene, and *Deadly Powers* is an important step in that direction.

—Barbara Ehrenreich

Acknowledgments

My footnotes should convey the measure of my indebtedness to previous scholars. But in particular, I would like to thank Adrienne Mayor, not only for her splendid examinations of how the discovery of fossilized dinosaur bones was encoded in storytelling and mythmaking in both the classical world and the New World, but also for the personal encouragement she gave me in the early stage of my research. I would also like to express my indebtedness to Cory Brester, who could always be depended upon to explain clearly and with good humor any computer problem that arose and make it go away.

Chapter 1

Predators and Myth

INTRODUCTION

The myths taught to us in school and college usually are about gods and heroes fighting, or falling in love, or both. Even when these stories end sadly, they have the power to comfort us because we see that the gods care about us intensely, and that the heroes and heroines fight and love each other with uncommon passion, gallantry, courage, and resourcefulness.

Deadly Powers is not about these kinds of myths. Instead, it is about myths that make us feel uncomfortable and a bit ashamed because they probe the most primal human fear—the fear of being ripped apart and eaten alive by an animal. The gods in these myths thirst—like carnivores—for human blood, and the humans live in nightmarish terror of being chased and swallowed by hideous monsters.

Wherever one looks, animal predators slither, run, and swoop their way through the mythic landscape in search of human flesh. Along with them are the fictional predators spawned by the mythic imagination—dragons, griffins, gorgons, furies, sirens, krakens, harpies, werewolves, vampires, ghouls, zombies, golems, and evil spirits, among others. The scarcely ennobling message of these myths is that humans are good to eat. This "unsavory" aspect of myth has been largely ignored by scholars—not even Joseph Campbell has anything to say about it. Yet

21

the threat posed by dangerous animals may be the oldest and most pervasive of all mythic themes.

In Egyptian myth, the giant serpent Apep (or Apophis) attempts to devour the sun god each night, and the lion goddess Sekhmet gets drunk on human blood, as does the Indian goddess Kali, who dresses in a tiger's skin and flashes long fangs. In Aztec myth, a ravenous alligator goddess, Tlaltecuhtli, possesses not only a great fanged maw but also gnashing mouths at her elbows and knees. And throughout the night she screams for the hearts of humans. In Hawaiian myth, dragons, giant birds, and enormous sharks regularly feed on human flesh.

Some myths suggest that in the earliest times, predators were so numerous and powerful that they threatened the very existence of humankind. In Hittite myth, a great serpent must be killed for the earth to be fertile. In Vedic Indian myth, a dragon must be dismembered if the waters of life are to flow. In Norse myth, humans can appear only after the gods have killed a giant wolf (Fenrir), a huge serpent (Jormungand), and a monstrous hound (Garm). The world of myth constitutes a veritable menagerie of fierce and hungry predators.

The fear of being chased and killed by an animal predator is not confined to ancient myths or tribal stories. Folklore and fairy tales also are filled with predatory agents—wolves, bears, ogres, giants—that eat hapless humans. And ever since Mary Shelley's *Frankenstein*, tens of thousands of novels, stories, and films have depicted predatory agents wreaking havoc on humans. This theme is treated almost obsessively in contemporary storytelling.

The film *The Ghost and the Darkness* (1996), based on a true story, is about two lions that killed over a hundred railroad workers in Africa at the end of the nineteenth century. In *Alligator* (1980), a giant reptile lives and kills in the sewers and waterways of Chicago. In *Anaconda* (1997, with follow-ups in 2004, 2007, 2008), a giant snake eludes capture and swallows researchers in South America. In *Attack of the Sabretooth* (2005), a genetically engineered reincarnation of a Pleistocene cat called *Smilodon* eats its way through the celebrants at the grand opening of a wild animal park. In the *Jaws* franchise (1975, 1978, 1983, 1987), a series of great white sharks have their way with bathers and boaters. In horror and thriller stories, all kinds of creatures—animals and animal-human hybrids—rend and tear human flesh, often with impunity.

Nowhere do predators take a greater toll on human life—or assume a greater variety of lethal forms—than in science fiction. Even when dressed up as a space alien, the predator is often a direct descendent of the monsters found in classical mythology. The slavering reptilian monster in the *Alien* franchise (1979, 1986, 1992, 1997, 2004) resembles the monster Scylla in Homer's *Odyssey*. The alien invader in *Predator* (1987, 1990) is essentially a well-armed and highly intelligent dragon. The winged predator that dines on rooftop sunbathers in *Q* (aka *The Winged Serpent*, 1982), is explicitly said to be Quetzalcoatl, the serpent-eagle god worshipped by the Aztecs.

The agents of death in science fiction run the gamut from reincarnated dinosaurs (*The Lost World*, 1925, 1960, 1993; *The Beast from 20,000 Fathoms*, 1953; *Jurassic Park*, 1993, 1997, 2001; *Godzilla*, twenty-five movies between 1954 and 2004), to mutant worms or "earth dragons" (*Tremors*, 1990, 1996, 2001, 2004), to giant rabbits (*Night of the Lepus*, 1972), to super-sized insects (*Them!* 1954), to carnivorous crustaceans (*Attack of the Crab Monsters*, 1957), to devious viruses (*The Andromeda Strain*, 1971), and even to peregrinating rock formations (*The Monolith Monsters*, 1957). There is no limit to what the mythic imagination is able to transform into a predatory agent. Nor is there any limit to its urge to perform this transformation. The number of these stories grows every day, as does the number of people who have read or viewed one or more of them.

So, why are we so fascinated with such an unsettling theme? Why have we unleashed predators to ravage the mythic landscape? Why do we haunt ourselves with the specter of being torn apart by wild animals?

Why do predators hunt and chase us in our dreams? Why do stories and myths provide such a congenial habitat for deadly powers?

The answers to these questions lie in the very *distant* past, at a time when the earliest members of our species could neither write nor even speak. *Deadly Powers* takes us back to this time to explain how our most ancient ancestors dealt with the threat posed by animal predators. *Deadly Powers* also takes us through the landscape of world myths to explain how our more recent ancestors mythologized animal predators in four basic ways to manage their primordial fear of becoming meat. At the end of this "safari," we will understand not only why our distant ancestors were compelled to tell stories about dangerous animals but also the role these animals played in the evolution of storytelling itself.

PICKING UP THE TRACKS
OF THE MYTHIC PREDATOR

The safari begins in the Pleistocene (the period from around two million to ten thousand years ago), because during this span of time there were more carnivores—both in terms of raw numbers and species—than at any time before or since. We begin here also because during this period, the human line was evolving in response to the selection pressures imposed by this predator-rich environment. Our brain, our emotions, our behaviors, our culture were being shaped by the need of our Pleistocene ancestors to survive amid a "variety of terrifying mammalian carnivores."[1]

Bear in mind that during most of these two million years, our ancestors did not have weapons other than sticks and stones (and an increasingly more crafty brain). Although we can't be sure about what early humans felt, it's reasonable to assume that they were racked by constant fear of being eaten alive by the carnivores that dominated the landscape. As sociologist Barbara Ehrenreich notes, "[T]he problem of predation by wild carnivores throws a new light on every aspect of human evolution, from group living to the relation between the sexes. No doubt many other aspects of human behavior and psychology will find, in time, at least speculative explanations in our prehistory as prey."[2] This primordial and visceral fear played a crucial role in the emergence of primordial "storytelling" and still shapes the tribal myths and urban legends of modern times. *Deadly Powers* will attempt to explain *in detail* how and why the animal predators of the Pleistocene got inside our heads and our stories.

TAKING A NEW PATH

Deadly Powers, I believe, is the first book to argue that fear of predators played a significant role in the evolution of storytelling. Although mythologist and author Joseph Campbell also traced the origin of myth back into the Paleolithic era (the term used to refer to human aspects of the Pleistocene), he believed that myth evolved to deal with the *guilt* felt by early humans when killing prey animals. Hunting guilt is certainly expressed in many myths, but before humans experienced *guilt*, they must have felt *fear*, because before we were hunters, we were the hunted. For a good chunk of the Paleolithic, our ancestors were essentially weaponless and did not pose a threat either to large herbivores or to dangerous carnivores. Our early ancestors were prey, not predators.

Another reason scholars find it hard to detect the influence of Pleistocene predators on the emergence of storytelling is that the interpretation of myth has been dominated by a psychological framework. The animal predators mentioned in myth are viewed as symbols of psychological states, as, for instance, expressions of the Freudian id or the Jungian Shadow of the collective unconscious. From these psychological perspectives, the deadly powers found in myth after myth do not represent actual predators but the unseemly inclinations and desires in our old mammalian brain. It's as if the mammals, raptors, and reptiles found throughout mythology never existed anywhere but in the human imagination.

To be sure, predators had to occupy the interior terrain of the human mind if they were ever to find their way into myths created by that mind. But before these predatory animals inhabited that interior terrain, they lived, for millions of years, in the real world inhabited by primates of the human line. Animal predators existed in their own right, and their significance and meaning were not arbitrarily conferred by the developing human mind but reflected life-and-death realities our forebears could hardly afford to ignore or whimsically fancify. Nature writer David Quammen sums up this life-and-death reality quite well: "Every once in a while, a monstrous carnivore emerged like doom from a forest or a river to kill someone and feed on the body. It was a familiar sort of disaster . . . that must have seemed freshly, shockingly gruesome each time, despite the familiarity. And it conveyed a certain message. Among the earliest forms of human self-consciousness was the awareness of being meat."[3]

Storytelling is universal because it reflects an adaptation that helped our species survive. We became a storytelling animal to deal with our predicament as a prey species—to address our fear of being hunted, killed, and eaten by predators. Like Scheherazade of the *Arabian Nights*, we told stories to stay alive. And, in a figurative sense, we still do. This means that there will be no end to stories in which ravenous beasts of one kind or another threaten to consume us, no end to the phantom of the predator haunting the human imagination. *Deadly Powers* gives animal predators their due as a force that affected the emergence of the storytelling imperative.

Let's begin, then, with a good close look at the actual predators that menaced our ancient ancestors, and that contributed—as strange as it may seem—to the emergence of storytelling and mythmaking.

Chapter 2

Bringers of Death
Predators of the Pleistocene and Beyond

INTRODUCTION

Although it's comforting and perhaps natural for us today to think that our ancient ancestors were a match for Pleistocene carnivores, this is not the view found in many myths, which convey a much darker picture of these ancient times.

A Winnebago story says that when the earth was new, animals were more powerful than humans and "hunted and ate" them.[1] A Sioux myth explains that when the earth was young, humans were devoured by "evil monsters" with "huge, piercing fangs."[2] In another Sioux myth, the first humans—"small, helpless, and pitiful"—had to be saved from water monsters that possessed "spikes at the tip of their powerful tails that could gouge out fearful wounds as they roared and thrashed."[3] An Iroquois myth says that "in days long past, evil monsters and spirits preyed upon humans.... On stormy nights they came out of their dens and prowled the earth."[4] The San of Southern Africa still believe that in primordial times, humans were beset by snakes, dangerous eagles, crocodiles, and other "bad ones."[5]

In many myths, humans were not just hunted; they were threatened with being wiped out. In an Apache myth the predatory "monsters" formed at the beginning of the world had to be killed if the first Indians were to survive.[6] In a Yuma myth, the gods again had to intervene because there were "too many" animals with "big teeth and claws" for humans to survive.[7] According to the Mayan book *Popol Vuh*, humans "would not be living today" had not the first pumas, jaguars, and anacondas been turned into stone by the gods.[8]

The first humans did not always survive the dangerous time of origin. When the Mayan creator gods decided that the first humans were grossly imperfect, they annihilated them, not by using water or fire but by using an eagle to "gouge out their eyes," a bat to cut off their heads, a jaguar to "devour their flesh," and a crocodile to "break and mangle their bones and their nerves, and ground and crumble their bones."[9]

Somehow the creators of these myths intuited a fundamental truth about early humans, a truth too often ignored or denied by scholars of myth. *Early humans were easy pickin's for Pleistocene carnivores.* Some scholars, however, are catching up to tribal wisdom. Nature writer Paul Shepard points out that "before we were eaters of animals we (monkey like) were their prey, subject to going inside them."[10] Donna Hart and Robert W. Sussman, two primatologists who have contributed to the emerging view of "man-the-*hunted*," amass fossil evidence that clearly shows that for several million years "hominids were preyed on by many large carnivores."[11] Paleozoologist Hans Kruuk sums up the situation: "[M]an-eating was . . . a normal aspect of day-to-day predation during the Pliocene and Pleistocene."[12]

And the situation may have been just as dire as myths suggest. According to archaeologist Brian Hayden, "[G]reat numbers of our ancestors must have been killed by the predators . . . that roamed the savannas."[13] He suggests that at one point in the Paleolithic, the entire human population may have numbered no more than a few thousand individuals.[14] This would mean that myths were on the right track when they said that our distant ancestors struggled to avoid extinction.

Even more developed humans could not escape the threat and fear of being eaten alive by ferocious beasts. As author George Constable points out, such a robust and intelligent species as weapon-bearing

Homo neanderthalensis, a successful hunter of big-game animals, was "presumably . . . toothsome prey" for carnivores.[15] "Before, and well into, the age of man-the-hunter," Barbara Ehrenreich notes, "there would have been man-the-hunted."[16] Even today, "tens of thousands of people throughout the world fall victim to animal predation."[17] Much of human evolution has to do with the fact that humans—along with other primates—"are a prey species."[18] It is no accident or exaggeration that in African myths, humans are casually referred to as the "meat without hair."[19]

Though true, these claims are devoid of *blood*—unable to convey what early humans were actually up against. We need to "see" the creatures that hunted, killed, and terrified our ancestors, and whose salient features were imprinted on the evolving human brain over millions of years, shaping the human psyche forevermore.

In the Pleistocene, as well as today, many *dangerous creatures* had the power to kill a human—from mammoths to insects. But a "predator" is an animal that *hunts and eats* its prey. To our ancient ancestors, a "predator" would have been not just another "dangerous animal" but a dangerous animal with special salience.

In the "bestiary" that follows, predators are categorized into three realms—those of the land, of the water, and of the air (roughly speaking, mammals, reptiles, and raptors). All of them had the opportunity and inclination to eat humans. (To keep things simple, I use common descriptive names instead of scientific ones.)

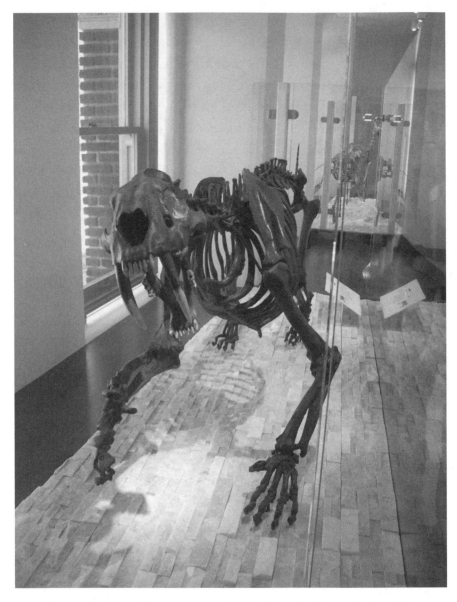

Smilodon was one of several big-cat species with saber-like teeth that populated the Pleistocene landscape throughout the world. Scientists make distinctions between the dirktooth,
the gracile sabertooth, the Idaho sabertooth, the false sabertooth, the scimitar cat, and so on.
The big cats of the Pleistocene were ferocious and effective predators. They coexisted with the
Homo line for several million years, becoming extinct about eleven thousand years ago. *Photo
courtesy of the Page Museum at the La Brea Tar Pits, Los Angeles, California.*

PART 1: ON DEADLY GROUND: PREDATORS THAT INHABITED THE LAND

THE KILLER CATS

Of all the predators that hunted and killed early humans, the most dangerous were the big cats. There were more of them in the Pleistocene than before or since.[20] The biggest were the gigantic sabertooths. They hunted throughout America, Africa, Europe, and Asia. The New World version, *Smilodon*, which ranged from western Canada to South America, had canine tusks ten inches long and weighed over seven hundred and fifty pounds, twice the weight of today's African lion.[21]

The *Smilodon* were quite numerous. The remains of over one thousand individual cats have been found in the La Brea Tar Pit in Los Angeles.[22] *Smilodon* went extinct only nine thousand years ago, so this killer greeted the first humans who migrated to the New World.[23] Another big-toothed cat—*Homotherium*—weighed in at six hundred pounds. It hunted in open forests and grasslands of both the New and

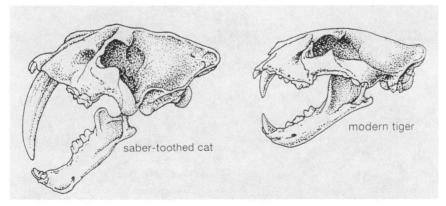

saber-toothed cat

modern tiger

The saber-toothed cats were bigger and stronger than later species, such as tigers. These predators were social animals that likely hunted in packs. *Reproduced from Ian M. Lange,* Ice Age Mammals of North America: A Guide to the Big, the Hairy, and the Bizarre *(Missoula, MT: Mountain Press, 2002). Illustration by Dorothy Norton. Courtesy of Dorothy Norton.*

Old Worlds, including Africa. It survived until just a few thousand years ago, posing a dire threat to humans for almost their entire history.[24]

Megantereon was a third form of saber-toothed cat. Weighing two hundred pounds more than a modern leopard, it could climb trees, and it hunted in forests and woodlands.[25] It thrived until the early Pleistocene, living in Eurasia, Africa, North America, and eventually South America.[26]

A fourth saber-toothed cat, *Dinofelis* ("terrible cat"), was seven feet long but could still climb trees, making it a "specialist in killing large primates, including our own near relatives and ancestors."[27] *Dinofelis* hunted and killed throughout North America, Europe, Asia, and Africa. It survived until about ten thousand years ago. This beast has been described as "our ancestors' worst nightmare."[28] Overall, it is something

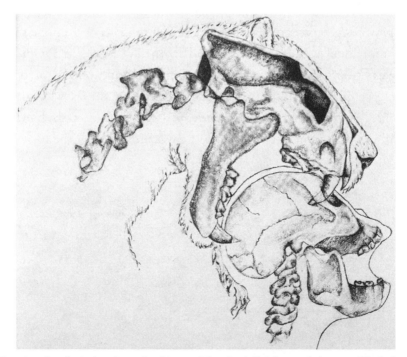

There is archaeological evidence that big cats did in fact kill and eat early humans. The holes in the skulls of some early hominid fossils match up perfectly with the fangs of big cats. *Reproduced from Donna Hart and Robert W. Sussman,* Man the Hunted: Primates, Predators, and Human Evolution *(New York: Westview Press, 2005). Drawing by C. Rudloff-Guilford. Courtesy of C. Rudloff-Guilford.*

of a miracle that our small hominid ancestors managed to survive "the predation of so many large-bodied, large-toothed felines."[29]

In addition to these now-extinct big cats, our ancestors were bedeviled by the feline carnivores that exist today—the leopard, the lion, the cheetah, the ocelot, the tiger, the jaguar, and the puma.

The leopard was, and still is, the most lethal killer of primates, including humans. The Pleistocene form, larger than today's leopard, ranged throughout Africa, the Middle East, China, and even Europe, where it flourished until ten thousand years ago.[30] There is hard evidence that leopards preyed on Australopithecines.

Though smaller than their Pleistocene ancestors, today's leopards usually kill with a powerful bite into the skull. "So ghostly silent is the hunting leopard that humans and dogs have been killed in their beds without waking others in the house."[31] The number of people killed by leopards in one area of modern-day Africa is said to be "horribly impressive."[32]

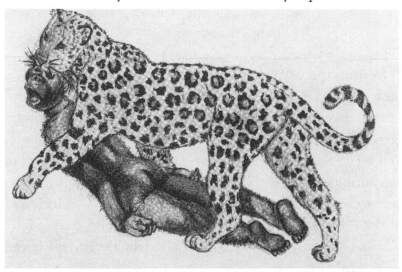

Archaeological evidence accumulated by C. K. Brain (*The Hunters or the Hunted? An Introduction to African Cave Taphonomy* [Chicago: University of Chicago Press], 1981) in South Africa proves that leopards preyed upon primates and early humans. Since leopards secure and eat their kills in trees, it is very likely that our ancient ancestors saw the torn and rotting bodies of their kith and kin hanging from many a branch. Reproduced from *Donna Hart and Robert W. Sussman,* Man the Hunted: Primates, Predators, and Human Evolution *(New York: Westview Press, 2005). Drawing by C. Rudloff-Guilford. Courtesy of C. Rudloff-Guilford.*

Leopards often kill humans for the sake of killing. One of the most notorious in this regard was the leopard of Masaguru, Tanzania. It killed twenty-six women and children, but not one of them was eaten. Another example, according to nature writer James Clarke, was a leopard in India that was alleged to have eaten four hundred people before it was shot. The leopard of Rudraprayag ate one hundred twenty-five. As recently as 1960, leopards in the Indian state of Bihar killed three hundred people, most of them children between six and ten years of age.[33] The Yoruba were so terrified of the leopard that they sang praises to the animal to appease it:

> Gentle hunter
> His tail plays on the ground
> While he crushes the skull.
> Beautiful death
> Who puts on a spotted robe when he
> Goes to his victim.[34]

Lions also preyed on our early ancestors. The Pleistocene lion, called the cave lion, was "gigantic," perhaps "the largest felid that ever existed."[35] (Except, of course, for "tigrons" and "ligers," the gigantic offspring of tigers and lions that occasionally interbreed in the wild or on game farms.) The cave lion was the most wide-ranging wild mammal of all time, inhabiting the deserts, mountains, Arctic steppes, woodlands, and grassy savannas of Africa, Europe, Asia, China, and the Americas as far south as Peru. Only Antarctica and the Pacific islands "escaped its teeth and claws."[36] There was very good reason why the ancient Egyptians commanded each other "[t]o be thou aware of the lion!"[37]

The cave lion survived into historical times in the Balkans, Asia Minor, and India, and the American version survived until ten thousand years ago. This awesome beast had plenty of time and opportunity to kill our early kin and earn its place in our nightmares and myths.

And in our art. Nowhere else in the galleries of Paleolithic art is there anything like the Lion Panel of Chauvet Cave (southern France, dating to about thirty-two thousand years ago), where the cave lion is depicted seventy-three times.[38] The power that the lion had over the burgeoning human imagination is also seen in the earliest art—sculptures of human bodies with lion heads.

Today's lion, though smaller than the Pleistocene version, can weigh up to a quarter ton and measure nearly ten feet from nose to tail tip. It can leap almost forty feet and, if necessary, climb trees. It is in Central Africa that lions have taken the highest toll of humans during modern times. In some parts of the continent, tribal peoples have a special drum to toll the news that another human has been eaten. By now almost everyone has heard of the Tsavo lions, which are featured in the 1996 film *The Ghost and the Darkness*.[39] The eight lions that hunted workers on the Nairobi railway killed about one hundred and twenty-five people, a relatively modest figure when compared to the man-eaters of Njombe (1945–47), which killed between a thousand and fifteen hundred people, a number representing "the greatest and most sustained record of man-eating ever known in Africa."[40]

No wonder that the frightening roar of the lion can be "heard" in many myths. "I will tell you a story of lions," says an African tale, "who are, as you know, second only to elephants in strength and power."[41] Another African myth tells of how a young lion killed all the other animals in the forest, including such large creatures as the ox and the camel. Then the lion boasts to a hapless woodcutter, "'There is no one as strong as I. Why, then, have you entered my forest? I shall devour you.'"[42] As Hans Kruuk observes, no other carnivore has provoked so many "fantasies, aspirations, admirations and fears" as has the lion.[43]

Tigers also added to the long nightmare of our ancient ancestors. Those that prowled the forests and savannas of the Pleistocene and Holocene were not only "gigantic," they could swim and climb trees.[44] Described as the "carnivore par excellence,"[45] Pleistocene tigers ranged from the Caspian Sea in the west through India and southeastern Asia (including Indonesia) to northern China and Siberia.[46] In North America, they existed along with cave lions during the last one hundred thousand years.[47]

Today's tigers weigh on average about six hundred pounds, with a few coming in at over seven hundred pounds. The longest modern tiger fang on record is 5½ inches with a girth of 3½ inches.[48] In the past—as now—tigers were "responsible for many human deaths."[49] "Tigers are able to clamp their jaws around the hips of a struggling man and carry him off the ground quite easily. Stories exist also of people being decapitated by a single blow from a tiger's paw."[50]

The most people recorded to have been killed by a single tiger were the four hundred thirty-six attributed to the tigress of Champawat (India). "Her toll was so enormous for such a relatively short period, and her kills so regular, that it appears she lived almost entirely upon a diet of human flesh."[51] "At a conservative estimate, tigers have consumed well over half a million Indians in the past four centuries. In the whole of Asia, the figure for the same period cannot be less than a million."[52] Women have been the most vulnerable, at least in northern India, because they typically go into the forests alone to gather firewood or down to the rivers to get water.[53]

Not surprisingly, the lethal powers of the tiger, in the words of nature writer Sy Montgomery, have evoked "a reverence, dread, and wonder accorded no other animal."[54] As a survivor of a tiger attack puts it, "When the tiger is about to attack you, . . . your blood goes cold out of fear. The teeth and the red portion of the eyes are mesmerizing. You cannot even utter the words 'help me.'"[55] Everywhere it roams, the tiger is credited with powers beyond those expected of any worldly animal. In the East—India, Malaysia, and so on—the tiger evokes such terror that it is worshipped as a god in an attempt to find a means of assuaging its predatory powers. Reverence may be most intense in Sundarbans (India), the largest tidal delta in the world. "Here, unlike any other place on earth, the tiger regularly hunts people. Hundreds die each year in the tiger's jaws. . . . Here the tiger is feared but not hated; here it is worshiped but not loved. For here the tiger is a sacred creature who rules an enchanted land."[56]

Like the other predators listed in this bestiary, "the tiger exposes the truth that we in the West try to ignore: we are all—chital and boar, frog and fish, astronaut and beggar—made of meat."[57] A Chinese proverb expresses our dread of the tiger in a wonderfully understated way: "Do not blame God for creating the tiger. Thank Him for not giving it wings."

The word *puma* comes from a Quechua word meaning "powerful animal." On average, the puma weighs about as much as the African leopard—from one hundred to one hundred seventy five pounds—and can be as long as nine feet. Strangely, the puma has more English names than any other big cat, being referred to variously as cougar, mountain lion, panther, painter, catamount, silver lion, purple panther, red tiger, brown lion, deer tiger, Mexican lion, American lion, mountain screamer, cat-of-the-mountains, and Indian devil.[58] The Pleistocene version was larger than today's and seems to have appeared around thirteen thousand years ago, giving it plenty of time to claw its way into tribal cultural memory. This cat exists throughout most of the world, as it did in the past.[59] Nowadays, the puma, because it can live close to cities, occasionally makes headlines by attacking hikers, joggers, and bicyclists out to enjoy a bit of nature.

Although the jaguar may have originated in Eurasia, the name *yaguara* is from Amazonia, where Guarani Indians spoke fearfully of a beast that killed with one leap. As with the other big cats, the Pleistocene jaguar was a "giant," weighing about three hundred pounds, 20 percent larger than today's version, which is the largest carnivore now living in Central America and South America.[60] Although now extinct, this giant jaguar has been called "the most formidable predatory felid" in the world.[61]

Jaguars ranged throughout Europe between seventy thousand and ten thousand years ago, but they were in the Americas more than two million years ago, being as common as the sabertooth cats.[62] In Mesoamerican sacrificial rites, it was to the jaguar god that the still pumping hearts of victims were "fed" to appease the creature's voracious appetite for human flesh and blood. This practice is encoded in the *Popol Vuh*, when the hero twins shout to the jaguars, "'Do not bite us! Here is what belongs to you.' . . . And quickly they threw some bones to the animals, which pounced upon the bones."[63]

Our Pleistocene ancestors had to contend with yet another feline predator, the giant cheetah.[64] Scholars believe that the cheetah arose in the New World and then spread to Africa, Europe, India, and China.[65] The European species lived until about five hundred thousand years ago, but the North American form may have survived until about ten thousand years ago. Of all the cats mentioned, the cheetah probably posed the least threat to ancient humans.

The great predatory cats have been called the "ultimate stalkers and ambushers" and "the most carnivorous of all carnivores."[66] In the Pleistocene, these big cats made their living killing and eating huge herbivores, but it is reasonable to assume that they were not averse to grabbing a risk-free easy meal in the form of a bipedal primate. Even today, in some parts of Africa, lions and leopards sometimes give up preying on game to indulge in the "easier . . . flesh of defenceless humans."[67] For several million years, these predators posed a constant threat to our ancestors, making them at once ever more sensitive to danger and ever more ingenious in creating cultural strategies to manage their fear of that danger. These strategies were etched, as we shall see, in myth after myth.

HYENAS, WOLVES, AND DOGS

Adding to the woes of our Pleistocene ancestors were the canine predators. Hunting in packs, they were as dangerous as any single big cat.

Hyenas

Although the hyena is anatomically closer to cats than to dogs, I include hyenas with the canine carnivores because they look and hunt like them.

One thinks of the hyena as an African predator, but at the beginning of human evolution, over one hundred species of hyena ranged throughout Europe, Asia, and Africa.[68] During the Pleistocene, the short-faced hyena—the largest hyena that ever existed—was "as big as a lion,"[69] weighing in at four hundred and fifty pounds. Today's hyenas, armed with canine teeth that can smash bones and rip flesh, are "fiercely aggressive hunters," especially at night.[70] Their jaws are so strong that they can leave tooth marks in forged steel.[71]

According to Hans Kruuk, an authority on this animal, Pleistocene hyenas constituted "a danger to early man."[72] The hominid bones found in South African caves indicate that hyenas chewed up the skeleton to get at the marrow and broke open the skull to get at the fatty brain tissue.[73]

Even today, the hyena is an especially effective predator of humans.[74] Those who manage to escape an attack may regret their survival because hyenas often rip off the face of human victims. Most of the time, the entire body of the victim is consumed, except for the skull.[75] At times, marauding packs of hyenas terrorize whole districts in Africa, taking so many lives—especially those of women and children—that people believe the animals must be witches in disguise.[76] This notion is reinforced by the animal's uncanny ability to sneak up on victims. One farmer who tracked two man-eating hyenas came to believe that he was up against lycanthropy, "for quite often victims would be taken from the midst of their sleeping families without a sound being heard." In some parts of Africa, the hyena is a greater man-eater than the leopard and lion together.[77]

The Dire Wolf was one of the most common predators of the Pleistocene, and its numbers were particularly plentiful in North America. The Dire Wolf was about a third larger than the wolf of today. It hunted in packs of up to fifty animals. *Photo courtesy of the Page Museum at the La Brea Tar Pits, Los Angeles, California.*

Wolves

Our ancient ancestors also fell prey to wolves, which hunted and ate humans throughout Europe, Asia, and the New World (from Alberta to Peru) "for as long as man and wolves have lived there."[78] The wolf that hunted our ancestors in the Pleistocene is called the *Dire Wolf.* It weighed on average one hundred and fifty pounds, and had the longest and most powerful teeth ever found in a canid.[79] The Dire Wolf stalked prey in North America as recently as eight thousand years ago. Of all the mammalian remains found in the La Brea Tar Pits, those of the Dire Wolf are the most abundant. The bones of the Dire Wolf have been found in caves that also contain the bones and artifacts of *Homo erectus* and *Homo sapiens*, although it is not clear from just this evidence exactly how often our ancestor entered these caves involuntarily.[80]

Not all wolves are as genial as the ones described by Canadian naturalist and writer Farley Mowat in his bestseller *Never Cry Wolf*. In his fascinating book *Man Is the Prey*, James Clarke relates several occasions when European wolves—driven by bloodlust or starvation—terrorized whole cities. Although the wolf was hunted to extinction in England and France during the eighteenth century, packs still roam Spain, Italy, Portugal, and the Balkans. In Siberia, in 1927, the village of Pilovo was besieged by hungry wolves that knocked down doors to attack terrified families. It took army troops to rescue the residents, although by the time they reached the village, almost every family had suffered a loss.[81]

Judging from myth, the wolf has a powerful presence in the human psyche. As author and mythographer Marina Warner explains, wolves haunt children's rhymes and tales in large part because in times of famine they posed a threat to humans well into the nineteenth century.[82] The wolf evoked fear even in well-armed and militaristic tribal peoples. In Norse myth, monstrous wolves tear and devour Skimir and his mighty horse, and, at Ragnarok, the wolves Fenrir and Managarm devour the sun and moon, "stain[ing] the heavens and earth with blood."[83] The wolf is often associated with evil, death, and destruction, as seen in the wolfskin cloak of Hades, the wolf ears of the Etruscan god of death, and the capacity of witches and warlocks to turn themselves into wolves or werewolves.[84]

Dogs

It's hard to think of "man's best friend" as posing a danger to human survival, but before wild dogs were domesticated about thirteen thousand years ago, they, too, hunted and ate humans. In some cultures, dogs are still feared, as the *Popol Vuh* indicates; "'Now we shall destroy you, now you shall feel the teeth of our mouths; we shall devour you,' said the dogs, and then they destroyed their faces."[85]

By the early Pleistocene, the dog family had evolved into several large forms, including cat-like dogs, hyena-like dogs, and bear-like dogs.[86] The bear dog, which weighed about two hundred pounds, was a strange blend of traits, having the hind legs of a large cat and the teeth of a wolf.[87] Remains of bear-like dogs have been unearthed in California.

There were also "plundering" dogs and "bone-crushing" dogs, both possessing "extremely powerful jaws and teeth."[88] In addition to these creatures, there were dholes, or red hunting dogs (technically not a true dog because of a difference in teeth between the species). In Pleistocene Europe, the hunting dog reached the size of a large wolf and was "highly predacious."[89] The dhole still exists in some parts of Europe, India, and Africa. "Nothing is sacred to a pack of dholes—not even the tiger, which it tears to pieces from time to time." Clearly, if a pack of these creatures can tear apart a tiger, it must have had no trouble with a weaponless bipedal primate. In Siberia today, they are feared as man-eaters.[90]

Dangerous canines are now represented by the African "devil dog," a creature that is a more successful group hunter than is the lion, and that has developed the knack of disemboweling its prey while on the run. Wherever our ancestors migrated, they would have encountered this family of "truly formidable predators."[91]

The primal fear of feral dogs is incarnated in such figures as Hecate, the "black bitch" of the Underworld; Sarameyau, the two hellhounds of Vedic mythology; the Norse god Odin's Geri and Freki; the Nordic hound Garm; Cerberus, the Greek guardian of Hades; the dog-like Furies; and Cheeroonear, the dog-like monster of the Australian Aborigines, who described in one myth "the youth and maidens clinging to the tree, and looking down toward the ground.... 'I see dogs are at their work killing the people.'"[92] Ku, the devouring Dogman of Hawaiian myth, "was very strong" and killed many people, carrying their bodies away "to feast upon them."[93]

BEARS

No catalog of Pleistocene predators would be complete without bears.

Although our ancestors had to deal with brown bears, polar bears, and black bears, the most dangerous bear by far was the short-faced bear (called the cave bear, perhaps an early form of grizzly bear). This "highly predacious" animal was "more carnivorous than the true bears."[94] Indeed, it has been declared "the most powerful predator of the American Pleistocene."[95]

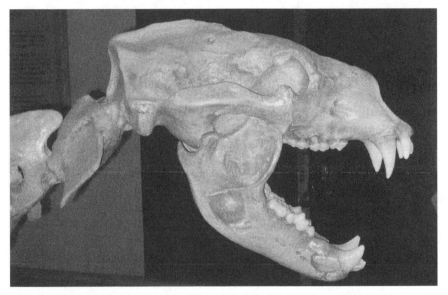

Though it hunted alone, the short-faced bear, often called the cave bear, was one of the most dangerous predators of the Pleistocene. It could weigh up to eighteen hundred pounds, and when it reared up, it would have towered over its two largest descendants, the grizzly bear and polar bear. *Photo by Adrienne Mayor, Fig. 14,* Fossil Legends of the First Americans *(Princeton, NJ: Princeton University Press, 2005).*

This bear was taller than the now-extinct California grizzly (*Ursus horribilis*)—standing five feet six inches from foot pad to top of head (when on all fours) and weighing more than two thousand pounds.[96] When it walked on two legs, it stood eleven feet high, a foot higher than a basketball hoop, dwarfing the modern grizzly.[97] It may have evolved into such a gigantic size to intimidate the other carnivores it competed with, such as the American lion, the scimitar-toothed cat, and the wolf pack.

This formidable predator ranged throughout Europe, Asia, and North and South America. The largest land predator in North America during the Ice Age, it survived until about eleven thousand years ago. It has been suggested that only when this species went extinct could humans migrate into North America.

Today, the species of bear that kills the most people in the world is the sloth bear, which is found in the jungles of India and Sri Lanka. Every year about one thousand five hundred Tibetans are killed by bears.[98]

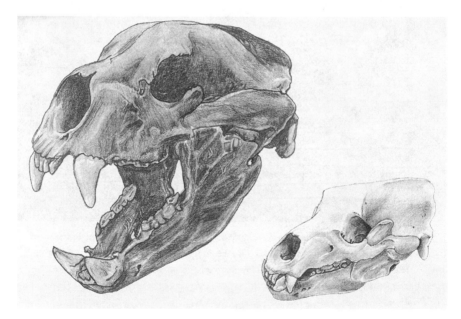

This illustration comparing the skull size of the short-faced bear with that of the grizzly should explain why this creature was feared and worshipped by our ancestors, and how the first myths about this predator species came about. *Reproduced from Adrienne Mayor,* Fossil Legends of the First Americans *(Princeton, NJ: Princeton University Press, 2005). Drawing by Patti-Kane-Vanni. Courtesy of Patti-Kan-Vanni.*

Although Native Americans respected and sometimes venerated the bear, they also feared it. In a Wasco myth, the Trickster figure Coyote warns humans about bears: "Don't go near them! They will tear you apart!"[99] A Modoc myth holds that when the Great Sky Spirit first made bears, he was so intimidated by their fierce appearance that he "sent them away from him to live in the forest at the base of the mountain."[100] According to a Cheyenne myth, bears acquired their taste for human blood because a young girl trained two bears to kill her abusive father by feeding them animal tissue. Ever since, "bears have eaten human flesh when they could."[101]

PART 2: UP FROM THE DEPTHS: PREDATORS OF THE WATER

I include in this section creatures that prey *in* or *around* water, such as constrictor snakes, crocodiles, and alligators, as well as sea creatures such as sharks and barracudas.

Every time our ancestors went near a watering hole, river, or lake, they risked winding up in the belly of the beast.

GIANT SNAKES

In the Pleistocene and early Holocene, boas, pythons, and anacondas—the giant constricting serpents—were larger and more numerous than today. How *much* larger is a point of controversy, but a snake skeleton dug up in Al Fayyum, Egypt, measured between forty-two and sixty-five feet long, which means that the snake may have had a diameter of eighteen inches and a weight exceeding eight hundred pounds.[102]

Did giant snakes, of whatever size, eat our ancient ancestors? Of course they did, even though there is no fossil evidence to prove it. Such attacks would likely leave no evidence, but we do know that giant snakes have always preyed on mammals; they have even swallowed porcupines.[103] In the environment in which the human line evolved, according to Anthony Stevens, big snakes were a constant source of danger, particularly at night.[104] Today they continue to kill primates, killing more adult monkeys than any other predator.[105] And these snakes still take quite a toll on humans. Accounts of python attacks on infants and children in Southeast Asia "are almost too numerous to recount individually."[106]

When a python strikes, its jaws are agape so it can fasten its teeth firmly in the prey, while the force of the thrust knocks the creature off-balance. At the same time, the python rolls itself over, twisting itself round and round, so that its body encircles the prey.[107] This process takes a while and often is noisy, as the prey screams and shrieks. A python kill will surely attract the attention of bystanders.

Judging from the "especially frightening mystique" of the snake, it must have made a powerful impression on our ancient ancestors.[108] Even today, throughout the world, "this awe-inspiring creature is experienced as numinous and sacred, inspiring reverence as well as dread."[109] The mythification of the snake as a god was pronounced in pre-Columbian Central America and Mexico, where hundreds of gigantic stones were carved in the form of snakes, usually shown with wide-open jaws inside of which is a human head. In ancient Mexico, a wooden instrument carved in the form of a large constrictor was used to hold down the heads of sacrificial victims having their hearts cut out.[110] Giant snakes haunted aboriginal Australians, whose myths recount the depredations of a monster called Julunggul. In one myth, Julunggul "opened his mouth and swallowed everything that lay within his coils—the baby, the two sisters, and the shelter disappeared into the vast maw."[111]

CROCODILES AND ALLIGATORS

Crocodilians can be found in saltwater and freshwater around the world and in all sizes, from dwarf crocodiles to giants weighing over a ton and capable of killing a Cape buffalo. The Indo-Pacific crocodile, which grows up to twenty-three feet and can weigh as much as two thousand pounds, is a super-predator, stalking and killing leopards and lions.[112] The crocodile's massive jaws are armed with seventy or so teeth, so once prey is seized it has almost no chance of escape. Crocodiles can outrun, out-hear, out-see, out-swim, out-sense, and outfight the strongest human.[113] They are the perfect "aquatic ambush predator."[114] Though the words of this nineteenth-century naturalist are a bit ornate, he puts it well when he writes that crocodiles and alligators are "forms so vast

The gaping jaws of a lunging crocodile or alligator were the last thing that millions of our kind ever saw over the vast expanse of human evolution. Cold-blooded, ferocious, unappeasable, and almost supernaturally stealthy, this reptilian survivor of the Age of Dinosaurs may be the most unnerving of all predators. The crocodile (pictured here) figures prominently in the myths of people who must coexist with it. *Worldwildlifewonders/Shutterstock.com.*

and terrible, as to more than realize the most exaggerated impression of reptilian power and ferocity which the florid imagination of man can conceive."[115]

It's reasonable to assume that crocodiles ate humans in the distant past just as they do today. The Nile croc is reputedly the biggest killer of humans on the African continent, responsible for more human deaths than lions, leopards, buffaloes, hippopotamuses, hyenas, rhinoceroses, and elephants combined.[116] According to one author, the crocodiles of the Sundarbans are "man-eating monsters of the worst kind," more deadly than the sharks that also infest the coastal waters.[117]

Most of those killed are women and children because women with children spend a great deal of time at rivers drawing water or washing clothes. One of the most horrifying collections of stomach contents taken from an African crocodile included eleven heavy brass arm rings, three wire armlets, wire anklets, a necklace, fourteen human arm and leg bones, and three human spinal columns.[118] Such horrific revelations have been encoded in myth. One Polynesian myth recounts the slitting open of the stomach of a "great lizard," exposing the "amazing sight" of headless, armless, legless "men, women, and children."[119] In 1970, it was estimated that crocodiles killed about one thousand people annually. The fear evoked by these creatures can be seen in a Bengali mantra directed at the "dangerous ones with sharp teeth." "Stay away for day and night," it pleads, "This mantra, like thunder, is a weapon in my hand, so I charge you in your mouth, in your teeth, to stay away for day and night."[120]

One myth explains the animosity between crocodiles and humans by saying that in the primordial past, a human killed the offspring of a friendly crocodile. Since this terrible event, crocodiles kill humans whenever they try to cross the river or come to drink, and humans kill crocodiles whenever they leave the water. According to one African myth, it is said that humans do not have to make offerings to the crocodile because this creature simply "takes what it wants."[121] An Australian myth recounts in detail an attack made by a man-crocodile on a canoe filled with people. Grabbing the canoe in its mouth, the crocodile shakes it until the people fall into the water. Frantically they try to swim to the shore as their tribespeople shout encouragement, but the croc is too quick. He darts from one victim to another, "his teeth coming together with a vicious snap, tearing them limb from limb, until all that remained were severed limbs and mutilated bodies drifting out to sea in the reddened water."[122]

The American crocodile and American alligator, which reside in coastal habitats, large rivers, and lakes within their range (southern Florida, Caribbean islands, eastern coast of Mexico), are also man-eaters. They were "a constant threat to the Indians [of Florida] who kept guard against them night and day."[123]

These survivors of the Age of Dinosaurs have so galvanized the human imagination that not only have they been transformed into demons, gods, and even benefactors, but they have also been fashioned into role models. The Bemba chiefs of (then) Rhodesia, thinking themselves descendants of the Crocodile Clan, would seize people "with their teeth and tear them to bits" as an actual crocodile would do.[124]

LIZARDS

In the past, the largest lizard was *Megalania*, which grew to almost thirty feet in length (as long as a python), and weighed more than two thousand pounds.[125] They thrived in Australia and some Pacific islands just fifty thousand years ago, about the time the continent was being colonized by humans, and they did not go extinct until about nineteen thousand years ago[126]—if in fact they did. There have been sightings of large lizards in the Australian Outback for some time. In July 1979, cryptozoologist Rex Gilroy examined thirty or more tracks from a farmer's field and said they looked like those of an enormous lizard, possibly *Megalania*. Living where and when it did, *Megalania* very likely consumed

While not as widespread as most other land predators, the Komodo dragon may have given rise to, or reinforced, the myth of the dragon. This creature not only scavenges but also hunts and is able to bring down very large animals, such as wild buffalo. This predator hunts in packs and can run as fast as a human in local terrain. Like all predators, the Komodo dragon converts a once-living creature into disarticulated bones and bloody offal. *Khaplin/Dreamstime.com.*

Homo sapiens. These creatures may have given rise to some of the dragon myths encountered around the world.

The descendant of *Megalania* is the Komodo dragon, a giant monitor lizard that grows to twelve feet long and weighs up to three hundred and sixty-five pounds.[127] This creature went undiscovered until 1912, well after it was first thought that these large lizards were extinct. The Komodo dragon has huge curved claws and teeth shaped like those of *Tyrannosaurus rex.* It is an ambush predator, catching the prey by the leg or throat, throwing it to the ground, and ripping out the intestines. It can swallow large prey in one or two gulps, eating anything, including other Komodo dragons, whether alive or dead.[128] It can climb trees, swim, or run, as the occasion demands; it can even outrun a human in the terrain in which it lives.[129]

This "ravenous" predator is now and likely was a threat to humans, often attacking without provocation.[130] In 1973, a Swiss tourist who sat down to relax while hiking through the Indonesian island of Komodo was attacked and eaten by a Komodo dragon.[131] All that was left was a piece of his camera. In March of 2009, an Indonesian fisherman was killed when he trespassed on one of the remote islands in the dragon's habitat. Incidents like these are few only because the Komodo lives in such a remote area. Most of the islands where the dragons live have no permanent human residents. It seems reasonable to assume that during the Pleistocene, the larger ancestor of today's Komodo dragon hunted and killed early humans when the opportunity arose.[132]

Giant Fish

Like poor Luca Brasi in *The Godfather*, many humans have wound up "sleeping with the fishes."

How could they have avoided it? Every time they entered or foraged around rivers, inlets, and bays, or braved the open seas to hunt or island hop, they risked being eaten by predatory fish—sharks, barracudas, killer whales, and a host of other "sea monsters." The wolf shark, thresher shark, and requiem shark (how aptly named!) still kill such water-going primates as the macaque, so it is highly likely that these predators harvested early humans in the same habitats.[133]

The great white shark grows to about fifteen feet and weighs up to seventeen hundred pounds, with the largest authenticated specimen (caught in 1987) being twenty-five feet long.[134] Sharks will eat anything, often hunting for food close to shore and striking humans in as little as two feet of water.[135] Island people, such as the Polynesians, were plagued by sharks, which, their myths insist, would attack people who dared to bathe or fish in the sea. The sharks would suddenly appear in their midst, "biting and tearing their limbs and dragging them down in the deep water."[136]

In the 1960s, a study sought to determine which single word has the greatest psychological impact on people. Researchers tested reactions to *spider, snake, death, rape, incest, murder,* and so on, but it was the word *shark* that elicited the greatest fear response, perhaps because in the "cold dead eyes" of the shark we recognize that we are nothing but meat. In his book *Great White Shark*, Jean-Michel Cousteau calls the shark "the most frightening animal on earth."[137]

Novelist Peter Benchley understood and brilliantly exploited this fear. It's the *jaws* of sharks that we find so terrifying. They open wide enough to swallow us whole, yet they are filled with dagger-shaped teeth that can chop us in half with one bite. Once grasped by these jaws, we suddenly disappear into the shark's dark cavity, only to reappear later as unrecognizable bits of shit.

One way we have tried to conquer our fear of the shark is by imagining that we can control it through veneration and worship. Strangely and hauntingly, there was a time in India (and elsewhere) when pilgrims, overcome with a fervor to sacrifice themselves, waded into the sea so that sharks could take them. The sharks obliged, reddening the water with the blood of the devout.[138]

Another dangerous fish that likely preyed on early humans is the barracuda. The large barracuda is found from Hawaii to the Red Sea, and from Brazil to northern Florida. According to wildlife author James Sweeney, the great barracuda is "an 8- to 10-foot power plant, with large, sharp canine teeth," and, like the shark, the barracuda "is a highly dangerous fish with an unpredictable nature." It has been described as "vicious" on the grounds that it often bites smaller fish only to then spit them out, apparently wanting not to eat them but just to kill them. Picture such an urge to kill in an eight-foot, torpedo-shaped body, noted for its speed and infallibility of aim, and it's clear why humans fear this creature.[139]

Farther from shore lurk the killer whales. Found around the world, they grow to about thirty feet.[140] They are well armed with ten to twelve large, conical, and exceedingly hard teeth that interlock, giving the killer whale a tremendous bite.[141]

Would a killer whale hunt and kill a human? Yes, it would. Adventurer Robert Scott saw a pack of killer whales attempt to knock a colleague and his sled dogs into the water by smashing their backs against the underside of the ice.[142] Eskimos have reported that as soon as killer whales see a kayak, they attack it. As one Eskimo hunter relates:

> So Eskimos try double hard to reach shore when killer whales are seen. The big sadness in all this is that young Eskimos show their smartness by learning, at a very early age, to handle kayak. They like to travel far and long on open sea. If caught by killer whale in the open, they disappear.[143]

Large bodies of water contain another predator rarely mentioned as such—the grouper. I've eaten plenty of grouper sandwiches at restaurants without ever imagining that under the right conditions, I would be on *their* menu. In Australia, newspapers "have factually reported incidents wherein *giant* groupers have attacked deep-sea divers or literally swallowed them whole—copper helmet, rubber suit, and lead shoes."[144] This article might seem like "Coast-to-Coast" material, but keep in mind that some groupers weigh two thousand pounds! (That's a lot of sandwiches.)

Of course, many other water creatures also kill and eat humans (such as the piranha), but the few I've mentioned should be enough to confirm my point that during the Pleistocene (and beyond!), humans faced lethal threats wherever they went in the natural environment.

PART 3: AERIAL TERROR: PREDATORS OF THE SKY

Among the predators that had the opportunity, ability, and inclination to kill our ancestors were those that swooped down from the sky, or would have, had they not been too immense to fly!

TERATORNS AND CONDORS

During the Ice Age, our ancestors had to be on guard against an immense aerial menace called *Teratornis* ("monster bird"). The teratorns were the "largest [flying] birds of all time," weighing about fifty pounds

This image comparing the sizes of the teratorn, condor, and eagle with the size of a fully grown male hunter lends credibility to stories and myths about giant birds carrying off humans. These ostensibly fictional accounts may reflect cultural memories of very real encounters with teratorns, as well as with other large raptors. *Reproduced from Adrienne Mayor,* Fossil Legends of the First Americans *(Princeton, NJ: Princeton University Press, 2005). Drawing by Rick Spears. Courtesy of Rich Spears.*

and having an average wingspan of fifteen feet. One subspecies, aptly named *Teratornis incredibilis*, had a wingspan of seventeen feet.[145]

Teratorns resembled eagles but had very long, strong hooked beaks for grabbing prey, which could have included "small humans."[146] These immense birds lived in the Americas until only "a few thousand years ago."[147] Remains of this bird have been found across the southern United States (and recently in Oregon), as well as in northern Mexico.

Intriguingly, there are Indian petroglyphs made between six hundred and a thousand years ago by the ancestors of the Hopi that show "a large bird carrying what appears to be a small, struggling man in its long beak." A Hopi elder said that a long time ago a giant bird used to swoop down on the pueblos and fly away with their children.[148]

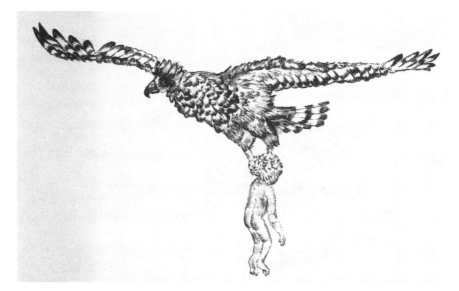

There is archaeological evidence that large raptors preyed upon protohumans. An *Australopithecus* skull thought to be that of a child was found near the town of Taung in South Africa in 1924. The skull has holes in it consistent with the talons of a large eagle. The skull has been dated to around two million years ago. With robust feet and talons, and the ability to strike victims with the force of a high-velocity bullet, eagles continue to prey on small primates and occasionally attack humans in Africa. *Reproduced from Donna Hart and Robert W. Sussman,* Man the Hunted: Primates, Predators, and Human Evolution *(New York: Westview Press, 2005). Drawing by C. Rudloff-Guilford. Courtesy of C. Rudloff-Guilford.*

A number of Native American myths encode a powerful fear of large and dangerous avian predators. One such myth from the Iroquois nation describes a monstrous bird that is nothing but a great flying head with wings growing from its cheeks. "Instead of teeth, the Flying Head had a mouth full of huge, piercing fangs with which it seized and devoured its prey. And everything was prey to this monster, every living being, including people."[149]

Another giant raptor was *Harpagornis* of New Zealand's South Island. Bigger than a condor, it had a wingspan of about ten feet. These "super-eagles" made their living hunting the huge but docile moa bird, but they may also have preyed on humans. One scholar wonders whether these super-eagles viewed the immigrant Maoris, as they first strode ashore more than seven hundred years ago, as "yet another group of tall bipeds worth sampling."[150] Perhaps it was this bird that gave rise to Hawaiian myths about a "great bird" with talon-tipped wings that hunted humans.

The California condor was also a powerful and dangerous sky predator, and it may have survived the Pleistocene extinctions in a somewhat smaller form.[151] This bird, with a wingspan of ten feet, may also have contributed to Native American stories about large birds carrying off humans.[152]

Several flightless birds were also capable of killing our ancient—and not so ancient—ancestors. The biggest of these so-called ratites is the now-extinct elephant bird (*Aepyornis*) of Madagascar, which weighed just short of half a ton. It stood about ten feet high and laid eggs the size of a two-gallon bucket. This "bird" became extinct only a few thousand years ago—within historical times—and may have given rise to the mythical roc (or rukh) of Arabic mythology.

Another feathered descendant of those velociraptors so menacingly brought to life in the novel and movie *Jurassic Park* was a six-foot-tall, three-hundred-fifty-pound predator that ruled the land for many thousands of years. Called *Titanis*, this bird had a neck as thick as a tree stump and a head that was two feet long, almost all beak. The feet were tipped with four-inch-long claws. It could probably run as fast as fifty miles per hour, though it may have burst upon its prey from the tall grass. It would have dispatched the prey by slashing it with its feet and ripping it apart with its massive beak.

Did *Titanis* rip apart humans? Such an event was thought to be chronologically impossible until Jon Baskin, a paleontologist at Texas A&M University (Kingsville) discovered *Titanis* remains in Texas that may be no older, and are perhaps younger, than fifteen thousand years. This date is very close to when humans arrived in the New World. By twelve thousand four hundred years ago, humans had already reached southern Chile. "With that in mind, it becomes easy to conjure a vision of humans meeting up with a resurrected dinosaur . . . face-to-face on a bright Texas prairie."[153]

During the Pleistocene, the alpha predator of much of South America was *Titanis*, a huge carnivorous, flightless bird that was eight feet tall, had hooks on its "wings," powerful talons, and a sharp beak that could crack coconuts. This creature, nicknamed "terror bird," crossed into North America when the continents joined about three million years ago. It is possible that the first humans who entered North America around thirteen thousand years ago may have encountered the last representatives of this daunting land predator. *Photo courtesy of Greg Turner (taken at the Florida Museum of Natural History at the University of Florida).*

EAGLES

Eagles have existed for millennia and probably behaved in the past as they do today—preying on midsize mammals, including monkeys, apes, and sometimes vulnerable humans. Raptors in Africa routinely hunt primates much larger than themselves by swooping down with incredible speed and extraordinary force, driving their talons into the skulls of their victims.

In the Pleistocene, hominids and early humans lived under the looming shadow of such gigantic (but now extinct) eagles as *Stephanoaetus mahery* and Haast's Eagle.[154] Haast's Eagles may have been larger than any eagle that exists today. But both of these giant predators went extinct as recently as two thousand years ago.

Contemporary eagles come in many sizes, with the largest ones— the Harpy Eagle, the Crowned Eagle, and the Martial Eagle—being "exceptionally powerful and rapacious."[155] All three have enormously robust feet and talons, allowing them to kill antelopes and monkeys many times the bird's own weight.[156]

The Harpy Eagle—which has been described as the "jaguar of the sky"[157]—has a foot spanning nine to ten inches equipped with massive dagger-like talons more than eleven inches long. "Such a foot is clearly adapted to dispatch large and powerful mammals, while the talons could be driven through the body of a young monkey to kill it almost instantly."[158] Primate anthropologist David E. Jones suggests that the talons of an attacking raptor so terrified early humans that they assigned them to the arch-predator of the human imagination—the dragon.[159]

Although not as big as the Martial Eagle in size or wingspan, the African Crowned Eagle—described as a "leopard with wings"[160]—has such powerful legs and feet that it is able to kill mammals up to four times its own weight.[161] "In other parts of Africa they are said to live almost entirely on forest monkeys"[162]

Eagles and hawks are still the major and most competent predators on nonhuman primates.[163] Given that in the past raptors were much bigger and more powerful, they probably had no reluctance attacking a four-foot-tall hominid sleeping in a tree perch. According to two authorities on this topic, "eagles with the power of the present-day crowned hawk-eagle were significant predators on young hominids."[164] Archaeologist Steven Mithen also believes that eagles "would have been a persistent threat to the hominids when foraging in environments with far less tree cover than those inhabited by the African apes today."[165] As mentioned previously, the skull of an Australopithecine Taung child (about two million years old) has holes in it that were made by the talons of a raptor, much like those of the modern Crowned Eagle.

This background helps explain the number of aerial predators that swoop through the mythic landscape. In Norse myth, the giant Thiassi assumes the form of a giant eagle to hunt down Loki (who himself takes the form of a falcon). Herakles is tasked to kill the man-eating Stymphalian birds. The Native American hero Szeukha kills a vicious, man-devouring eagle, bringing back to life "all the people the great eagle had abducted and killed."[166] The Shoshoni were hunted by a great bird called Nunyenunc.[167] In Creek myth, "a huge blue bird" devoured people until it was killed.[168] Many Native American tribes worship and fear the "great mystery bird of the heavens," the Thunderbird, "a hundred times as big as the largest eagles."[169] In the *Popol Vuh*, the hero twins of Mayan myth kill the monster bird Vucub-Caquix. The predator bird of Fiji—Ngani-vatu—seizes and devours humans in its cave.[170] Another predator of Polynesian myth is Punga-rehu, a bird that catches its victims as they go to fetch water.[171] In African myth, the monster bird Oom Leeuw is always looking for something to kill with its "iron claws."[172] In Hopi myth, Man-Eagle, a "frightful monster," seizes women and girls in "his sharp talons" and takes them to "his home above the clouds," where he abuses them "before eating them up."[173]

No doubt these creatures, like other mythic animals, were imbued by tribal peoples with all kinds of psychological functions and social meanings. But these "mythic" aerial predators cannot be dismissed merely as symbols of something else, such as lightning, storm clouds, or volcano plumes. These creatures are the shadows of actual predators that once were big enough to kill our ancestors, and that still have the power to evoke in us the primal fear of *dying by predator*. If humans have been telling animal stories for about two hundred thousand years (see chapters 4 and 5), there would have been ample opportunity for aerial killers to earn a place in the bestiary housed within the human imagination.

CONCLUSION

These, then, are the predators that menaced our distant ancestors. These are the same animals whose features and behaviors, as we shall later see, were mimed and imitated as part of humanity's first fledgling efforts at storytelling. And these are the creatures that—in the alembic of the mythic imagination—were transformed into the bizarre hybrid "monsters" that terrorize and devour humans in myth after myth, story after story, from ancient times until today.

This detailed account of Pleistocene (and later) predators should make clear that early humans were not the alpha predators of their environment. For about 99 percent of our time as a species, we would have been at a disastrous disadvantage when confronting Pleistocene carnivores. Myths reflect this understanding. In one Polynesian myth, for example, the stomach of a great bird—Hotu-puku—is opened up to reveal not only the bodies of its victims but also their "clubs" and "spears"—"all were within the belly of the *taniiwha*, as if the monster were a stored armory of war."[174]

Our ancient ancestors were not defenseless, but they hardly were the confident and dangerous "hunters" imagined by so many students of myth. Even if our ancient ancestors were not eaten *that* often, they understood that they were always on the menu.

In saying this, I am not attempting to *demonize* predators. To survive, these awe-inspiring creatures evolved extraordinary abilities to feed themselves, and it is a historical fact that for a vast expanse of time, they have often fed themselves on human beings. It is also a historical fact that in response to this threat, the genus *Homo* evolved a wide assortment of defensive (and sometimes aggressive) "weapons" to avoid becoming food. Yet, though I have no wish to demonize predators, I also must confess to being less objective in this matter than the woman in Abraham Lincoln's anecdote, who, upon seeing her husband in a life-and-death struggle with a bear, shouts out, "Go to it husband! Go to it bear!"

Refocusing attention on this disturbing, less-than-glorious aspect of human evolution has vast implications for understanding the nature and content of myth, and the emergence of primal storytelling as a survival strategy.

The stage is now set for exploring how these predators got into the heads and hearts of early humans, and how, once there, they helped shape and galvanize the developing creative impulses of the human mind.

Chapter 3

Be Afraid, Be Very Afraid
Fear and Survival in the Pleistocene

INTRODUCTION

Though scholars rarely mention it, myths often are about fear.

In Mayan myth, the original tribes that gathered at night on a mountain top to await the rising of the first sun were too afraid to sleep. Their hearts "were filled with fear" because the jungle was filled with dangerous animals. At the rising of the sun, "the puma, the jaguar, the snake, the cantil, and the hobgoblin" were transformed by the gods into stone, and the people were released from dread.[1]

According to Polynesian myth, islanders are terrified of the Whiro, a ravening beast that hunts them by night.[2] In Australian myth, people keep guard "to give the warning if the whowie should appear in their camp."[3] The Quechua of northern Ecuador are afraid to leave their huts after sundown because of carnivorous spirits that might attack them. In Africa, cannibalistic ghosts assume the form of "predators or dangerous animals" to kill anyone who strays away from home after the sun goes down.[4] In a Brule Sioux myth, people are afraid of the water monster Uncegila.[5]

If myths are the language of the soul, then the soul speaking to us is anxious and fearful, haunted by the dreadful prospect of being killed and eaten by voracious predators. Bear in mind that these myths were created by humans who by this time in history were armed with lethal weapons. Imagine, if you can, the terror felt by our Paleolithic ancestors—who were armed with only innate fear reactions and cunning, when "the terror of being ripped apart and devoured was never farther away than the darkness beyond the campfire's warmth." The original trauma—not a single event but a long-standing condition—was brought on by living in an environment where one continuously feared "being hunted by animals, and eaten."[6]

Fear is often regarded as a negative emotion, as something to be avoided and to be ashamed about. But in the Pleistocene it was the key to survival. It was also the basis, I believe, of storytelling and myth-making. The fear system hardwired into the primate line provided early humans with behaviors that could be used to act out stories that could not be verbally narrated. How this all came about will be explained in the next two chapters. First, let us take a close look at our life-sustaining fear system, at its neurochemical features, at the things that trigger its defensive reactions, and at how these reactions help us avoid violent death. The ancient Greeks of Sparta seemed to have understood this, for in the heart of their city they built a temple dedicated to fear.[7]

THE GIFT OF FEAR

When primates climbed down from the trees, they entered a landscape filled with large and skilled killers. They also entered a race to evolve survival skills as fast as their predators were evolving hunting skills. Natural selection favored any human trait or ability that reduced the chance of being killed so that one's genes could be passed on through generations. Our ancient ancestors survived only because they evolved the ability to recognize which animals to fear, when to fear them, and how to react to them. This "knowledge" was earned the hard way, through millions of years of being hunted and eaten.

There is no mistaking the grimace of fear in other primates because it is hardwired into us as well. Curiously, the expression of fear is not all that different from the expression of aggression—mouth open, teeth exposed, and so on. The face of fear is depicted throughout world art, though it is sometimes reassuringly interpreted as expressing "concern" or "pain." *Sloth 92/ Dreamstime.com.*

"Fear" is not a simple emotion but a rather complex neural-chemical system that unfolds in stages. A potential danger must first be detected by one or more of the senses and then interpreted or identified as a danger. A predator can evoke any of several "emotions" depending on the context: alertness, concern, wariness, uneasiness, apprehension, anxiety, distress, alarm, horror, terror, or panic. The term *fear* can be used to cover this spectrum or to refer to just those feelings that are intense enough to trigger stereotypical defense reactions (freeze, flight, fight, appeasement).

Once tripped, the neural-chemical system galvanizes the resources of the brain and body to deal with the potentially life-threatening situation. Electrical/chemical functions send information from the sense organ(s) to the thalamus and then to the amygdala, where the information is further assessed and endowed with emotion (the amygdala is a relatively small brain area located deep inside the middle part of the temporal lobe, and is a very old structure found in all mammalian brains). The amygdala is good at assessing stimuli because it is the storehouse of memories of past encounters with dangerous things and events.

The amygdala sends out an alert to the central and autonomic nervous systems that triggers the release of certain stress hormones from the pituitary and adrenal glands (such as adrenaline) and also activates specific defense reactions (I call them "survival strategies"). Breathing and heart rate increase, blood pressure goes up, adrenalin is secreted, energy stores are mobilized in the liver and released in the bloodstream, sweat glands secrete, pupils dilate, blood is redistributed from the internal organs to the large muscles and the brain—all to prepare the body "to fight like a demon or run like hell."[8] This process is important because it helps explain why we often find frightening stories about dangerous animals *pleasurable*. More on this later.

Anybody who has been really scared knows that the body goes through these powerful changes almost instantaneously. When suddenly attacked, we don't have time to think things through. This was the optimal design for creatures trying to survive in a predator-rich environment. But to survive, it is not enough that we feel fear. The fear must be translated into appropriate *behaviors*. These same defensive/survival behaviors can be found throughout the mammal class since natural selection determined them to be the most successful ways for a prey animal to survive a confrontation with a predator.[9] In this sense, "fear" is indistinguishable from the repertoire of defensive or protective behaviors triggered by threat or danger. In a very real sense, the defensive repertoire of an animal "forms a system as vital as its cardiovascular or reproductive system."[10]

PART 1: TRIGGERS OF FEAR

How did our ancestors know which animals to fear? Did they learn from experience? Or were they blessed with some sort of inherited memory of specific predators?

Experience certainly taught hard lessons, but evolution also helped by priming our species to react anxiously or fearfully *not* to specific predators but to a *general set* of physical stimuli (or "releasers") closely associated with dangerous animals. As Hans Kruuk puts it, "[W]e have a strong instinctive response to the killer attributes of large predators."[11]

Even newborn chicks have a physiological sensitivity to specific environmental stimuli. They will scurry in fright when a cardboard cutout of a hawk that has been placed on a string moves across a barnyard. But if the cutout is made to go backward or if the shape is changed to resemble a non-predatory bird, the chicks show no fear. The chicks have been programmed by evolution to fear a certain *shape* and *trajectory of motion* rather than a specific predator.

What were the predator features that triggered the fear reaction of our ancestors? And why should we care? These stimuli are important to us because Paleolithic storytellers likely used them as "stage props" to enact "tales" about predators. The same stimuli are used even today by storytellers to tell their frightening tales.

THE PREDATOR FACE

Almost all predators (save raptors) attack headfirst. And even in the case of raptors, which attack with legs extended, the head—with its glaring yellow eyes and sharp curved beak—is prominently framed by extended talons. From the perspective of the terrified victim, it must seem as if the wings grow from the raptor's head. This may explain the Native American monster called the Flying Head. For ancient primates and for us today, the most powerful signal of possible annihilation is a dangerous predator staring us straight in the face.

The Staring Eye

Although the face of the attacking predator is probably experienced holistically, evolution has primed us to fear certain features of it, most crucially, "a fixed and direct stare."[12] The reason is simple: before attacking, predators stare at their prey. In the Pleistocene, being stared at by an animal was a strong indication that one was being hunted.[13] As a result, "fear of two staring eyes is widespread throughout the animal kingdom."[14]

Certain kinds of predator eyes are particularly alarming to humans. Leopards, lions, cheetahs, and jaguars have a layer of reflective cells on the back of the retina (the *tapetum lucidum*) that bounces light off the back of the eye and directs it forward to stimulate the retinal cells a second time. This feature allows these cats to hunt effectively at night (precisely the time when humans feel the most fear because they have the most to fear). The reflection gives the impression that the predator's eyes are actually sending out light to magically find its prey despite the darkness. Poet

We don't have to think twice to know this expression signals imminent attack. Humans have reported being frozen by the fear it evokes. Like other predators, the tiger is both feared and worshipped by those who must live with it. *Kitch Bain/Shutterstock.com.*

William Blake evoked this effect when he famously wrote "Tyger, tyger burning bright / in the forests of the night." In many European languages, the word for *dragon* suggests penetrating gaze or sharp-sightedness. "In paintings of dragons worldwide, the eyes are most typically wide open, bright, fiery, and large."[15] In a Chinese folktale, a horrible monster bars the way of a traveler. "Its awful eyes popped out like a grasshopper's or a crab's. The staring eyes were bright and shining like torches."[16]

Intriguingly, some prey species have coopted this fear stimulus to intimidate their predators! Moths, for example, have evolved large "eyespots" on their wings to scare off birds (I use a tethered balloon with large eyespots on it to scare off birds from raiding my raspberry patch.) Other prey species have also evolved "terrifying masks" to bluff or trick the animals that prey on them.[17] Of course, these prey species didn't go about acquiring these fear stimuli consciously. The acquisition was the result of natural selection. When these traits appeared accidentally within members of a prey species as a result, let's say, of mutation, these traits imbued the members with a slightly better chance of deterring predators, and so of passing on the mutant genes that accounted for the appearance of the traits. As a result of this process, some prey species managed to coopt the fear-inducing traits of aggressive predator species as a survival strategy. The very signs that warned and frightened them came to protect them. From a mythic perspective, the prey could be seen as *imitating* and *mocking* the predator.

Our ancestors were required by circumstances to be sharp observers of nature. It is not expecting too much of them to assume that they noticed that weak and vulnerable creatures were defensively assuming a predator trait to appear more menacing than they were. There, before their eyes, fear triggers were being *imitated to enhance survival*. With more conscious intent, our ancestors may have done the same thing when they incorporated fear triggers into storytelling.

Even today, one of the most effective devices in developing countries for discouraging a predator from attacking from behind is to wear on the back of one's head a mask with exaggerated wide eyes.[18] Even today, in Africa, the typical response to a greeting from a stranger is "I see you."

Naturally occurring examples of prey species coopting the traits of predators may have given early humans the idea to do the same, but now it was with conscious intent. In order to communicate about predators, to create narratives and stories about them, our distant ancestors would have had to imitate—however crudely—the essential features that define predators. In essence, they were coopting the fear-inducing traits of predators to enhance their own survival.

The Predator Mouth

The eyes merely guide the predator to the prey. It is the *maw* that does the dirty work—rending, tearing, crunching, dismembering, and swallowing the prey. Even the big snakes—though they don't rend or tear—attack with their mouth to grip the prey before crushing and swallowing it. This is why the "blood-smeared mouth" is the organ most associated with violence.[19] The feature is a powerful fear trigger that figures prominently in mythic depictions of deadly powers, as in the Chinese folktale "The Horse Mountain Ghost," in which the ghost's "horrible mouth stretched from ear to ear and looked like a bowl of blood. Protruding from this foul orifice were rows and rows of very long and pointed teeth."[20]

Our ancient ancestors probably did not dread "death" or "mortality" in the abstract sense but rather the existential fact of being torn apart and eaten. This dread is expressed in the many myths that vividly describe the stomach contents of monstrous predators. In an Australian myth, the evil Cheeroonear vomits up what remained of the humans he recently ate—"heads and feet of infants that had been swallowed whole." Villagers gather around the spot and "to their horror they saw skulls and feet and hands of babies. Before them was the solution of the disappearance of their people."[21] As nature writer David Quammen explains in *Monster of God*, "[T]he worms of the graveyard don't scare us the way

Over a couple million years, our ancestors saw members of their species, as well as other animals, disappear into the maw of the predator. Great snakes can swallow a creature as big as a
wildebeest. Crocodiles tear apart their prey and swallow large chunks of it. Some big fish can
ingest a human in one swallow. No doubt there were rare times when someone managed to
escape from the predator's mouth and lived to create a story about the miracle. *OlivesJean
Michel/Shutterstock.com.*

the crocodiles of East Alligator River do. We can contemplate being
nightcrawler food without feeling all manner of primordial dread.... It
pales in comparison with the experience of ... being prey."[22] It is only
when in the mouth of a predator that we are compelled to feel, as a survivor of a crocodile "death roll" put it, the "total terror ... of a terrible
death."[23]

The Iroquois expressed this fear through the surreal image of the
Flying Head. According to one story, in days long past, humans were
preyed upon by a "scowling, snarling head without a body," four times

the size of a human. Two huge wings grew from its cheeks, and with these wings the head could soar and dive in pursuit of food. Its mouth was full of "huge, piercing fangs with which it seized and devoured its prey. And everything was prey to this monster, every living being, including people."[24]

The predator face—with its teeth and maw—was imitated in all kinds of cultural productions, from masks worn at ceremonies to architectural elements of buildings. Even when used to "protect" buildings (such as temples) from intruders, such images must have activated at some level the hardwired visceral fear of dying by carnivore. *aaleksander/Shutterstock.com.*

The Hopi have a strikingly similar story about a girl who, crazed by the taste of her own blood, devours *herself* until only her head is left, at which point the disembodied head attacks village after village, devouring everyone in them.[25] In the Middle Ages, the elemental horror of the predator found expression in the gaping maw of Hell's Mouth, which swallowed sinners by the cartload. As classicist Walter Burkert suggests, almost every abyss or yawning gap "is a memorable projection of anxieties linked to the image of devouring jaws."[26]

Even when death is regarded in a more spiritual way, it is often associated with being consumed by a predator. In Polynesia, for example, death is equated with being "devoured." "For when a person died it was customary to say he was eaten up by the gods, and this may have originated the belief in the common mind, which is apt to be extremely literal, that the souls of the dead were devoured by Miru."[27] In Greek mythology, Time, the universal devourer, is depicted as a giant python who, in the powerful words of the poet Ovid, closes its "envenomed jaws and little by little consume[s] all things in a lingering death."[28]

As psychologist Pascal Boyer suggests, our ancient ancestors saw so many creatures killed by predators that they likely viewed any dead body as being "the victim of a successful predation."[29]

Predator Teeth

The maw of the predator triggers fear not only because it swallows but because it chews. The shark is often seen as the ultimate predator because it has twenty-six upper teeth and twenty-four lower ones, and behind each of these are ranks of gleaming replacements, each a triangular serrated blade well shaped for "stabbing and slicing the tough hide of a sea lion or a seal."[30] Also, as I have noted, several big cats in the Pleistocene had not only sharp teeth but also enormous dagger-like tusks.

Exposed teeth trigger fear in all mammals, which then exploit this response to intimidate and frighten even members of their own species.

Though even human teeth "remember wolf," as William Golding put it in *The Inheritors*, human teeth don't have the same power to make us shudder as do the long, sharp, and often numerous teeth of animal carnivores. Research has shown that a stiletto shape devoid of context is enough to trigger a pang of fear. Warriors have often carried or worn the teeth of predators in order to acquire their killing power. *Lukasz Misiek/Shutterstock.com.*

Although this mythic creature is called a dragon, it illustrates the most salient attribute of almost all predators— numerous long pointed teeth. It is the feature always incorporated into any depiction or imitation of a predator or a monster. By their teeth we shall know them. *Joy Stein/ Shutterstock .com.*

Primates are especially intimidated by bared teeth.[31] To scare adversaries, baboons actually pull down their lower lips to fully expose their very long upper canines.[32] Early humans, being primates, would have reacted powerfully to the sight of teeth.

Even today, sharp, conical, jagged, and serrated shapes evoke in us more anxiety than rounded or curved shapes. Ethologist Irenaus Eibl-Eibesfeldt believes that this fear reaction reflects an "innate response to the tooth pattern of a predator's teeth."[33]

By using animal teeth and pointed stones, early storytellers probably exploited this innate response to conjure up a semblance of the predator during an enacted performance. Eventually, this fear trigger became a prominent feature of terror masks and of almost all mythic descriptions of predators and monsters.

As anthropologist David Gilmore notes, whatever the peculiar anatomical features of a given monster, the creature is always depicted as having a cavernous mouth brimming with fearsome teeth or fangs. (Just think of the double-mouthed creature in Ridley Scott's sci-fi film *Alien*.) "These anatomical assets are used to rip and tear humans, to bite and rend and devour."[34] Remember what the dogs said to the hero twins of the *Popol Vuh*: "Now we shall destroy you, now you shall feel the teeth of our mouths; we shall devour you."[35] No wonder that in some myths, predators are referred to as "the ancients who tear and rend."

Whatever else they may symbolize, teeth evoke our primal fear of dying by carnivore.

The Predator Tongue

Fear is also triggered at the sight of a tongue—especially when it is depicted in the shape of a dagger or shark tooth.

In Russian folktales, the witch Baba-Yaga catches her victims with her tongue.[36] The Hindu goddess Kali is often depicted with her saber-shaped tongue extended to lick up the blood of her victims. In Polyne-

The extended pinkish tongue is a fear trigger because it exposes the teeth and throat of the mammalian predator and is used to lick up blood. *James Laurie/Shutterstock.com.*

sian culture, warriors stick out their tongues to frighten the enemy. The deadly striking and jabbing weapon of the Maori—the *taiaha*—has at one end two faces with four large shell eyes and long, carved protruding tongues.[37]

Our ancient ancestors were primed by evolution to associate these features with a potential threat to their lives. To feel fear, they did not have to identify the specific kind of animal—they simply had to notice any of these physical features: staring eyes, an open mouth, flashing sharp teeth, a lolling tongue—these all spelled "danger," "predator." One Hawaiian myth conjures up all these fear triggers in its depiction of a monster who confronts a young girl in the jungle: "[Ku-aha-ilo's] eyes flashed and he opened his mouth. His tongue was thrusting viciously from side to side. His red mouth was like the pit of Pele. His teeth were gnashing, his tail lashing. Hiilei stood paralyzed by fear."[38]

More than any other tribal culture, the Maori exploited the extended tongue to evoke fear in their enemies and galvanize themselves to kill them with the ruthlessness of a predator. Maori warriors even tattooed dribble lines around their mouths to simulate dripping blood. Imitating the predator can transform one into a "predator." *Sherpe/Shutterstock.com.*

Since ancestral humans were primed to associate these physical features with dangerous animals, it would have been quite natural for them to use these features to mimic or imitate the appearance of predators during gestural communication and enacted storytelling. In essence, our language-less ancient ancestors made props of the very features that frightened them. As moths did with eyespots, our distant forebears likely appropriated features of the predator to counter the predator.

The predator face, however, does not exhaust the natural fear triggers that early storytellers would have been able to exploit.

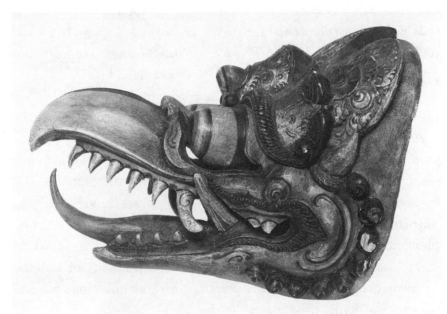

This powerful tribal mask was used in African ceremonies to conjure a mythic bird predator god. This mythic monster has a beak resembling that of *Titanis*, but its teeth in profile conjure up the image of a crocodile. One can surmise the depth of fear that engendered such a grotesque composite of fear triggers. *CreativeHQ/Shutterstock.com*.

FEAR OF MENACING MOVEMENTS

The face of the predator is not always the first thing that *alerts* the prey to danger. Although predators usually attack headfirst, they don't always attack head-on. Many spring from ambush, surprising the prey from behind. The prey has a split second to react in the right way to the *motion* and *trajectory* of the predator as it attacks.

Natural selection has programmed prey species to interpret certain movements as threatening. Any sudden motion, especially when the moving agent (or object) is close not only startles but frightens. So, too, do movement trajectories that promise a direct encounter between prey and predator. Prey animals are more afraid of creatures coming directly at them than those approaching obliquely on a "miss" trajectory. Toddlers are even afraid of a toy animal when it approaches them in a stalking motion. Infants become tense when a shadow grows larger and relax when it grows smaller. The phrase "danger looms" captures our primal fear of anything that quickly fills our visual field.[39]

One scholar has suggested that the apparently innate fear that primates have of snakes is really an "innate fear of intense, sudden or unexpected movement."[40] Fear researcher Isaac Marks also notes that the writhing and rearing motions of snakes provoke terror even in young children who have never seen a snake or known the word. In one instance, the snakelike form and movement of waving fronds of seaweed were enough to throw a child into a panic.[41] In Greek mythology, Tisiphone scares to death two enemies simply by throwing two snakes on them: "The reptiles landed and glided over the breasts of Ino and Athamas, breathing their noxious breath . . . without inflicting a physical wound. The deadly effect was felt in the mind."[42]

An intense awareness of the threatening movements of predators prepared the ground for the earliest form of storytelling—storytelling that was acted out. To conjure images of predators, storytellers would have mimicked not only their essential features but also the way they moved. Once again, a fear stimulus—in this case menacing motion—was exploited by early humans to manage their fear of predators.

FEAR OF BLOOD

When carnivores kill, they create an awful lot of blood (only the big snakes swallow the prey whole). The prey is torn open and pulled apart, with its intestines, heart, lungs, glands, and other soft tissue spilled on the ground until devoured or carried off.

At a kill site, blood and tissue cover the ground and cake the face and fur of the feeding predators. Blood also marks the trails away from the site and coats the body parts left uneaten. The scent of blood saturates the air and is constantly refreshed by new kills.

Given the incredible number of animals that died in the Pleistocene, our ancient ancestors must have seen and smelled an awful lot of blood—some of it, of course, their own. It has been suggested that saber-toothed cats used their long teeth to stab their victims so they would eventually bleed to death.[43]

Although the blood at a crocodile kill site is quickly washed away, a croc attack is still a blood-soaked event. Crocs repeatedly toss the prey into the air to chomp on different parts of it, or they thrash the body back and forth or smash it against the bank to dismember it. It takes only a few minutes for a croc to break down even the largest mammals into swallowable chunks. During this thrashing and churning, blood and tissue fly everywhere. It would be hard even for Hollywood special-effects artists to make it look more gruesome.

Myths drip with blood—or flow with it, as in the *Popol Vuh*, where the hero twins must cross a "river of blood."[44] The Roman poet Ovid often took particular delight in highlighting the sanguinary aspects of the violence found in many of his myths. In one, the snapping jaws of a wolf are described as "horribly smeared with foam and with clotted blood, while his glaring eyes were ablaze with a fiery glow.... He had to destroy the whole of the herd and to get his teeth into every animal.... Blood streamed on the beach, in the shallow waves, in the swamp where the bellows of pain still echoes.... He was rabid with blood's sweet taste."[45]

Natural selection has primed us to react powerfully not only to the sight of blood but also to the color red. Red is the primary color with the longest wavelength perceptible to the human retina. We had to notice and react to this color when it flowed from our bodies. No wonder that red was the first color (in the form of ocher, a red-colored ore used as a pigment) consistently used for body decoration and religious worship, including burial rites. In many animal species, red is a signal of high testosterone levels and so is associated with strength and dominance. In sports, athletes who wear red are more victorious than those who wear other colors. We view the color as a symbol of life and danger, and we emotionally associate it with cruelty, fire, ferocity, anger, excitement, and intense energy.[46] Use of the color red as a warning sign is not a mere "cultural construction" or an arbitrary or accidental decision but an expression of an inherited sensitivity to the color of life and death.

That mythmakers were quite aware of the peculiar power of red to evoke fear is made clear by a myth of the Dogon people (Africa). When the Jackal first sees a red ant, he is so struck by the color that he borrows the "costume" from the ant so he can wear it to his father's funeral. But when he appears in it, "everyone ran away in fright." This fear reaction delighted the Jackal, so he hid the costume from the ant. But a bird found it and, thinking it was raw meat, carried it off. The bird hid the red costume in a tree. There it was found by a female spirit, "one of the little red people," who took the costume and wore it into the village. "Terrified, all the men ran away. This gave the woman power over the men, and she exercised it."[47]

The voracious, dagger-tongued goddess Kali is often shown with blood dripping from her mouth. The Celtic god Cuchulainn is luridly described as bathed in a "red mist, like a fog of vaporized blood," with "a column of thick dark red blood sprouting high into the air from the center of his crown." "His mouth opened huge and red, gaping back to his throat's edge and his jaw gnashed together in bites that would kill a beast."[48] In Hindu myth, red is the favorite color of the ancient tiger god.[49] In a Yoruba myth, the teeth of the leopard Ajanuku "are red in color," and its eyes "turn a deep, deep, and a bright, bright red."[50]

Maori warriors, who thrust their tongue out to intimidate their enemies, tattoo their mouth and chin to suggest blood dripping from the lips, called "dribble lines."[51] This practice is another example of a natural fear stimulus being coopted and made into a defense mechanism that deters aggression and enhances survival. As Colonel Kurtz of *Apocalypse Now* would have understood, Maori warriors made fear their friend.

FEAR OF BONES

Predators create more than blood—they create bones. In the *Popol Vuh*, the crocodile god Tucumbalam breaks and mangles the bones of its victims and "ground(s) and crumble(s) their bones."[52]

For several million years, our ancestors trekked through a landscape littered with the skeletal remains of animals. Not all of these creatures had died violently, of course, but our ancestors were not forensic scientists and would not have been able to tell the difference, since all bones eventually would have been gnawed, crunched, and scattered by scavengers. Every disarticulated skeleton would have reminded our ancestors of the terrible power of the predator to transform a living creature into lifeless shapes and shards. The animal predator was the first great Master of Metamorphosis.

Bear in mind that many of these bones would have been those of *predators*. The skull of a large carnivore is an impressive sight even to our eyes, but it must have been a chilling experience in the Pleistocene, when such skulls were massive, five to fifteen times the size of a *Homo* skull. And, of course, the skulls—devoid of flesh and life—would have been examined unhurriedly. A close scrutiny of the killing tools of a saber-toothed cat, of a cave lion, or of a cave bear must have been unnerving.

If the skulls and bones of run-of-the-mill Pleistocene predators were upsetting, imagine how our ancestors felt when they came across the massive skulls and skeletons of *extinct dinosaurs*—such as the remains of a pterosaur, which had a wingspan of up to forty feet—or an allosaur, a fifty-foot eating machine with bladelike, saw-edged teeth eight inches long riveted inside a six-foot-long skull that weighed almost a ton. Such "close encounters" with the remains of terrifying predators surely must have lit up the "fear neurons" of the *Homo erectus* amygdala, especially since *erectus* would have had no idea that these remains belonged to creatures long extinct. Even today, tribal people are terrified when they discover large bones because they believe that the bones belong to creatures that still exist.[53] It is also widely believed that bones house the vital force of the creature they come from and so have the potential to engender a "new life," a process dramatized in the popular dinosaur film *Jurassic Park*.[54]

The impact that dinosaur bones had on the human imagination has been illuminated by geo-mythologist Adrienne Mayor. In *The First*

Predators, like the hyenas pictured, are the greatest magicians, transforming living creatures into piles of bloody bones. The transformation is a noisy business and a messy one, littering the landscape with harsh reminders of what it means to die by carnivore. *p.Schwarz/Shutterstock.com.*

Our ancestors were not hunted and eaten by Jurassic dinosaurs, but in a sense they lived among them. Wandering humans must have encountered all kinds of fossil bones, including those belonging to such terrifying prehuman predators as *Tyrannosaurus rex*. Our ancestors would have had no way of knowing that the monstrous skulls filled with nine-inch teeth belonged to predators long extinct. *RodBeverly/Shutterstock.com.*

Fossil Hunters: Paleontology in Greek and Roman Times and *Fossil Legends of the First Americans*, Mayor argues that the discovery of fossilized dinosaur bones often provoked people—people with modern brains—to create stories and myths about where the bones came from and what they signified. For example, the bones of dinosaurs gave rise to Lakota myths about the monster Unktehi. In one myth, the bones of Beaver were used to counteract the menace posed by monster bones.[55] What we see in this myth (and in many others cited in Mayor's two books on fossil legends) is an attempt by mythmakers to assuage fear through storytelling. As we shall see, fear management was the primordial function of storytelling in the Paleolithic, and for good reason.

One can surmise that if modern humans felt the need to create comforting stories about frightfully large bones and menacing skulls, so, too, did our Paleolithic ancestors. Primordial storytellers likely used bones and skulls as props to conjure up the image of the animal that they were acting out. Perhaps some *comfort* was to be found in the skull of a *dead* predator, whatever the story it was being used to enact.

FEAR OF SOUNDS

The Pleistocene environment is easier to "see" than to "hear," but that shouldn't make us deaf to the fact that many of the sounds on the savanna would have chilled the blood of our distant ancestors, as they chill our blood today. Though it hardly needs to be said, we are deeply disturbed when we hear creatures "screaming in agony or panic."[56]

All prey animals emit alarm and distress calls. Vervet monkeys, for example, have at least four distinctive alarm calls for different types of predators, each call indicating the kind of predator that threatens, and each call releasing the appropriate defensive behavior—scampering up the tree, scampering down the tree, staying put, and so on.[57] Our ancestors must have heard such cries and calls all the time. They could not have afforded to simply tune them out because what menaced other animals menaced humans, too. This survival wisdom is explicitly encoded in an Australian myth about brothers who "heard the warning notes of birds as they stirred in the bushes and trees, and they knew that this was a sign of danger."[58] So, even when not in immediate danger, our ancestors would have been made anxious by the frightening sounds made by the animals around them.

Some scholars believe that alarm calls contributed to the emergence of speech. Hominids and early humans were under a survival imperative to develop communication skills that enabled them to better avoid and fend off attacks from carnivores. "It is the ability to warn others, hail others, and keep together by exchanging sounds that protected hominids. Anatomically modern human speech may not be solely a result of predation, but there is little question that vocal communication is a result of predation and is used as a protective tool by all primates, including hominids."[59]

This possibility has significant implications for understanding the emergence of storytelling. In the words of Hans Kruuk, one of the functions of "art and especially literature" is to "send alarm signals to our conspecifics. . . . These alarm signals have been embellished and magnified, and they have acquired their own significance and started their own life, but in their roots the original function can still be discerned, and it still serves to warn us."[60] Put another way, primordial storytelling was a way for distressed humans to manage their fear of dangerous predators.

Ancient humans would have been frightened not only by warning and distress cries but by the noises made by predators during the kill. To freeze their prey, many raptors emit a "sonic shrill" when coming in for the kill.[61] Big cats make a "loud and frightening noise" when they lunge at their prey. In most cases, "the noise of the predator is very intense."[62] Only big snakes and reptiles strike silently, although they make noise as their movements disturb vegetation or water. In response to the sounds emitted or made by dangerous animals, natural selection has wired into humans and other primates what fear specialist Isaac Marks calls "prepotent auditory triggers of fear."[63] This means that fear is automatically triggered by such sounds as roaring, flapping, hissing, and so on. It is reasonable to assume that these fear stimuli were used by the first storytellers to conjure up images of predators during the first fledgling attempts to depict and communicate about them. Once again, as with the other fear triggers, like eye spots, fearful sounds were coopted by the prey to enhance their survival.

The predator isn't the only one making noise during the kill—the animal being killed is hardly quiet. Some of them snort, some bellow, some bray, some screech, some bleat, some shriek, some scream, some squeal, and some wail, as they protest being clawed, bitten, eviscerated, and dismembered. Whatever the sound, there is no mistaking what it signifies—the terror and agony of violent death.

Although predators have evolved techniques for stifling these noises, the kill sometimes takes much longer than the predator would like, and the agonized sounds of violent death fill the air. Crocodiles usually kill as silently and as efficiently as any predator on the planet, but not always. One croc attack on a baboon led to an ordeal that lasted almost an hour, with the baboon screeching at the top of his lungs for the entire time.[64] Its distress screams provoked an (unsuccessful) rescue attempt by members of his troop, which added their own shrieks and squeals to the drama of death being played out at the water's edge.

In one instance, two cheetahs took over forty-five minutes to finally subdue a bellowing and snorting wildebeest.[65] In another, a pride of lions took over an hour to kill a buffalo, despite the fact that a lioness had her jaws locked on his snout the entire time. Another lion attack on a Cape buffalo unfolded over seven hours, with members of the herd repeatedly trying to drive off the lions with noisy charges at them.[66] A man in East Africa screamed for help for fifteen minutes as he was literally being eaten alive.[67] No doubt many of our ancestors screamed their life away as well.

The big snakes kill so slowly that the prey has plenty of time to screech, howl, or bellow. Two primatologists were drawn to the kill site of a python by the screams of a baboon troop that was trying to frighten the snake into releasing another baboon.[68] Once again, the Roman poet Ovid shows his understanding of the fear triggers hardwired into the primate line: "From here a succession of crashes and howls could be heard, to the terror of neighboring farms, when a huge and sinister monster, a wolf, emerged from the marsh reeds. . . . Blood streamed on the beach, in the shallow waves, in the swamp where the bellows of pain still echoes."[69]

The agonized death of the prey animal does not end the ghastly sounds of predation. The kill site is filled with growls and snarls of pack predators as they tussle over the feeding order and as opportunistic scavengers try to drive off those already feeding. Hyenas are especially noisy, "with an enormous range of often very loud sounds . . . including Africa's most evocative sound, the 'whoop.'"[70] A big-game hunter has written of the hyena, "One has to hear them eating the bones of some carcass in the veld or hear them sniggering, giggling, moaning, shrieking, and screaming with 'laughter' to appreciate the horror that they can engender."[71]

Even when not killing and eating, predators emit a range of sounds that trigger fear. Big cats constantly howl and roar in order to warn competitors and to communicate with pride members. Predators also make aggressive noises when mating, fighting over mating partners, threatening competitors, and battling for status, with some confrontations taking place over several hours. Male lions typically let rip a series of twenty to twenty-five roars at a time, while females roar about fifteen times.[72] The roar of a male lion can be heard five miles away. Leopards emit a series of eight to ten rasping grunts that sound like someone sawing wood. Cheetahs can't roar, but they can moan.[73] Wild dogs bark, and hyenas howl and whoop. As one African poem says of the lion, "You whose roar frightens the dreams out of the heads of sleeping warriors!"[74]

Our ancestors must have *heard* predators more often than they actually saw them. Imagine the unnerving racket made by hundreds of noisy Pleistocene predators within a radius of a mile or so. This round-the-clock din of shrieks and howls and moans of an agonizing death surely kept our ancestors on edge every moment of their lives. Each growl, each panicked screech or bellow reminded them that they, too, were in danger of being transformed into bones and blood stains.

But this fear drove our distant ancestors to seek a remedy. Even before they were able to speak, they were able to imitate the sounds made by predators in order to communicate about, and enact stories about, the deadly powers they dreaded. Eventually, humans commanded these sounds to excite themselves into a killing frenzy and to transform themselves into the very predators they feared, as is shown in the *Popol Vuh*: whenever a stranger or two came into view, "the tribal leaders began to shout on the mountain-tops, howling like a coyote, screaming like a mountain cat, imitating the roaring of the puma and jaguar." The people know what this means: "what they want is to make an end of us."[75]

FEAR OF SIGNS

The first commandment of Pleistocene prey must have been: "Be thou aware of the predator!" Survival depended on detecting any cue or sign that a predator was nearby. Perhaps it was the "redemptive" value of sign reading that led to the belief that "divination"—the interpretation of signs—was a "divine activity."[76]

Some signs—such as the ones we've been examining—automatically trigger fear because they are closely associated with predators. But other signs are not as clear-cut. To survive, early humans had to *learn* to interpret such subtle signs as slither or claw prints, feeding remains, disturbed vegetation, excrement, tufts of hair, feathers, odors, spittle, scratches and rubbings, diggings, nests, and so on. When they were in doubt about the sign, our ancestors probably did the smart thing—they assumed that a dangerous animal was present because if it wasn't, nothing was lost, but if it was, a lot was gained.

The evolutionary imperative to be aware of predator signs meant that our ancestors had to have predators on the brain, even to the point of assuming their presence when none could be seen. This imperative had a couple of important effects.

First, it proliferated "predators" as a *felt*, if not always perceived, phenomenon. Certain signs alone would have been enough to make our ancestors feel endangered. This effect increased the overall amount of fear that permeated the minds and souls of our forbears. The more fear, the greater the need to manage—control, direct, assuage—the fear. Storytelling emerged in part to perform this fear-management function.

The second effect of the evolutionary imperative was to select for humans who were able to *imagine an image of the predator* merely on the basis of signs. In other words, the Pleistocene environment selected for humans able to conjure up in their mind's eye a representation of a "predator" when no predator was seen or heard.

Moreover, this ability to imagine an unseen or absent predator was crucial to the development of mimetic storytelling. To communicate information about a predator, an ancient storyteller would have imitated the signs, sounds, and behaviors of the predator, using signs that would conjure up in the minds of onlookers a memory image of an actual predator. Those humans would have had a better chance of surviving and passing along their genes to future generations.

This mental feat sounds absurdly elemental to us now, but it was a hard-earned cognitive development for our ancestors, enabling them to manage their fear of the dangerous animals that hunted and ate them for millions of years. Within the storytelling circle, the "predator," as well as the disturbing emotions triggered by it, could be symbolically controlled.

FEAR OF DARKNESS AND NIGHT

In a myth of the Miwok Indians, a group of warriors come to the edge of the Land of Darkness. "'This blackness is frightful,' they said. 'This land is darker than dark. . . . We will not go down there.'"[77] In the *Popol Vuh*, the first people await the coming of the day with "anxiety in their hearts and stomachs." They begin to cry when they cannot see the sunrise. But then the sun came up, and everyone is happy, "and all turned their eyes to where the sun was rising."[78]

When adults are asked by researchers to recall their earliest fears, they respond "dread of darkness."[79] If fear of the dark "is a universal human characteristic,"[80] as psychotherapist Anthony Stevens believes, what I've said about our ancestors' experience with Pleistocene predators could explain why. While humans find it hard to see in the dark, and so are more vulnerable, many predators see better in it and hunt precisely when their prey are visually handicapped. In ancient times, lions, leopards, and hyenas must have turned the grasslands and woodlands into killing fields at night (the big snakes hunt all the time). Even today, humans are chilled by the sight of "a pride of lions silhouetted in the dusk, padding off in single file as they begin their nighttime hunt."[81] Both literally and figuratively, "night is peopled with all kinds of malignant beings."[82]

Perhaps the behavior of contemporary nonhuman primates gives an indication of what our ancestors may have done, and felt, eons ago. As night descends, primates (save for gorillas) look for safety in the trees, where they build their beds, sequestering the young in the highest branches. Once ensconced, the adults engage in group drumming and vocalization. English professor Dudley Young, in his provocative book *Origins of the Sacred*, suggests that this behavior is an effort to overcome their fear of the creeping darkness. That is, their ritualistic drumming and shouting are forms of fear management, reassuring the group of its unity and perhaps frightening away lurking predators.[83] Remnants of this primordial fear-management strategy can be found in African Bantu night drumming, the Catholic Vespers and Angelus, the Protestant Evensong, "Taps," and prayers at bedtime designed to "protect us from the perils and dangers of this night."[84]

In our own time, fully armed Masai lion hunters are afraid of the dark and will not sleep on the Serengeti Plain without being surrounded by fires. But even fire's protective magic is uncertain, as the man-eaters of Tsavo made clear (1898). They often ate their victims within the glow of the bonfires meant to scare them off.[85] Without weapons and the ability to control fire (an achievement that took over a million years), our savanna-dwelling early ancestors were as vulnerable at night as it was possible to be.

In myth, shadows are often associated with the perils of darkness and night. In some cultures, sorcerers are said to kill their quarry by conjuring a night-shadow spirit, often a dead relative of the victim. Some sorcerers claim to be able to carry off the victim's soul by biting the person's shadow. The association between darkness and death is found in all cultures.[86]

Darkness also provides a congenial milieu for the nurturing of created, imaginary terrors. "In the absence of sharp visual details and with the ability to move uncurtailed, the mind is free to conjure up images . . . upon the slenderest perceptual cues."[87] It is at night when the natural opiates of the human brain are at their highest and prime us to imagine monsters and predators that are not there and could never have existed.[88] There is an account of the panic caused in an Australian village when, in the middle of the night, someone cried out "*kurdaicha*!" the name of one of the many animal-human evil spirits inhabiting the aboriginal world. Frantically weeping men, women, and children rushed to a local mission building for protection from this invisible night stalker.[89]

I suspect that the earliest stories were enacted around a hearth fire at night, perhaps within the perennial darkness of a cave. As darkness fell, group members would have gathered together for safety, food sharing, and socializing. With the flames casting shadows on the trees or walls, storytellers would have been inspired to use various fear triggers to conjure up their life-preserving stories of predators, while real ones lurked just outside the glow of the flames. The setting would have imbued these performances with riveting and unforgettable power. Of course, this cannot be known for sure, but we do know that it was in such dark and remote sites that later humans took extraordinary pains to paint their "stories" about the animals they hunted, worshipped, and feared. And even today it is within a darkened theater that we most successfully evoke the primordial fears of the Pleistocene.

PART 2: SURVIVAL STRATEGIES AND DEFENSIVE BEHAVIORS

INTRODUCTION

Fear elicits defensive *behaviors* that animals can call upon to deal with danger. These behaviors are usually categorized as freezing, fleeing (escaping), fighting, and appeasing, although each category embraces a range of physical responses. These responses help animals not only to survive an attack but also to manage the fears associated with the attack. In engaging in these behaviors, animals are not only saving their bodies but also lessening the fear hormones coursing through their bodies. These behaviors, then, should be regarded as part of the repertoire of fear-management strategies that we evolved to keep our potent fears within healthful bounds.

I would further assert that fear stimuli and the survival strategies they triggered provided early humans with the essential elements for communicating about, and telling "stories" about, animal predators. Before the emergence of language, the first stories must have been acted out, and these enactments would have required the exploitation of the fear stimuli and of the emotions and reactions naturally evoked during an encounter with a real predator. What I'm suggesting is that story-telling extended into culture the survival and fear-management programs that were already wired into our brains and bodies.

FREEZING

When animals detect a predator, their first reaction is almost always to freeze to avoid being noticed and to gain time to focus their minds on the danger. Some animals can remain still for hours. Should the danger become imminently life threatening, the prey will break out of this strategy for another one—such as flight.[90]

Although it's not easy to remain immobile in frightening circumstances, often it is the best strategy because some predators—such as big cats—have a hard time picking out a stationary object and are evolutionarily primed to "chase" any agent moving rapidly away from them. In really terrifying situations, the prey animal may undergo extreme immobility, called the "death feint" or "terror paralysis." This is the state that overtakes prey animals when they are in the clutches of the predator, when the last recourse is to act and look dead. What is operating is a last-ditch bit of survival wisdom wired into the prey's neural chemistry by millions of years of evolution. To survive an attack from Wolverine, the crafty Beaver Man "pretend he's dead. Beaver Man is smart. He pretend he die."[91]

At some point in our evolution, we became able to consciously control this terror paralysis, or at least to mimic it. When attacked by a grizzly, for example, humans are able to force themselves, as Beaver Man did, to consciously "play dead" by falling to the ground, doubling up, covering one's head, and remaining motionless, even while being mauled and bitten. The definition of *willpower* is the ability to remain motionless while your scalp is being ripped off. Exactly when humans developed the ability to control this innate survival strategy is impossible to know for sure. What is clear is that the ability to control or "imitate" innate or reflexive behaviors is at the core of mimetic performance and storytelling.

FLEEING

Flight covers a range of behaviors that run the gamut from slowly backing up to running away like a bat outta hell. This is not a simple reflex. To know when, where, and how fast to move requires deep intuitive knowledge about the typical attack pattern of that specific kind of predator. Even though they possessed a less-than-modern-size brain, early humans, as several scholars have argued, must have possessed a considerable amount of "natural knowledge" about predator attack behavior.[92] They would have used this knowledge to counsel each other about the best ways to avoid and to escape from predators. At first, this counseling would have been done through mime and enacted performances, but eventually it was embedded in stories and myths—from folk and fairy tales to modern films.

FIGHTING

Fighting—or *defensive aggression*—covers a range of survival behaviors, some of which do not require that the prey animal actually engage in hand-to-claw combat. For instance, the purpose of a threat or defensive display of aggression is to deter the fear-provoking agent by bluffing a counterthreat. These displays may cause the predator to hesitate just long enough to allow the prey to escape, or they may actually frighten the predator from going any further. This is, in essence, the survival strategy that lies behind all those instances, cited earlier, in which animals and humans have appropriated predator threat-stimuli to ward off predators (eye spots, dribble lines, and so on). Early storytellers probably did the same thing to allay fear. They employed objects and colors to imitate the most frightening and defining features of animal predators. Before the evolution of spoken language, it was only by imitating predators that early humans could communicate about them to enhance survival.

The threat displays of early humans were probably not that different from those used by contemporary primates when faced with predators. Male baboons, for example, bare their very sharp teeth or rush at the predator, only to quickly withdraw before any physical encounter. Other apes break branches, pull up small trees, and thump their chest as if it were a drum.[93] Chimpanzees brandish sticks to "dispel fear."[94] It is tempting to find in these apparently instinctual primate behaviors a foreshadowing of the *power sticks*—the magic wands, the royal staffs, and so on—that humans have used to ward off and control all kinds of menacing and powerful forces. Early humans may have used leg or arm bones to the same effect. Animal bones would have been sturdier than branches, and, as we've seen, would have been freighted with powerful feelings and associations. Appropriating the bones of a *dead* carnivore to deter a living one might have had a consoling and empowering emotional effect.

Massing

For many prey animals, and certainly for humans, the most powerful threat display (or defensive posturing) is simply to band together in a group. I call this *massing* (which is not the same as *mobbing*, or group physical assault).

By massing together, individuals become, from the *predator's* point of view, a big beast with many heads, perhaps too many to take on. Research has shown that when attacking a large group of prey animals, "predators take longer to hunt and are less successful, showing more fear and hesitation in attacking."[95] Should the predator attack, the sudden fracturing of the massive "oneness" into many scampering parts often confuses the predator, preventing it from targeting any one individual in optimum time.[96] As Barbara Ehrenreich puts it, "Millennia of terror seem to have left us with another 'Darwinian algorithm': that in the face of danger, we need to cleave together, becoming a new, many-headed creature larger than our individual selves."[97]

Mobbing

When in a group, even grass-grazing ungulates occasionally take on predators to defend themselves. Primates can be particularly aggressive, and successful. For example, a group of apes sometimes charges predators using sticks, thorn bushes, and stones.[98] Capuchin monkeys mob threatening boas "quite viciously."[99] Baboons mob and chase cheetahs and jackals, and will attack—or counterattack—even lions and leopards.[100] Of the eleven documented instances where a leopard attacked a group of baboons, the leopard was killed four times.[101] (How many baboons were killed was not recorded.)

Our primate pride tempts us to overestimate the effectiveness of mobbing. While some predators are deterred by being mobbed, others stick to their agenda and kill the mobbers. This is why primates, when dealing with especially dangerous predators, mob "only at a distance, often for prolonged periods,"[102] and resort to this strategy less than one-fourth of the time.[103] Keep in mind that our Paleolithic ancestors for the most part were puny weaklings compared to present-day chimps, baboons, and gibbons.

The contagious bravery arising from group solidarity occasionally provokes a single member of the group to engage in an individual act of courage. In an experiment using a stuffed leopard, a single chimp picked up a stick, rushed at the "leopard," and whacked it. Then another chimp, aroused by this example, uprooted a small tree and did the same thing. One by one, all the members of the troop attacked the leopard, "screaming and hooting to keep up their collective adrenaline rush."[104] Each chimp became, in a way, a "hero." Had the stuffed leopard been real, one or more of the chimps might even have become (what we would call) a sacrificial martyr. What internal processes and forces provoke such behavior, and how might these relate to storytelling?

Let's begin with the "intoxication" arising from what Donna Hart and Robert Sussman call the "collective adrenaline rush." Fear unleashes adrenaline and other hormones that reduce pain, enhance tolerance of stress, stimulate the immune system, increase endurance, and generally endow the body with almost "magical" powers. Clearly, this natural opiate system evolved to enable animals to struggle or fight in life-threatening situations despite severe pain, fatigue, and blood loss. In short, fear energizes, making a creature feel *vital, alive,* and *powerful.* These feelings are intensified during collective defense—or mobbing— when one's own feelings are heightened by contagious reinforcement. In other words, we are rewarded for engaging in collective behavior by being flushed with pleasurable feelings of power and solidarity.[105]

The chemicals released by fear—whether the fear is real or imagined—not only give us a sense of potency; they induce an altered state of consciousness, sometimes involving visual and auditory hallucinations. As medical anthropologist Alondra Oubre explains, when neurons in the region of the temporal lobe are "hyper-excited" by messages from the amygdala—the site of emotions and *fear assessment*—they trigger the release of endorphins (natural opiates in the brain) that "induce a visceral state of euphoria."[106]

The euphoria of danger!

The presence in the blood of these euphoria-inducing chemicals helps explain why—once the dire threat has been survived—we suddenly experience joy, elation, even ecstasy—what Marina Warner calls the "high of surviving."[107] As Michael James Winkelman puts it, release from fear produces "a sense of great energy, which may be interpreted as light, pure god, or unitive feelings of reunion with the true self."[108] Safe in suburbs and high-rises, we can scarcely imagine the "survival high" felt by ancient humans after they fended off a pack of hyenas with nothing but sticks, stones, screams, and group solidarity, but this repeated experience may have had momentous consequences for such ritual behaviors as group dance and group storytelling.

The intense fear of predators ironically nurtured in our line, I believe, an *addictive desire* to experience *survival euphoria.* We literally got hooked on the feelings and emotions arising from the opioids released by fear and danger. Perhaps there is something in the primate genome that prepared us to become danger junkies. Sykes' monkeys have been observed deliberately antagonizing the very eagles that prey on them. Are they seeking excitement—the thrill of danger? Even certain ungulates have been known to

invite pursuit from predators, perhaps to relieve the tension of a threatening situation while still in control of it.[109]

Certainly we love to tempt fate in all kinds of life-threatening
ways—as when, for instance, we continually put ourselves at the mercy
of predators (as is seen in the 2005 documentary *Grizzly Man*, in which
Timothy Treadwell lived—and ultimately died—among the wild bears
of Alaska). One can see this desire in tribal initiation rites (especially
surrounding the shaman), in which simulated predator attacks are consciously exploited to induce ecstatic states of consciousness in initiates,
engendering a feeling of transfiguring "One-ness" with the group and its
values.[110] As Winkelman writes, "[O]pioids are specifically elicited by
situations of helplessness, which has survival value in improving
endurance and conserving energy in emergencies. Ritually induced
release of opioids is triggered by the terrifying experiences enacted by the
shaman." In short, the shaman conjures up, almost always through some
sort of performance of an attack by a predatory agent (actual or supernatural), a "horror scenario" designed to trigger the release of the ravishing emotions associated with an actual predator attack.[111]

The desire to experience the euphoric emotions associated with
predator attack encouraged the emergence of storytelling. Enacting
predators around the hearth fire was a way for our early ancestors to
recapture—in a safe though diluted way—the emotions that flooded
through them during an actual confrontation with a carnivore. In the
enactment, the "predator" would have been "driven off" or "killed,"
rekindling in the ritual participants the survival euphoria they felt
during the life-and-death struggle. These enactments had the additional
benefit of strengthening the emotional bonds so crucial to group survival in the Pleistocene.

Enacted confrontations with predators can be found in many cultural genres, from carnivals and circuses to novels and movies. In carnivals, a monster is defeated by joyous collective action—mobbing. As
Ehrenreich summarizes, many cultural events and rituals "allow us to

recapture the elemental potency of the group united against the beast."[112] In fiction after fiction, a "predator" of some kind pursues its human prey, only to be eventually killed (but not always), so that the audience members can experience "vicariously" both fear and relief from fear. The imago of the menacing animal predator is an archetype unfortunately ignored by both Campbell and Jung.

APPEASING

Appeasing, the last fear-management strategy (or defense reaction) is an intriguing one. Many animals, when they are threatened by a more dominant *group member*, attempt to defuse the danger by displaying some kind of subaltern, placating, mollifying, or assuaging behavior, something that says, "I am no threat."

Monkeys and apes appease each other by grooming, prostrating, lowering their eyes, and smiling in a peculiar way (sometimes called the "fear grin").[113] Canines and felines typically roll on their back, or bow their head and expose their throat. Humans do the same thing by falling to the ground, bowing the head, or kneeling. To stop aggression, Walter Burkert explains, "one has to be small and humble, *humilis*, which originally meant 'close to the soil.'"[114] The human repertoire of aggression-suppressing behaviors also includes spitting on oneself and tearing one's clothes, self-wounding, and touching what is feared (such as the Greek act of *hiketes*, or grabbing the knees of one's would-be killer). These behaviors put the powerful one at ease by showing that the supplicant is too powerless to pose a threat, or that he has already been attacked. Clearly, appeasement is not only a survival strategy but a fear-management strategy as well.

While appeasement behavior makes a lot of sense as a strategy for minimizing violence between members of the same group (who share the same interpretations of gestures), it would seem to be a suicidal way to turn off the "kill switch" of a hungry predator. But maybe not. Recall the discussion about "freezing" and "terror paralysis." As noted early, a potential victim can sometimes stay alive by playing dead or just remaining motionless. There are many real-life accounts of hikers and hunters deterring an attack by a dangerous carnivore by literally *prostrating* themselves to it. It's as if the victim were actually offering himself to the predator. Apparently, this sudden, *non-evasive* strategy disconcerts some chase-primed predators, "magically" turning off their chase-and-kill impulses. Once again, survival wisdom has been recorded in myth. According to an Aboriginal myth, it is said that all children are taught that if they should happen to be captured by a monster, "they should offer no resistance, because they have a better chance of escape."[115]

Since prostration is a natural response, it's reasonable to assume that our ancient ancestors used it when attacked by a predator—and lived to talk about it. Could this survival behavior—salvation through abasement—be the source of worshipful prostration before fearful supernatural agents? Intriguingly, the same pose used throughout the ancient Mediterranean cultures to indicate prayer—arms in the "stick 'em up" position—is the same pose we use to indicate submission and being unarmed.

There is another way to appease a predator. Give it what it wants—flesh. Baboon males engage in this ultimate form of predator appeasement by *sacrificing* themselves in the troop's defense. Other animals also offer themselves to the predator in defense of the group. Zebra stallions sometimes separate themselves from the herd to give the mares and foals a chance to escape from lions. This behavior may be related to the tactic often used by prey species to feign injury in order to lure the predator away from more vulnerable members of the group. This form of "submission" is called *deflection*.

Sometimes the group itself selects the member to be offered to the predator. In one remarkable instance, a Cape buffalo was literally offered by one of its own to appease a relentless pride of lions. According to two wildlife photographers who witnessed the event, the attack on the single buffalo had been going on for six hours, with the herd fending off the attacks on this one bull. Finally, another bull walked up to the injured animal and began to attack him too, "hitting him over and over on the side and locking horns with him, finally flipping him. . . . The attacking bull . . . gave him one more head butt on the ground. Then he turned his back on the injured bull, and left." Within moments, the lions killed the male as the herd watched.[116]

Could this impulse to appease a threatening agent through prostration or flesh offering be the seed of ritual blood sacrifice? I think so, and I will discuss this topic later.

One of the functions of early storytelling may have been to "appease" the predator through symbolic enactment of prostration or flesh sacrifice. Such enactments may have been the precursor of magic rituals meant to "fend off" or dissuade threatening agents. These enactments would have helped manage the group's collective fear of the predator by making them feel they had some control over the dangerous creatures stalking them.

CONCLUSION

For our ancient ancestors, the Pleistocene was a reign of terror, a never-ending assault by huge monsters, as in the film *Cloverfield*, during which time they knew that they were little more than "meat walking around on two legs."[117]

Famed American novelist Jack London (*White Fang, The Sea Wolf*) understood the dangers that beset primordial humanity and captured them powerfully in his imaginative novel of prehistoric humanity *Before Adam* (1906). The main character has inherited the "germ plasm" of an ancient ancestor that allows him to tap into the experience of primordial humanity. His dreams are filled with fear, "the fear that was rampant in the younger world...the fear that reigned supreme in that period known as the Mid-Pleistocene."[118] Like early humans, the main character wanders in his dreams through primeval forests as a "timid, hunted creature, starting at the least sound, frightened of my own shadow, keyed up, ever alert and vigilant, ready on the instant to dash away in mad flight for my life. For I was the prey of all manner of fierce life that dwelt in the forest, and it was in ecstasies of fear that I fled before the hunting monsters."[119]

The key to survival was being good at knowing which animals to fear, when to fear them, and how to react to them. Fear, in the Pleistocene, was not a "negative" emotion, as we moderns tend to deem it, but a "blessing." Without it, or with not enough of it, the *Homo* line might have suffered the same fate as *Australopithecus*—extinction by predator, whether the predator was an animal or a more dangerous primate.

But there is a dark side to this selection process, even in the Pleistocene. As evolution worked to make our species smarter, it also worked to make us even more anxious and fearful. Smarter brains would better remember past threats and better envision new and future ones. Fear, anxiety, and stress, if prolonged, can have pathological consequences, interfering with brain functions and even causing brain damage as a result of repeated and sustained doses of stress hormones.[120] It was good to feel fear, but it was also good *not to need* to feel fear, or to feel just the *right amount* for the situation. Fear had to be managed, not just felt.

As I see it, the "fear system" not only helps humans survive immediate physical threat but also helps them *manage* their fear. Every element of it—from predator detection through sign reading to predator appeasement—helps humans avoid, alleviate, or transcend this feeling. Even freezing at the first sight of a predator is a fear-management strategy, because it is a way to avoid the more intense fear of being attacked and chased. Similarly, mobbing transforms panic into power. The need to manage fear became more pressing as early humans developed the capacity—thanks to the evolution of the brain—to *imagine* "predators" that were even more awesome than the ones that actually ate their flesh—*monstrous* predators with supernatural powers (the "tragedy of cognition"). It was the need to manage fear that drove the emergence of storytelling.

Storytelling was a cultural adaptation that grew from, and continued the work of, the innate fear system. Like this system, mimetic storytelling helped early humans manage their fears of being consumed by predators by using the elements of that system—fear stimuli and survival behaviors—to enact stories about predators—stories that informed, warmed, consoled, and inspired.

Chapter 4

Performing the Predator
Mimetic Storytelling in the Paleolithic

INTRODUCTION

Artist and philosopher Nancy Aiken points out that at some point in the distant past, our ancient ancestors discovered "that they could reliably and consistently control the emotions, and, thereby the actions of others of their kind by evoking the releasing effects of biologically relevant stimuli."[1] Those biologically relevant stimuli are the fear triggers we have just examined. In other words, our ancient ancestors learned that they could use symbolic images—bones, skulls, teeth, stones that resemble claws—to trigger, to evoke, the feelings and emotions hardwired by evolution into the primate line. This realization—no doubt emerging over an expanse of time—was the foundation of storytelling. We can never know for sure exactly when the first stories were told, but there are good reasons for believing that rudimentary stories were being told *before* our line had developed the power of grammatical speech. These stories would have been acted out by exploiting the fear triggers that enabled our ancestors to detect and to defensively react to the predators that menaced them every moment of every day. The essential elements of such an ancient enacted performance can be inferred from a tale of the African Baganda people.

A cow is running from a lion when it meets a shaman-Trickster figure, who assures the cow that he has the power to save it from the lion.

The shaman-Trickster secures a red flower that is shaped like the heart of an animal, puts milk into a pot, and finally puts into another pot some blood from the cow. When the lion appears, the shaman dashes the pot of blood on the lion's breast, saying, "I have killed you. Isn't this your blood?" Then he strikes the lion with the flower, shouting, "Isn't this your heart? I have killed you." Finally, he bashes the lion over the head with the pot of milk, saying, "Let me crush in your head and brains, and finish you off." This performance is so convincing that the lion— thinking itself injured—runs away in terror.[2]

The lion has been terrified by fabricated *imitations* of its blood, heart, and brains. The Trickster-performer has used symbols to create a powerful mimetic performance—an enacted story—that cons the lion into feeling fear. In this myth, the predator is driven off not by weapons or mob action but by a clever manipulation of fear triggers that help to *enact a story* that the lion does not know *is* merely a story.

But the Baranda do. What are they saying to themselves in this myth? On the simplest level, the myth teaches or reminds people that predators *can* be deflected through blood and meat offerings, and that they *can* be discouraged by the sight of a noisy and aggressive human. But a more intriguing message can be found here.

This story is also about the power of storytelling to drive off not actual predators but the *fear* of actual predators. The same fear stimuli that frighten humans are manipulated by the shaman-storyteller to frighten the lion, thus reversing the normal flow of fear. In real life, of course, lions wallow in blood, hearts, and brains. It is only in a story— through the power of metaphor and imitation—that "lions" can be frightened by such things or imagined to be.

This tale reflects the essence of one of my central claims. I contend that our ancient ancestors—using vocalizations and imitative behaviors—were able to tell stories about dangerous beasts even before the evolution of modern language. This rudimentary form of storytelling evolved as a cultural survival tool because it enabled our ancestors not only to communicate important information about predators but to mitigate, redirect, and control their fear of them. It very well may have been in the early Paleolithic, almost two million years ago, that the archetype of the Predator entered the human *imagination*, haunting it, terrifying it, fascinating it, and exciting it ever since.

MIND AND MIMETIC CULTURE

Let's now look at the evidence supporting the claim that around two million years ago, humans with a brain half the size of ours were smart enough to imitate predators as a survival strategy. The evidence is sparse and speculative but also rather intriguing.

According to neuropsychologist Merlin Donald, nearly two million years ago early humans—*Homo ergaster*, *Homo habilis*, and *Homo erectus*—were smart enough to have evolved what he calls a "mimetic culture."[3] Donald uses the word *mimesis* to describe a voluntary, willed effort to call up (or represent) through mime and imitation an event, object, or behavior that was experienced or *imagined*. A toolmaker who "sees" in the mind's eye a new way to shape a hand-axe, and then acts to create that envisioned hand-axe, is engaging in mimesis. So, too, is a learner who imitates what the axe maker did.

For early humans, chipping away at a rock with another rock was not a matter of hit-and-miss guesswork. The toolmaker had to know which stones to use, where to find them, how to hold them, and how to strike—up to sixty times—with the best effect. Throughout the process, the toolmaker had to hold in his mind an image of the finished product and know when chipping had finally achieved that image.

Moreover, this skill (as well as other skills) had to be passed on to the next generation without the benefit of grammatical speech. The gradual improvement of toolmaking in the early Pleistocene, Donald argues, could have occurred only if the "individual who 'invented' the [better] tool could remember and reenact or reproduce the operations involved and then communicate them to others."[4] This transmission process was achieved through mimesis.

In essence, early humans were able to think imaginatively and symbolically (if not yet "mythically"): to see in a round rock a sharp-edged point, to mentally represent a future event (simulation), to plan for the future, and to teach and learn complex skills across generations. Mimesis allowed early humans to cooperatively tackle large-scale challenges and enterprises, to create new types of tools, to colonize new landscapes, to use and control fire, to develop hunting skills, and to devise new cultural behaviors and forms. This is why Donald calls it a mimetic *culture*.

MIMETIC COMMUNICATION AS PERFORMANCE

In a mimetic culture, communication was through signs and gestures made by the arms, legs, hands, and face.[5] By using body language, early humans were able to reenact and represent, according to Donald, a wide range of objects, events, and relationships.[6] A long sequence of such mimetic behaviors amounted to a performance, not unlike a skit by the French mime Marcel Marceau.

Monsieur Marceau, however, kept absolutely silent, whereas our ancient ancestors must have uttered sounds as they manipulated their bodies. Donald calls these utterances "vocal mimesis" because they would have imitated (he believes) the sounds of nature, from waterfalls to the "calls and cries" of animals—both predator and prey.[7] These reproductions of "relevant environmental sounds," according to Donald, would have allowed early humans to represent a wide variety of objects, situations, and events.[8] They also would have provided the foundation for enacted stories about dangerous animals.

The Australian Aborigines have a sweet little story honoring the enchanting powers of sound and vocal mimesis to affect the emotions and behaviors of onlookers. Once there was a frog that could draw together all the animal tribes—birds, kangaroos, eagle-hawks, snakes, reptiles, even insects—merely through his astounding power to imitate their songs and "mimic any peculiar gesture of an individual or tribe." He even had the power to imitate the sights and sounds of nature—the wind, lightning and thunder, the sound of rain and hail, the roar of a cataract. When he imitated these sounds and noises, he was so convincing that the animals ran for cover. "After a few days' entertainment the animals, the birds, the reptiles, and the insect all went away to their homes, and for many days afterward they spoke to each other of the wonderful things they had seen and heard."[9] In American Indian culture, storytellers who could perfectly mimic the voices of animals were much sought after and prized.[10] Even today, when African bushmen tell their animals stories, they actually mimic the mouth formations of the animals, pronouncing the words as though the animals themselves were pronouncing them.[11]

Archaeologist Stanley Mithen goes a bit further than Donald by claiming that mimetic performance may have involved more than imitation of environmental sounds. Although early humans had not yet evolved a fully developed spoken language, Mithen acknowledges, they may have possessed a "proto-language," the precursor of a more grammatically sophisticated language.[12] This proto-language was "holistic, manipulative, multi-modal, musical and mimetic."[13] A basic utterance was a complete message in itself (such as, "hunt with me"). Mithen believes that such utterances were used primarily to allay suspicion, warn of danger, command, threaten, request, and appease.[14] Such utterances would have accompanied imitative behaviors to make the performance more meaningful and memorable; that is, more *dramatic*.

And maybe even more *musical*. Mithen believes that these primitive utterances used rhythm, intonation, melody, timbre, and pitch to better represent what was being imitated.[15] In short, early humans sang and danced their mimetic communications, another reason to describe such communications as *performances* and *mini-dramas*.[16]

Mimetic performance not only represented things, it aroused *emotions* associated with the things represented.[17] As far as we can tell, then, early humans not only pointed and postured, they stomped, bellowed, howled, keened, drummed, chanted, and trilled their meanings and feelings. As anthropologist Barbara King notes, "[E]arly prehistory was steeped in hominid emotion; it had to be. Our ancestors survived in challenging conditions. . . . They *felt* their lives."[18] Mimetic performance likely was able to express and evoke the full range of human emotions, from joy and triumph to grief, anger, and terror.[19] These powerfully emotional spectacles were reproducible from memory without the need of a direct or even recent stimulus.[20] Repeated often enough, a particular performance could become ritualized, perhaps even archetypal, with its conventional display rules and associated emotions.

Mimetic performances were not only emotional and pleasurable; they were useful because they enhanced group cohesion. As Mithen explains, such "joint music-making served to facilitate cooperative behavior by advertising one's willingness to cooperate, and by creating shared emotional states leading to 'boundary loss'/ 'we-ness' / 'coupling' / 'in-group bias.'"[21] There is a neurochemical substratum for this feeling of "we-ness." These activities release endogenous opioids that mediate "complex forms of attachment" and social bonding.[22] Strong bonds were essential to survival in the Pleistocene because they enabled the group to face threats as a cohesive unit. This bit of survival wisdom is reflected in an Eskimo myth about the "great, horrible" monster called Thrashing Spirit. Though a vicious predator, it does not attack "people who were singing in their feasting-house."[23] In other words, group activity—with its noise and energy—deterred predators. In was in this and other ways that mimetic performance could be said to have served the "concrete, pragmatic ends of a fragile, survival-oriented society."[24]

To sum up, almost two million years ago *H. ergaster*, *H. habilis*, and

H. erectus had at their disposal a sophisticated means of relating information, expressing emotions, and narrating events—in short, of telling "stories."

PRIMAL STORYTELLING

The human mind is a narrative mind. Narrative arises naturally from our mental representations of whatever happens around us. At its simplest, a narrative "story" is an account of related events organized in temporal order (this happened, then this happened, then this happened). A story does not have to be spoken or written, it can be *enacted*, as the killing of Gonzago is enacted in Shakespeare's *Hamlet* to imitate the "actual" murder of Hamlet's father.

How would a "story" have been told in the Pleistocene? Let's begin with a simple discovery narrative. Mr. and Mrs. *Homo ergaster* have found a fine flint quarry or a ripe fruit tree. To communicate what they found and where they found it, they imitate walking and/or climbing in a certain direction and then mime behaviors associated with the object—such as flaking in the case of the flint or eating in the case of the fruit tree, with a few grins, hoots, and jig steps added to encourage others to follow the benefactors back to the treasure. This narrative pantomime tells a story of discovery at the same time that it communicates survival information.

Over time these enacted narratives became more and more sophisticated until they became mini-dramas, the ancient precursor of pantomime, ritual dance, and other forms of mimetic representation.[25] It could be said that the very first enacted narratives and mini-dramas had a certain element of "fictiveness" about them in that they enacted something not actually present but remembered or imagined. This may be low-grade fictiveness, but it is fictiveness nevertheless.

What this means is that almost two million years ago, early humans, even without a fully developed grammar and lexicon, were likely managing to tell stories—emotion-laden mini-dramas—that warned, excited, informed, and alerted group members about the threats and opportunities in their environment. In performing these stories, early humans were fashioning the essential elements of all later storytelling, as well as developing a crucial survival tool that enabled them to cope with the most salient menace in their environment—animals out to eat them.

ENTER THE PREDATOR

Both Merlin Donald and Steven Mithen believe, as I do, that mimetic performances were about animals, but where I differ from them is that they believe the performances were about the animals that humans hunted, not about the animals that *hunted humans*. Admittedly, myths eventually did become preoccupied with hunting power, hunting magic, and hunting guilt (precisely those myths that preoccupied Joseph Campbell and many other scholars), but we must bear in mind that for most of our evolution, we were a prey species, not (as we have become) the alpha predator of the planet.

Once again the nineteenth-century writer Charles Gould can be called upon for an astute assessment of the prehistoric conditions of primal storytelling: Early man "co-existed with animals which . . . excelled in magnitude and ferocity most of those which in savage countries dispute his empire at the present day. Is it not reasonable to suppose that his combats with these would form the most important topic of conversation, of tradition, and of primitive song, and that graphic accounts of such struggles, and of the terrible nature of the foes encountered, would be handed down from father to son, with a fidelity of description and an accuracy of memory unsuspected by us?"[26]

To enact a story about a predator, the storyteller would have had to "look" and "act" like one, no doubt using the natural fear triggers and survival behaviors wired into the primate line to accomplish this. A storyteller might have gotten on all fours, opened his or her mouth to expose teeth, glared, reared, flapped arms, stalked, lunged, or charged. Sensitive to the power of signs, the storyteller, to intensify the performance, eventually must have used "props" such as bones or sticks in the mouth to simulate the incisors of saber-toothed cats, or shells over the eyes to accentuate the predator stare, or the skulls of actual predators to make the audience cringe. Red ocher, a color associated with the most ancient of human ceremony, may have been used to signal blood. These props likely were the foundation for the ceremonial "terror masks" used much later in human evolution to produce fear during tribal rituals. A combination of these items would have made any performance gripping and memorable. Even today these images are used in art and other cultural venues "to trigger an emotion on the fear continuum."[27] Think how easy it was for old Don Corleone to frighten his grandson in the garden merely by wedging a slice of fruit under his upper lip.

Vocal mimesis also played a part in performing the predator. The sounds imitated would have ranged from familiar and automatic alarm cries to the chilling noises made by predators and prey as they hunted and died. Growls, howls, hisses, snarls, barks, roars, snorts, bellows, shrieks, screams of agony—any or all could have been vocalized during the performance. As Charles Darwin recognized, the ability to imitate the threatening sounds of predators would have been a valuable asset to our Pleistocene ancestors.[28]

All this is guesswork, of course, but guesswork that is supported by the storytelling practices of basically contemporary Stone Age tribes. In Indonesia, for example, tribal storytellers create an "ogre" by tying a piece of string around the nose, tongue and chin, and placing a bent stick into each nostril, then boar tusks under the upper lips, and feathers on the head and body.[29] To imitate the roar of lions, they swing on a rope hollow bones with holes in them. In Africa, the best storytellers are those who bring their stories to life "by imitating a range of human and animal voices, by accompanying the story with a variety of sounds, squawks, screams, and by providing suitable singing, dancing, and gestures."[30] Among the !Kung, these elements are repeated over and over again to create "drama and excitement."[31]

The imitation of predators in the Pleistocene could be thought of as *cultural crypsis*—the copying in self-defense of a trait of an aggressor (as

Some masks give the fear-triggering features of the predator a more human semblance, as in the image shown above, in which the top of the mask is decorated with skull-like human heads. However this African mask may have been used and whatever it may have meant to the people who created it, it reflects a primal human fear of creatures with sharp teeth and gaping mouths who are staring at us. Predator-face masks likely derive from the efforts of very ancient storytellers to imitate the appearance of carnivores by using bones and grimaces. *eans/Shutterstock.com*

in the case of protective eye spots). Of course, the point of mimicking these features during performance would not have been to scare off actual predators as the moth is trying to do, but to drive away another danger—the *fear evoked by actual predators*. As Marina Warner puts it, "[M]yth summons specters from the shadows and enfleshes them" to confront them with countervailing "devices created by make-believe and art."[32] Even today, as remote as we are from the prospect of dying by carnivore, we use popular media to conjure up fictional representations of dangerous animals to defy and transcend our lingering fear of them and to feel the primordial and pleasurable "rush and high" they evoke.[33]

Some tribal members must have been better than others at enacting the predator. Those who were may have been seen by members of the tribe as having a special, maybe even supernatural, power. In Native American myths, the person with this special power is called a Transformer. The first Transformer is credited with having imposed on animals their present shapes. Intriguingly, these myths also insist that originally, the animals were also humans, a notion that might reflect the transformative power of mimetic performance, where the storyteller would indeed have imposed an animal appearance on a human form.

The awesome, terrifying power of enactment—not unlike that found in the African myth I explored at the beginning of this chapter—is acknowledged in a Hopi myth about hero twins who behead and skin a monster. To play a trick on their grandmother, they use the head, hair, and skin of the creature to make themselves look like him. "So frightened was the old woman that she ran about the house urinating and defecating from fear, finally collapsing in a heap." Being good-hearted, the twins revive her, and she forgives them.[34] The grandmother, of course, was reacting in precisely the way any vulnerable member of the primate line is liable to react when threatened by a predator.

Paleolithic Transformers could be considered not only the first actors and storytellers but also the first *animal masters* and *shamans*. Certainly in more recent tribal cultures, animal masters and shamans

have the power, it is thought, both to control and to become animals—
often predatory animals. To strengthen this notion, they dress in animal
skins, wear animal heads and masks, behave and sound like animals, and
often keep animals as "familiars." In hunting tribes such as the Ojibwa,
it is the sorcerer-shaman who is thought to control through *imitation*
the prey animals sought by the hunting party.[35] And shamans are
thought to secure the safety of hunters either by impersonating dangerous animals—and absorbing, cannibal-like, their powers—or by surviving a symbolic encounter with a predator, thus acquiring the power to
extend his protective magic to the group.[36] Shamanism very likely
evolved from rudimentary storytelling.

I want to revisit that Hawaiian story recounting a young girl's confrontation with a dragon. Again, as in the story that begins this chapter,
the predator is driven away not through violence but through *simulation*. The girl has been instructed by her grandmother to *show* no fear
when menaced by a dragon, who will use—Hiilei is warned—all the fear
triggers associated with the predator to terrorize her. And the dragon
does: "[H]is eyes flashed and he opened his mouth. His tongue was
thrusting viciously from side to side. His red mouth was like the pit of
Pele. His teeth were gnashing, his tail lashing." Despite these fear
stimuli, the young girl "hid her fear and called a welcome to this dragon."
She passes the test. Suddenly, and almost magically, this fearsome
dragon "fell into pieces, which all became nothing. The fragments flew
in all directions. While Hiilei was watching this, all the evil disappeared
and a handsome man stood before her."[37]

This tale can be read in several ways, of course, but it strikes me as a
story that reflects an initiation rite using the imitation and manipulation
of fear stimuli to test the courage of the young. During the actual ritual,
the young would have watched with awe and relief as the "monsters"
before them "fell into pieces"—that is, as the adults stripped off their
ceremonial animal costumes and fear masks to embrace the children
who braved the ordeal.

As psychotherapist Anthony Stevens observes, many myths and rituals "arose out of the anxieties that inevitably afflicted human beings living in the environmental circumstances in which our species evolved and lived for most of its existence."[38] To put this more plainly, the threat posed by Pleistocene predators contributed to the emergence of such culturally evolved survival strategies as storytelling and rituals of social cohesion.

MIMETIC STORYTELLING AS A SURVIVAL STRATEGY (1)

Though mimetic storytelling must have been enthralling and pleasurable, it was not "entertainment" as we understand the concept. It was a survival tool for both the individual and the group. For instance, by exploiting innate fear triggers, mimetic performance revived memories (stored in the amygdala) of past encounters with predators, reminding everyone especially the old, cursed with fading memories—about the features of local predators.

This activation may have been fine-tuned. Our ancient ancestors likely repressed (as we still do today) truly horrific or terrifying memories of encounters with predators. When a traumatic event is too stressful—that is, when it triggers an overabundance of adrenaline—the memory of the event can become fuzzy rather than vivid. "It is thus completely possible that one might have poor conscious memory of a traumatic experience, but at the same time form very powerful implicit, unconscious emotional memories through amygdala-mediated fear conditioning."[39] It was the task of mimetic performance to create the right amount of stress to therapeutically reactivate the traumatic memories safely stored in the amygdala without flooding onlookers with stress hormones that could physically harm them if unvented. Primal storytellers did not want to reduce members of the group to defecating grandmothers.

Mimetic performance also would have helped imprint vivid images of dangerous animals. Children, for instance, would have learned about predators not only by watching adults react to *real ones* but also by watching adults react to *simulations* of them. The ability to learn through simulation was crucial to our survival struggle during the Pleistocene, for—as H. Clark Barrett observes—"an individual who could only learn about predators through direct encounter would be unlikely to leave many offspring."[40] These primordial enactments functioned like the terror-tales that we still tell children in order to make them wary and to warn them about specific environmental hazards that threaten their survival. Nowhere is this function more obvious than in folk and fairy tales, which warn children about the dangerous predators—both human and animal—that lurk, sometimes disguised as grandmothers, throughout the environment. Even today, the !Kung of the Kalahari use mime, gesture, dance, and chant to sharpen the survival skills of their children. In one ritual, males pretend to be lions and hyenas, growling, springing, even slipping into the camp at night to bite children who pretend to be asleep and then jump up shouting and waving their arms to scare the predator away.[41]

The !Kung's ceremonial enactment of predators has several functions. It tells the young which carnivores are the most dangerous, it demonstrates how these animals sound and hunt, it rehearses successful antipredator behaviors—such as alarm calls and aggressive mobbing—and it "celebrates" the conquest of an "enemy." If the !Kung use *their* mimetic skills to enact predators as a survival strategy, then so, too, may have early humans, who had the same mimetic capacity as the !Kung and a lot more reason to be afraid of dangerous animals.

Ethologist Hans Kruuk sums things up rather well when he says that "at its most basic our art, literature, heraldry and many of their derivates have a role of instruction . . . and as such they are an important extension of the learning part of our anti-predator behavior. In a purely biological sense, through art and especially through literature, we can send alarm signals to our conspecifics."[42]

MIMETIC STORYTELLING
AS A SURVIVAL STRATEGY (2)

Mimetic storytelling, which exploited the emotional impact of hard-wired fear triggers, had the power to evoke essentially the same powerful emotions evoked by a real predator. Of course, onlookers understood that the storyteller, however good the impersonation, was not a real animal. But the fear triggers exploited during the enactment would have worked their emotional magic on the limbic system nevertheless, just as they still do today when we flinch and shudder and scream while watching a scary movie.[43] By stimulating defensive impulses and emotions, performances kindled essentially the same feelings of group cohesion and connectedness that the group members felt when they bonded together to mob an actual predator.

As I noted earlier, during a confrontation with a predator, our ancestors were flooded with a variety of hormones that made them physically stronger, less sensitive to pain, suffused with energy and excitement, and emboldened with courage. These chemical-emotional effects were *exhilarating*, *pleasurable*, and perhaps *addictive*.

There was nothing in the daily life of our Pleistocene ancestors that offered them as ravishing, galvanizing, or thrilling an experience as a communal stand against a pack of roaring carnivores. Unfortunately, the pleasurable and transformative emotions evoked by such an encounter were fleeting, unpredictable, and fraught with risk. It was the task of mimetic performance, I believe, to recapture and revive these emotions, but to do so safely. By enacting encounters with predators, especially ones in which humans triumphed, early humans were able to enjoy the social and emotional benefits of a (remembered or imagined) predator attack without running any risk. But even if the enactment depicted an agonizing scene of carnage from real life, it would have had survival value, not only by underscoring the importance of being wary but by bonding group members through enactment itself and through the sharing of grief.

DREAMING OF THE "BAD ONES"

A commonly reported dream is about being attacked by an animal. In dreams about physical threat, an animal is the culprit 82 percent of the time for males, and 77 percent of the time for females.[44] Generally speaking, in dreams that could be recalled, more bad things than good things happen to the dreamer, suggesting that during sleep the world is felt to be threatening, unfriendly, and hostile.[45] It seems to have been so for the Aztecs, who dreamed of the "Bad Ones"; that is, dangerous predators. "An eagle is standing on top of me. A jaguar is standing on top of me. A wolf is standing on top of me. A rattlesnake is lying on top of me."[46]

Did dangerous animals also haunt the dreams of our ancient ancestors? And if so, did "dreaming the predator" contribute to "performing the predator"? A case can be made for answering yes to both questions.

The research of Jonathan Winson suggests that the brain system that produces dreams has a very ancient lineage and contributes to human survival. In *Brain & Psyche*, Winson claims that animals (depending on the role) use REM sleep to rehearse predator or prey behavior.[47] For example, in a laboratory setting, a napping cat "acted out attack and fear behavior—which in my view could represent activities being processed neurally during REM sleep as part of a laying down, integration, or rehearsal of predatory experience."[48]

Like Winson, dream researcher Antti Revonsuo believes that the ability to dream evolved as an "ancient threat-simulation system," one that enabled early humans to prepare for threatening events such as encounters with "large carnivores":[49]

> Behavioral strategies to avoid contact with such animals and to escape or hide if attacked by them obviously were of high survival value. . . . Dreaming simulates and rehearses these ancestral threat-avoidance programs in order to maintain their efficiency, because the cost of a single failure to respond appropriately when the danger is real may be

fatal, while the costs of repeated threat simulation during sleep are rather low.[50]

Our ancient ancestors, in short, had the ability to imaginatively "represent" and imitate dangerous animals within the dream state. They must have dreamt a lot about predators, given research that shows that the more a person is threatened by dangerous animals while awake, the more the person dreams about these animals and the more "dominating" and "realistic" the dreams become.[51] During a dream, our ancestors would have gone over their traumatic experiences with predators, likely envisioning themselves as somehow escaping or avoiding them. This is to say that dreaming was an *internal mimetic performance* where our ancestors could "rehearse" the behaviors that would keep them alive in the waking world. This fear-management strategy may very well have led early humans to act out in public the internal stories about the "bad ones" haunting their dreams.

IMITATION AS MAGICAL INCANTATION

As anthropologist Bronislaw Malinowski (1884–1942) observes, "[W]e find magic where the element of danger is conspicuous."[52] In *The Golden Bough*, James George Frazer identifies two basic principles, or techniques, underlying the practice of magic. The first is the law of similarity, which assumes that *like produces like*, and that *the effect resembles its cause*. The second is the law of contact or contagion, which assumes that *things that once were in contact with each other continue to influence each other at a distance after the contact is over*. Frazer calls magic that is based on the law of similarity "imitative," or "mimetic," magic.[53]

In mimetic magic, the created image is thought to somehow capture the essence of the object it represents, so that what is done to the image is thought to be done to the object (immediately or in the future).

When an act of symbolizing, whether through drawing or mimetic enactment, "represents" what is absent, it gives the object a sort of life and reality. The more realistic the image or enactment, the more vivid and powerful the impression that the object has been summoned and is thus under control. Again, it is not the actual thing itself that is invoked through mimesis but the essence or spirit of the thing that it made to appear before us "through the metaphors and symbols that 'give to airy nothing a local habitation and a name.'"[54]

Hunting peoples have long used imitative magic to "summon" and "control" the animals they hunt. Typically, an image of the prey animal is drawn so that it can be pierced by spears or arrows in the belief that this mimetic enactment will influence future events. Ojibwa hunters, for example, chant the following words over a drawn depiction of the prey animal, "I shoot you in the heart, I shoot you in the heart, O beast! I hit your heart."[55]

Mimetic *picture* magic apparently was practiced at least thirty thousand years ago, and very likely much earlier, though these depictions did not survive the ravages of time. The many (and extraordinarily beautiful) depictions of game animals found in the painted caves of Europe suggest, at the very least, that Paleolithic hunters were using picture magic to encourage the earth to provide them with abundant prey. There is evidence as well that about fifty thousand years ago (if not longer) our Paleolithic ancestors threw spears at *clay models* of cave bears, either to exorcize their fear of these formidable predators or to increase their hopes of hunting them successfully.[56] The hunters of the Ice Age (about twelve thousand years ago) often depicted dangerous animals without eyes, ears, or horns; this was apparently done in an attempt to rob them of their power.[57] This was the purpose of a magical practice engaged in by Egyptians. A papyrus on sorcery urges the fearful to draw pictures of threatening creatures without their dangerous body parts—the head, in the case of a snake; the tail, in the case of a scorpion.

Essentially weaponless, early humans also must have felt an urgent need to somehow neutralize the lethal power of animals, to bring them under *symbolic control*. Mimetic storytelling was not simply a device for communicating survival information. It was a form of sympathetic magic in which the terrifying "predator" could be lured into symbolic existence and so subjected to the will of its rebellious prey.[58] In mimetic performance, early humans turned the tables on predators by symbolically and ritualistically scaring and killing *them*. This is the point of the Baganda story about the lion. And it is also the message of an intriguing myth told by the Ashanti of Africa.

At the beginning of the world, only the Sky-God had the power to tell stories. One day Ananse the Spider-Trickster went to the Sky-God to "buy the stories which the sky-god owned." But the price was high: Ananse had to capture "the python, the leopard, the bush-spirit and the hornets."[59] He captures each of these dangerous creatures by weaving a story that entraps it. The most difficult to ensnare are the evil bush spirits, who are trapped by means of a story involving a "large wooden [tar] doll, the size of Ananse himself." True to his word, the Sky-God gives all his stories to Ananse, the Trickster-Storyteller, who has demonstrated his power to control dangerous creatures through words. And it is the desperate belief that words can control predators that we find in this Bengali mantra:

> Male and female sharks,
> Male and female crocodiles, dangerous ones with sharp teeth,
> If you come to bite or attack, I charge you:
> Stay away for day and night,
> This mantra, like thunder, is a weapon in my hand,
> So I charge you in your mouth, in your teeth,
> To stay away for day and night.[60]

In a myth of the Shona of Zimbabwe, a hunter encounters a large pride of frightening lions, who displayed their "long and sharp teeth" every time they yawned. But the resourceful hunter manages his fear of the lions by playing a tune on his lute that makes the lions dance, "and as they danced he passed through them and continued on his way."[61] In this instance, it is music, not words, that controls the predator, but still it is a performance that works the magic.

The alleged power of storytelling to manipulate actual predators was—of course—imaginary and ineffective. But that didn't matter, because the real value of mimetic performance was its power to control fear. *That* is what needed to be managed. Merely thinking that they had some measure of control over predators imbued our ancient ancestors with more confidence and power—rendering them less fearful. Storytelling was like a psychological stockade behind which threatened people could live with less fear. This belief that the behavior of predators could be controlled not only increased their resolve and solidarity; it also contributed to the gradual transformation of humans into the alpha predator of the planet.

Before our ancestors could become formidable killers, they first had to *imagine themselves* to be formidable killers. Each time they enacted predators to render them harmless, they were engaging in a meta-initiation rite that, over a vast expanse of time, eventually transformed us from the *hunted* to the *hunter*, from *prey* to *predator*. So, although mimetic storytelling had no effect on predators, it did have a transformative effect over the long haul on the human psyche and on human behavior. This transformation is discussed in detail in chapter 9.

CONCLUSION

According to mythologist Joseph Campbell, the fundamental purpose of myth and rite is to protect people from "psychological dangers" by "conjuring forth the life energies of the individual and his group to meet and surpass the danger."[62] This is exactly what mimetic storytelling did for our ancient ancestors. Fear of the predator had to be *controlled* or *managed*—avoided altogether when possible, reduced or redirected when possible, or channeled into strategic life-enhancing attitudes and behaviors.

Mimetic storytelling evolved as a response to this need. It arose from, and was an extension of, those physiological reactions that served the survival needs of our ancestors. It performed the same function as the natural defense system discussed in the previous chapter—helping humans respond effectively to the threats and fears posed by predators. At the hearth fire, perhaps deep within a cave, our ancestors imitated predators to control and conquer their fear of them. By imitating, mimicking, simulating, and impersonating the very animals that frightened them, they were able to imbue themselves with greater resolve, more courage, heightened physical strength, and a more intense sense of group solidarity. The mimetic evocation of threat and fear was done to manage threat and fear. Storytelling, by protecting early humans from the potentially debilitating effects of fear, was a *meta*-antipredator behavior, serving the survival needs of an endangered species by embracing and exploiting the whole realm of survival strategies biologically available to our species. Storytelling did for our ancestors what it did for Scheherazade—it saved their lives.

Chapter 5

The Emergence of the Mythmaking Mind

INTRODUCTION

I n Native American myths, bears are able to walk on two feet and talk to people—they are even able to marry them. In Norse myth, two huge wolves chase the sun as it moves across the sky every day. In Aboriginal myth, a monstrous dog eats so many people that it has to store the body parts in a pelican-like pouch hanging beneath its jaws. In African myth, a lion caught in a trap agrees not to prey on people if a woodcutter frees him, and in another tale, a crocodile confers with other animals before deciding whether to eat a fisherman who befriended it.

These "predators," of course, are *not* the ones that actually hunted and haunted our ancient ancestors; they are not the material creatures imitated by our ancient ancestors. These creatures are *mythic*. By this I mean something more than that they are found in myths. I mean that these creatures are anomalous, strange, counter-natural in one way or another. They have physical features not found in nature, and they do things that real animals cannot do—such as talk, reason, and bargain.

If these mythic creatures don't seem all that strange to us, it is because our brain—the *Homo sapiens* brain—created them. Our brain is wonderfully inventive, capable of yoking bits and pieces from here and there to create physically impossible but still recognizable hybrid creatures even more menacing in appearance than the creatures that draw real blood from real people.

This brain of ours—blessed and cursed with the ability to think mythically—came into existence around two hundred thousand years ago. Its emergence brought about the transition from mimetic culture to *mythic culture*, transforming storytelling from an enacted performance accompanied by vocalization to a spoken performance accompanied by action. As a result of this momentous transformation, all humans can be said to now live in a "mythic world, however ignorant of it they may be."[1]

How and why did things change? What happened to the human brain to make it capable of mythic thinking? What drove us to imagine "predators" that were at once more physically intimidating than actual predators and yet could be bargained with and worshipped? Tracking down the answers to these questions will take us into some thick, difficult, and unexplored terrain.

THE ANCIENT ROOTS OF MYTHIC THINKING

Mythmaking (as we know it) became possible only when the human mind had achieved a tipping point that unleashed the imaginative and inventive powers of the *Homo sapiens* brain. That tipping point was the acquisition of language. Possessing both a modern language and an active creative imagination enabled humans to invent and transmit the complex and creative oral narratives that we call myths. But keep in mind that mimesis persisted as a predominant form of expression and communication "even following the emergence of language as a general communication tool."[2]

Before the human mind evolved the ability to think mythically and to orally narrate myths, it possessed the essential, fundamental cognitive abilities that eventually coalesced to form the mythic mind—the mind capable of imagining (and often believing in the existence of) counter-factual and counter-intuitive agents and events. These essential, funda-mental abilities are: *anthropomorphism* (attributing human traits to nonhuman creatures and things), *animism* (attributing life to inanimate objects), and *metamorphism* (the belief that a creature or object can be transformed into a totally different thing while still preserving its essence). These mental operations—each a defining feature of mythic thinking—emerged, I believe, as by-products of two even more funda-mental mental operations that were crucial to the struggle of our distant ancestors to survive in the dangerous environment of the Pleistocene. These two operations are the Agency-Detection Device (ADD) and the Theory of Mind Mechanism (ToMM). Understanding these two oper-ations will help us understand how our brain was primed to evolve a mythic imagination.

The Agency-Detection Device (ADD) enabled our ancestors to detect "agency" at the slightest provocation. An "agent" is defined as anything that moves or appears to move by itself. In a dangerous envi-ronment, the survival of early humans depended on this detection system being easily activated. It is far safer to over-detect than to under-detect a predator, better to *imagine* a predator that may not be there than to overlook one that is. This system, which works unconsciously, "is the fundamental mechanism of fear," orchestrating its behavioral, physi-ological, and conscious manifestations.[3]

As soon as ADD identifies—or thinks it has identified—an agent, the Theory of Mind Mechanism (ToMM) imbues that agent with a mind—with feelings, desires, and intentions.[4] If a rock falls, it has fallen because it wants to. It was easy to view animals as humanlike because they exhibit many behaviors and emotions that humans also exhibit, such as searching for something to eat when hungry. These two cogni-tive biases evolved because they had survival value: they encouraged our ancestors to pay close attention to cues emitted by a predator that might reveal its mood or future actions. "Attributing desire to a leopard on the ancestral plains of Africa is a very useful notion to possess if you spot one that is looking at you from some distance away."5

The survival value of these mental operations that we now take for granted is honored in many myths. One Sioux myth explains how the mud hen became a good detector of predators. When the Trickster Iktomi goes hunting for ducks, a "smart one" does not trust Iktomi's protestation that his stick is for beating out a pleasant tune; he thought it was for beating ducks to death. Although to look at Iktomi means losing one's sight, the smart duck peeks with only one eye. "'Take off! Take off!' he cried to the other ducks." As a result of his sacrifice, the smart duck becomes a mud hen, and to this day mud hens "swim alone, away from other ducks, always on the lookout, diving beneath the water as soon as they see or hear anyone approaching, thinking it might be wicked Iktomi with a new bag of tricks. Better to be a live, ugly mud hen than a pretty, dead duck."6

In another Native American myth, Iktomi is the one who boasts of having exceptional predator detection skills. Before Iktomi is allowed to join a tribe, a suspicious chief examines his predator-detection qualifications. "Can you spy an enemy from far, far away? Can you hear an enemy creeping stealthily up on your camp? Can you detect the scent of grizzlies, wolves, or cougars creeping up on our herd?"7 When Iktomi answers yes to all questions, this Trickster is viewed as a valued member of the tribe.

The survival benefit of intuiting what is in the mind of predators is also honored in myths. It is the mythical transformer Glooskap's ability to "read what was going on in another person's mind" that allows him to detect the murderous intentions of an "evil sorcerer."8 In another myth, Great Rabbit keeps himself from becoming a meal of Wildcat because of his active Theory of Mind Mechanism: "[N]ow Great Rabbit can sense what others are thinking from a long way off, so he already knew that Wildcat was after him. He made up his mind that he would use his magic power against Wildcat's strength."9 This little story sums up the trajectory of humanity's tense relationship with predators—the almost magical abilities of the human mind to overcome the terrible strength of dangerous animals.

In the operation of ADD and ToMM, we find, I believe, the cognitive foundation of *anthropomorphism*, the defining characteristic of mythic thinking. All the animals (and many other agents and objects) depicted in myths have been anthropomorphized in some way and to some degree. That is, they have been given—or have been thought to possess—one or more human traits.

The first *hard* archaeological evidence of anthropomorphic thinking is relatively recent, occurring in the Upper Paleolithic about forty thousand to thirty thousand years ago. It is within this time frame that graphic depictions of "hybrid" creatures mixing animal and human characteristics have been dated. The most famous of these are the bison with human legs found in the Chauvet Cave; the celebrated "Sorcerer" figure from the cave of Trois-Frères, which has human legs and hands but the back and ears of an herbivore, the antlers of a reindeer, the tail of a horse, and the phallus of a feline; and the ivory statuette with a body of a human and the head of a lion from a cave in Germany, which archaeologist Steven Mithen regards as the oldest known work of art.[10] Although it is tempting to conclude that these anthropomorphs or zoomorphs (depending on one's point of view) signal the birth of mythic thinking, they more likely signal the birth of the *skills* needed to express mythic thinking in painting and carving. If, as Mithen believes, *Homo ergaster* and *Homo erectus* acted out the role of animals, imitating their sounds and movements, then our distant relatives were engaging in something like anthropomorphic or zoomorphic thinking and behavior over a million years ago.

What's intriguing about ADD is that it is primed to go off even when no agent—or predator—has been detected. A sign, a trace, a track, a sound, a motion—almost anything can induce the human mind to assume the presence of an agent even though it is unseen. In the dangerous landscape of the Pleistocene, it was always "best to anticipate and fear the worst of all likely possibilities: the presence of a deviously intelligent predator."[11]

This hyperactive tendency of the Agency-Detection Device contributed to the emergence of the mythic imagination. It induced our
ancient ancestors to *imagine* agents, especially predatory agents, when
none were there. Of course, it could be said that it was "memory" not
"imagination" that our ancestors were relying on when faced with a sign
or mark possibly portending disaster. But in an ambiguous situation,
where the sign did not reveal the *nature* of the predator to be feared, our
ancestors could not have *remembered* a *specific* predator.

In unclear situations like these, what "predator" would our ancient
ancestors have "imagined"? A crawling predator? A flying one? A running one? Each type of predator requires a different type of response. I
think that our ancient ancestors may have *imagined* a composite, hybrid
predator—a *mythic* predator—one that combined the lethal traits—or
fear stimuli—of different species. This hybrid image didn't specify a particular kind of predator but signified a "very dangerous animal," and
although the hybrid image would have been enough to make one fearful,
it would not have been specific enough to trigger a potentially disastrous—because too specific—survival response. It simply served to put
the prey on high alert. This ability to imagine a hybrid predator may
explain the strange combination of features that make up the mythic
"dragon," a sort of generic predator with the composite traits of a big cat,
a huge snake, and a raptor. I am not saying that early humans must have
imagined a "dragon" in ambiguous situations, but only that they may
have created in their imaginations a fearful hybrid well before they
evolved the ability to carve or paint one.

The Agency-Detection Device and the Theory of Mind Mechanism
also provide the foundation for another crucial feature of myth—*animism*.
Animism, which comes from the Latin word for "soul" or "breath," is the
belief that every object is alive and hence capable of being interacted
with, for good or for ill.[12] In a sense, animism extends anthropomorphic
thinking to everything in the environment—animals, plants, atmos-
pheric phenomena, even natural or human-made objects such as rocks

and swords. As eighteenth-century Scottish philosopher David Hume noted, it is a "universal tendency" with humans "to transfer to every object, those qualities, with which they are familiarly acquainted, and of which they are intimately conscious. We find faces in the clouds; and, by a natural propensity, if not corrected by experience and reflection, ascribe male or good-will to everything that hurts or pleases us. . . . Trees, mountains and streams are personified, and the inanimate parts of nature acquire sentiment and passion."[13]

There is no limit to what the mythic imagination can animate or "transform" into a predator. In Native American mythology, *inyan*, or rock, was deemed to be the most ancient being, "old beyond imagination, ageless, eternal," the origin of life itself.[14] Rocks can also be transformed into premeditating killers, as they are in the sci-fi film *The Monolith Monsters* (1957). Even "griddles and pots" can take on life and become predators, as they do in the Mayan *Popol Vuh*, where they rebel against being "put on the fire . . . as though we felt no pain."[15]

Animism has both negative and positive effects. For one thing, it increases the number and kinds of malignant agents that threaten and frighten humans, such as angry griddles! But it also makes it possible for people to establish human relationships with everything. This is why it is comforting and reassuring to believe—as the Greek philosopher Thales put it—that "everything is full of gods."[16] But the situation is comforting only to the extent that one knows how to mollify and propitiate these potentially angry gods.

The third aspect of mythic thinking is *metamorphism*, the belief that a being or object can be transformed into an entirely different physical form. Metamorphosis is based on the assumption that the same substance is shared by all people and objects (which is true, of course, at the atomic level). Because people and things share the same substance, they can exchange their exterior forms or shapes, taking on totally different ones without entirely relinquishing their original nature. No doubt this belief was reinforced by the dramatic transformations that actually take place in the life cycles of certain reptiles and insects, but it is rooted in the mental operations of ADD and ToMM, and in the anthropomorphic animism they produce. Myth and magic "are universally present because the human mind has evolved to think in these ways."[17]

In myth and folklore, the most dramatic shape changing entails the transformation of a human into a predatory hybrid creature both human and animal, such as a werewolf, were-bear, were-shark, were-lion, and so on (*were* meaning "man"). For tribal peoples, such creatures seem to be everywhere because it is natural to assume that a particularly intelligent animal—one that displays the remarkable cleverness of a human—is animated by a human spirit lurking within, or that it is at least under the control of a human whose identity may be hidden. In Maya and Aztec culture, a jaguar was thought to become even more formidable when a shaman decided to inhabit its body, for now the animal possessed the skills and knowledge of the shaman (and the shaman, of course, the skills and knowledge of the predator).

According to Todd Tremlin, a scholar who studies the cognitive foundations of religion, ADD and ToMM account for "some of the most creative operations of human intelligence—from the attention needed to survive in hostile and competitive environments to the sensitivity and cunning involved in interpersonal intercourse to the conceptual framework behind lots of imaginative thought."[18] It has been said that "monsters" spurred the development of the human imagination, but it is more accurate to say that the emergence of the mythic imagination spurred the creation of monsters.

MYTHIC THINKING AND THE MODULAR MIND

Although anthropomorphism, animism, and metamorphism constitute the essential elements of mythic thinking, they do not quite explain such mythic creatures as flying lions and vampires that do not die. As Joseph Campbell wondered, where do such counter-natural creatures come from in the human mind? "Whence the images of nightmare and of dream?"[19] These mythic creatures are best explained as violations of mental domains that evolved to contain reliable and lifesaving information about the real world.

To survive, our ancient ancestors would have needed a certain amount of basic and reliable knowledge about how the world works. Given the modest size and reticulation of the early hominid brain, this information probably was stored in separate compartments, called, variously, "ontological categories," "domains," "modules," or "intelligences." For instance, one compartment processed and stored information about people, another about animals, another about toolmaking, another about natural objects (rivers, mountains, and so on), and another about plants. Each faculty or domain had evolved to deal with specific problems arising in the Pleistocene environment, such as recognizing faces, identifying cheaters in social exchanges, and detecting predators. Neurological research has confirmed that even the modern brain, which is considerably more complex in design and function than the brain of early humans, is "organized into discrete modules of cognitive abilities."[20] For instance, children seem to be born "with content-rich intuitive knowledge models in physics (tool use), biology (animal behavior), psychology (social relations and mind), and language acquisition."[21]

Although these domains contained information that our distant ancestors had to find useful and reliable, the domains evolved not to discover scientific truths about the natural world but to deal practically with the opportunities and threats in the Pleistocene environment. It was not necessary that early humans be *always right* about the way the world worked, but it was necessary that they not be *always wrong*. As Scott Atran puts it, if our ancient ancestors did not perceive the world fairly accurately, then how could they have "avoided falling off cliffs or being eaten by wild animals at every turn?"[22] Generally speaking, a grip on baseline reality was good enough.

Although each of these separate domains had survival value, they were likely functionally isolated from each other, with the part devoted to toolmaking dedicated only to toolmaking, the part devoted to understanding animals isolated from the domain devoted to social interaction between humans, and so on. This functional isolation would mean that our ancient ancestors were unable to consistently *violate or integrate* the information sequestered in modular structures. There likely was no crossover, no hybridizing of concepts. In essence, our ancient ancestors did not possess the brain power, or the need, to imagine such counterfactual creatures and events as flying pythons or slithering eagles, even though they did have the mental capacity to "imagine" the presence of a real predator without seeing or even hearing one.

But everything changed at some point in the Middle Paleolithic—perhaps as early as two hundred and fifty thousand years ago, but certainly by fifty thousand years ago. The human mind—now the mind of *Homo sapiens*—evolved the power to integrate information produced by, and stored in, these previously compartmentalized knowledge/skill domains. Archaeologist Steven Mithen has called this synthesizing power "cognitive fluidity." Cognitive fluidity enabled humans to link diverse domains of information and reasoning and to imagine the world as a single environment, encompassing humans, animals, and plants. As a result, even hunter-gatherers living an almost Stone Age life are able to think of the world in a highly integrated way, with an interpenetration "of natural world modules and social world modules manifested in an ideology and metaphysics that there is a single environment that encompasses humans, animals, and plants in a living nature."[23] According to Mithen, it was the emergence of cognitive fluidity that ushered in such crucial cultural activities as religion, art, and mythmaking.

Many forces contributed to the emergence of cognitive fluidity and the integrating imagination. Certainly ADD and ToMM played a crucial role, but so, too, did the altered states of consciousness associated with ritual behavior and shamanism. Medical anthropologist Alondra

Oubre believes that Australopithecines, even before the appearance of *Homo erectus*, induced in themselves neurochemical changes to create a euphoric and visionary state of mind.[24] She calls this state of mind "transcendental consciousness." During these states, protohumans "may have entered a new world of fantasy and surrealistic hypnagogic imagery of a metacorporeal existence."[25] In short, even protohumans may have created counter-intuitive and counter-factual creatures and events—semi-mythic beings. Whether or not some rudimentary form of ritual- or drug-induced mythic consciousness goes back this far, it almost surely came about as the result of two related Middle Paleolithic events: the evolution of a larger and more reticulated brain and the acquisition of grammatical language, both of which together unleashed all kinds of imaginative powers.

According to the modular view, mythic thinking results not from abandoning the domains of intuitive knowledge but by *violating* their boundaries. A counter-intuitive or counter-factual creature—a god or devil—is created by our imagination by mixing helpful and reliable bits of knowledge about different types of entities in the real world. The concept of the vampire is a mythic creation because it mixes human and animal traits and because it violates the biological fact that all humans (as well as animals) must eventually die (vampires can be killed only by special means).

This modular view of myth does not contradict what I've said about anthropomorphism, animism, and metamorphism. In their early stages of development, these concepts did not require that our ancient forebears think that a lion was actually an ancestor, only that the lion was motivated by intentions, feelings, and desires understandable to a human mind. It was only much later that humans—now *Homo sapiens*—developed the imaginative ability to think that an actual human could take the form of a lion.

LANGUAGE AND THE EMERGENCE OF MYTHIC CULTURE

Steven Mithen (among others) believes that the artistic achievements of the Upper Paleolithic show that cognitive fluidity and mythic thinking emerged around forty thousand years ago. But for neuropsychologist Merlin Donald, these achievements signal not the emergence of myth-making but the emergence of graphic skills used to depict "mythic ideas that were already the governing cognitive constructs of human society."[26] According to Donald, mythic ideas existed as early as the Middle Paleolithic, almost one hundred and fifty thousand years before the cultural explosion that produced the painted caves of Europe. These mythic concepts were the products of *language*.

Donald contends that it was around two hundred thousand years ago that the early modern brain developed the capacity to construct a language based on syntax and a lexicon. This transformation was the result of several spurts in brain development that occurred through the Paleolithic, the last resulting in about a 20 percent increase in overall brain volume.[27] Thanks to this development, humans now were able to advance from holistic communication, which represented episodic events, to communication that used separate words to refer to the wealth of objects and events in the world, and that had a way—syntax—to compose these words into claims of infinite variety (including claims about claims about claims, and so on).

This development released the creative and integrative powers inherent in the brain of *Homo sapiens*. As Donald puts it, the manipulation of words and concepts triggered "mythic inventiveness, by which events could be mentally restructured, interrelated, and reshaped in the mind's eye."[28] Adopting Mithen's term, the human mind became cognitively fluid.

With language, humans were able to *reflect* upon *reflection* at ever-higher levels of abstraction, since syntax and discrete words kept these levels separate and manageable. Language-based metacognition—thinking about thinking—is the font of imaginative thought, enabling us "to conceive of imaginary beings and alternative worlds."[29] The wide-ranging effects of metacognition are explained by Scott Atran:

> It lets us enjoy novels *as fiction* that can emotionally arouse us without actually threatening us. It lets us think about being in different situations and deciding which are best for the purposes at hand *without our having to actually live through (or die in) the situations we imagine*. . . . It enables us to become aware of our experienced past and imagined future *as past or future events that are distinct from the present that we represent to ourselves* and so permits us to reflect on our own existence.[30]

Donald points out that language not only enabled our human ancestors to engage in metacognition; it allowed them to vet the results of metacognition. Using *oral narrative*, the vehicle for mythmaking, our ancestors were able to examine, reflect upon, and discuss the ideas, experiences, and feelings important to the community. Different narratives likely competed for acceptance by the group. With the passage of time, they winnowed which of the competing narratives best suited the group's survival needs.[31] A narrative that proved its survival value over time is what Donald calls a "myth."

The group, Donald believes, is held together by one fundamental *meta-myth*, usually a myth of origin. The meta-myth integrates information from the various knowledge domains to provide tribal members with a comprehensive interpretation of the world, an interpretation that explains and sanctions all aspects of existence. Every decision is influenced by myth, and every event and object, every animal, plant, and social custom, right down to clothing, food, shelter, and family life, is situated and explained by myth. Myth not only regulates behavior and enshrines knowledge; it constrains "the perception of reality and channels the thought skills of its adherents." The validating function of myth is so crucial to survival that myths are imbued with "deadly seriousness"; "a person who violates a tribal taboo may die of fear or stress within days, or be ostracized, or put to death."[32]

Mythic culture provided the first *Homo sapiens* with a unified, collectively held, and authoritative system of explanatory and regulatory metaphors. Through myth, the human mind expanded its reach beyond the mimetic reconstruction of episodes "to a comprehensive modeling of the entire human universe. Causal explanation, prediction, control—myth constitutes an attempt at all three, and every aspect of life is permeated by myth."[33]

If this view of myth is largely correct, as I think it is, it creates a couple of paradoxes. First, although mythic thinking was unleashed by the brain's burgeoning imaginative and creative capabilities, it wound up frustrating the expression of these capabilities by establishing and protecting an authoritative vision of reality. And, second, although the imagination enabled the creation of more effective cultural devices for dealing with fear, it also added to and intensified fear.

Let me see if I can resolve these paradoxes, or at least render them slightly less paradoxical.

THE TRAGEDY OF THE IMAGINATION— PROLIFERATING FEARS

There is no disputing the survival value of creative thinking. A "flexible" and "open" mind stands a better chance of solving problems than an inflexible and closed one because it can imagine alternative scenarios, build models, form hypotheses, and generate "as-if" situations, thus enabling people to think through possibilities without physical risk.

But as we became smarter and more imaginative, we became ever more anxious and fearful by anticipating traumatic experiences that might never occur. As humanistic geographer Yi-Fu Tuan explains,

"[I]magination adds immeasurably to the kinds and intensity of fear in the human world. . . . To apprehend is to risk apprehensiveness. If we did not know so much, we would have less fear."[34] The imagination is able to conjure up "preternatural evils unique to the human species," by combining, for example, the killing features of various carnivores into a hybrid "monster" that is bigger and more ferocious than anything in nature.[35] The imagination also exacerbates the mind's natural bias to detect signs of predators even when none are seen. As a result of our imagination, we humans come to inhabit what Carl Sagan describes as a "demon-haunted world" filled with all kinds of threatening creatures— from animal monsters to witches, ghosts, ghouls, and vampires.

This is the world of most tribal people, past and present. In Ghana, for example, houses, trucks, canoes, and workers' toolboxes are decorated with such legends as "Trust no man," "Enemies everywhere around me," and "Fear men and play with snakes."[36] Halfway around the globe, the Eskimo people also live in a constant state of anxiety, bedeviled by all manner of strange, violent, and wild spirits—dwarves, giants, ten-legged polar bears, ghosts, monstrous fish, even giant worms.[37] The Aztecs lived in dread of the gods extinguishing their civilization and sacrificed countless humans to placate divine wrath. Add to these the existential fears that gradually came to haunt human consciousness, from the fear of death, which came to be viewed as an omnivorous agent that spared no one and could not be appeased, to the fear of disease, starvation, loneliness, and social shaming. Humans fear things that a rat could never conceptualize.[38] The capacity to envision all kinds of distant or nonexistent threats has been called the "Tragedy of Cognition."[39]

A restlessly creative mind is a mixed blessing in another way as well. It makes possible socially subversive activities such as lying, deception, and a programmatic contempt for social norms. The same mind that could invent a new tool could also invent a new rule, but not always a helpful one. Small groups struggling to exist within a dangerous environment cannot afford *too much* "creativity," especially when it is directed at social norms that sustain the group. This fear of restless energy may explain the ambiguous depiction of warriors and Tricksters in many myths. People understood that a warrior powerful enough to protect the group was also powerful enough to destroy it, and that the Trickster—who inventively connives to survive no matter what—endangered social trust and cooperation if imitated by too many in the group. It is only in the West that the impulse to "subvert" or "transgress" boundaries can be blithely endorsed and exercised. Endangered people have to defend those boundaries or die. The easier it was to imagine threats, the more pressing the need to create—that is, to *imagine*—cultural devices to deal with these *imagined* threats.

Back to resolving the paradox.

MYTHMAKING AS FEAR MANAGEMENT

A certain level of fear is tonic, but *too much* is toxic. Fear stresses the immune system, and at phobic levels it inhibits normal and life-sustaining behavior. Humans, after all, have to mate, rear young, find food, establish and maintain social bonds, and play. To live, we must take risks. This is especially true for our ancestors, who could no more have survived the Pleistocene by constantly cringing in caves than by "tra-la-la-ing" through the predator-filled landscape. As Hart and Sussman put it, "[P]rey species cannot live in a state of terrified panic all the time—the stress would kill them before the predators did!"[40]

As I see it, mythmaking performed a crucial survival function for our Paleolithic ancestors. It served to harness the fear-proliferating imaginative energies unleashed by the acquisition of language as well as by metacognition. Mythmaking channeled and constrained the creative imagination to protect society from its fear-mongering excesses. The channeling and constraining was achieved in part by the very nature of language. Words and syntax not only facilitate the creative symbolic manipulation of objects and events, as Donald points out, but they also capture these objects and events in symbolizing structures. A lexicon and syntax allowed for inchoate fears and anxieties engendered or intensified by the creative imagination to be constrained and managed. Our fore-bears must have known the difference between a real lion, an image of a lion, and the word *lion*, because if they didn't, we wouldn't be here. What the word *lion* allowed them to do—to oversimplify—was to gain a little more control over the emotions evoked by real and even imagined lions.

Myths could be described as containers for fear. All things that caused fear—from real predators to havoc-wreaking warriors, double-dealing Tricksters, flesh-consuming monsters, and boundary-breaking Bacchantes—could be conjured up symbolically in order to be placed within the safe boundaries of a story, where the fearful agents and events could be examined, subdued, or exorcized. Mythmaking was a way of restraining a fear-mongering imagination too apt to run amok.

Myths function to manage fear in another way as well. As Donald points out, myths present a comprehensive and authoritative account of experience—explaining away calamities and suffering, showing people how to appease and befriend supernatural forces and agents, and helping them stay within the protective embrace of the group. By erasing or mit-igating potentially unnerving existential doubts and uncertainties, myths humanize the cosmos, rendering it understandable and control-lable. Yes, we can imagine and believe in the most terrifying creatures and events, but at the same time we can imagine comforting ways to deal with them as well.

It is impossible to know if people were aware that myth had these effects, but they may have been. Take, for example, the Hawaiian myth about Kamakau—literally, "the afraid one." His overactive fearful imag-ination detected threats everywhere, in the clouds, in the trees, in old lava flows—everywhere. He was so haunted by these fears that he could not be an effective chief. But suddenly his active imagination detected in the configurations of a lava flow *not threatening images* but the countenance of "a god of protection and empowerment." "It seemed to his vivid imagination as if ten thousand good spirits were gathered in the heavens to fight for him. He leaped to his feet, strength came back into the wearied muscles, a new will-power took possession of him, and he cried: 'I will not die! I will not die!'"[41] The same imagination that can trammel us with fears can also release us from their ensnarement, as this very myth did for those who heard it told around the campfire.

Recall the Hawaiian myth about the young maiden Hiilei, who had to face down the dragon. When she encounters the monster during a walk in the dark tropical forest, she is "paralyzed with fear." But despite the dragon's marshalling of fear stimuli, Hiilei is able to follow the advice of her grandmother—show no fear. Hiilei "hid her fear and called a welcome to this dragon." What's intriguing about this story is its self-conscious acknowledgment that the terrifying "dragon" is a creation of Hiilei's fearful imagination, for as soon as she shows no fear by bidding the monster a welcome, "the dragon fell into pieces, and the fragments flew in all directions."[42] It is Alice blurting out, "You're nothing but a pack of cards!"

It would seem, then, that mythmakers were aware, at some level, that story and myth could be used to alleviate the negative effects of the fear-mongering imagination.

STORYTELLING IN THE MIDDLE PALEOLITHIC

Who told the stories and myths of the Middle Paleolithic? How were they told? What were they about? Let me offer some plausible answers to these intriguing questions.

In the Middle Paleolithic, storytelling and mythmaking still would have been partly mimetic, but the mimetic components would have been supplemented by oral narration. The narratives still must have been mostly about predators since *Homo sapiens* remained, essentially, a prey species (though this was soon to change).

What changed in the Middle Paleolithic was that now predators (and other topics) could be *mythologized*; that is, imbued with counter-intuitive and counter-factual features—given characteristics unthinkable in mimetic performance, where enacted portrayals were rooted in realistic event perception and limited to what an early human could manage through body movement, vocalizing, and props.

Over time, it must have become apparent that some people were better than others at creating, dramatizing, and narrating stories. This recognition led to the emergence of the role of tribal "storyteller." Although we cannot know for sure, there is reason to believe that the storytellers of the Middle Paleolithic may not have been that different from the "shamans" of Stone-Age cultures studied by anthropologists. For one thing, mimesis is fundamental to shamanistic thought and practice. Shamans often use animal-like grunts and growls to convince onlookers that they can talk to animals; they chant, sing, dance, and drum to enact their traumatic soul journey that almost always entails a life and death struggle with an animal predator or supernatural creature of some kind.[43] For another, the shaman is often a healer, not just of physical wounds and disease but of emotional troubles, such as anxiety and fear. As one expert explains, the shamans' ritual drama includes the "enactment and resolution of threats and conflict" to help manage these emotions.[44] In the same way as did the early storyteller, the shaman used performance to release people from what endangered them, forces both external and internal.

Let's take a closer look at a typical shaman tale. It usually recounts the shaman's visionary journey through supernatural realms filled with powerful and often threatening animals or monsters that attack the shaman, slashing and devouring his body piece by piece.[45] In fact, most shamans are initiated into their role by being attacked and "devoured" by a predator. In Eskimo myth, the shaman is "eaten by the bear and vomited up again," enabling the shaman to become master of the bear and "endowed with magical and healing power and with eyes that see hidden things."[46] Even a life-threatening attack by a walrus can create a shaman. "The walrus," as one myth has it, "having failed to kill him, became his helping spirit."[47] In Yąnomamö society, shamans are initiated into their calling by a "violent spirit encounter with a huge, supernatural jaguar" conjured up by hallucinogenic snuff. The initiate, covered with painted jaguar spots and tufts of Harpy Eagle down, falls into an ecstatic trance and travels deep into the rain forest until he comes face to face with Omaokohe, animal master of all the big cats. The jaguar strips the candidate of human flesh without injuring the bones and provides him with sacred flesh, along with now-magical organs. The new organs enable the initiate to sing powerful curing songs and understand the language of animals.[48]

The shaman is the *archetypal survivor*, blessed, not destroyed, by the rending power of the carnivore. The shaman's dramatic and moving account of his terrifying encounter with predators likely releases in village members the same flood of opioid neuropeptides released by the stress of an actual attack.[49] In other words, the shaman—like the mimetic storyteller of the early Paleolithic—has the power to evoke the ravishing ecstasy of survival.

But the shaman may take the enactment of dangerous animals a step further than the Paleolithic storyteller did. The storyteller *imitated* a natural predator, but the shaman, thanks to the mythic imagination, often believes he has *become* an animal predator, and so do his or her village members. For example, in pre-Columbian South America, shamans were thought to magically transform themselves into were-jaguars, the most feared of the predators. To encourage this belief—and the power it gave them—shamans dressed in jaguar skins, wore necklaces of jaguar teeth, and growled like jaguars during rituals.[50] When a shaman died, his or her soul was thought to take the form of a jaguar or to possess the body of one that was nearby. Any jaguar was believed to be a reincarnation of a dead shaman.

Although were-jaguar shamans may have frightened people, they were considered necessary since illness was thought to be caused by animals, and so the graver the illness, the more powerful the animal needed to combat it. As one contemporary shaman explains, when the people fall ill, "they must call upon me, for I am the black jaguar. I drive away the illness. They have to call on me. I am the tapir-jaguar. It is me they have to invoke if they wish to frighten it [the illness] away. I am the puma jaguar. I too am here. I extract the illness from their backs. It is me they have to call. I am the multi-colored jaguar. I too am here."[51] The shaman, in essence, creates a powerful story about himself as a *were-predator*.

The shaman protects people from more than sickness. As Pascal Boyer puts it, "Shamanism is all about . . . chasing spirits away or avoiding predation by dangerous witches."[52] The shaman readies himself to take on all evil forces by donning a hideous ceremonial mask designed to "scare angry spirits."[53] In other words, the shaman is at the center of a self-referential story in which the shaman functions as a fear manager, allaying the anxieties and fears of tribal members through a shrewd manipulation of fear stimuli. The shaman continues, I believe, the essential work of the Paleolithic storyteller.

But the shaman-as-predator did not reassure tribal members that they were safe from evil forces. As Dudley Young suggests, the shaman's ceremonial fright-mask functioned at times not only to scare off angry spirits but to *encourage* these spirits to welcome the shaman into their demonic domain.[54] It says, "I am one of you!" Shamans can go bad, and they can use their supernatural animal powers to kill not only the tribe's enemies but also its members. Needless to say, the shaman as were-predator evokes intense dread in those around him. In a tale told by the Kwakiutl of British Columbia, spirit wolves visit a person undergoing transformation into a shaman and warn him, "Friend, take care of the shaman power. Now you can cure the sick and make sick those in your tribe whom you wish to die. They will all fear you."[55]

When shamans succumb to the temptation to "go predator," they almost always kill under the guise of (or by means of) a dangerous animal—a lion, a leopard, a hyena, a tiger, a jaguar, or a crocodile. In one Eskimo myth, a shaman turns against his village, murdering hunters and children. "He stomps around, festooned with amulets, bones, and tusks. His hair appears electrified, disgusting snot and saliva blow from his face with gale force." Although he is eventually killed, "today in some northern villages the shaman's drum-dance and his animal-growl chants can still be heard."[56]

The fear evoked in tribal peoples by bad shamans is so intense that they resort to extraordinary measures to counter the threat. An African tribe called the Lele is so afraid of shamans who take the form of were-leopards that it creates a countervailing savior figure who also assumes the form of a leopard. "His nimble feline intelligence is a match for the leopard-sorcerer and his train of vengeful familiars. All will be well if a village is adequately protected by its official diviners."[57]

Obviously, this desperate effort to allay fear of a shamanistic were-leopard is doomed to increase that fear. This bitter irony is not lost on the Lele, who realize that the power of the good diviner is essentially the same as that of the sorcerer and so can be turned against them once again.[58] Thanks to the ceaseless operation of the mythic imagination, there is no way for humans to escape the fear of predation.

To summarize, the flourishing of the mythic imagination in the Middle Paleolithic transformed the role of the mimetic storyteller into that of the *mythmaking* shaman-storyteller. Of course, the shaman-storyteller continued to imitate actual animals as a way to manage fear. But with full *cognitive fluidity*, the storyteller now could imagine other predators not found in the natural world—were-predators, monsters, and so on. Those with the most active and visionary imaginations probably were the ones selected to fulfill the role of storyteller. The storyteller increased his or her own innate imaginary powers by using psychotropic agents and activities to induce visions of even more powerful and fearful creatures. "The purposeful use of narcotics and hallucinogens to invoke animal spirit assistants or divinities with animal attributes is well attested in sorcery, shamanistic and other ritual contexts in quite unrelated cultures."[59] It is worth noting that in the Amazon, the drug used by shamans during ceremonies was called the jaguar's drug and was kept in a hollow jaguar bone.[60]

In the gradual evolution of the storyteller into the shaman, we see *the mythic imagination working on itself*. The shaman is the storyteller *self-mythologized*, a "mythic" hybrid creature capable of all kinds of counter-factual and counter-intuitive activities, from taking on the identity of a predator to journeying into supernatural realms. The shaman-storyteller is a *symbol of the mythic imagination itself*, an imagination that could transform anything, command the most dangerous threats to human existence, and by so doing, both suppress and activate primal fear.

WERE WOMEN THE FIRST STORYTELLERS?

There are good reasons to think that women were the first storytellers.

As caregivers of children, women had more occasions and greater incentive to engage in dramatic gesturing and evocative vocalizations to entertain, comfort, and connect with newborns. Natural selection favored mothers who knew how to soothe and quiet their babies with both voice and gesture when predators were searching and sniffing for prey.[61] A reflection of this Paleolithic form of mother-infant communication may be found in "motherese" or "baby talk," a combination of singing, clucking, whispering, patter and prattle, coos, and babble that is both dramatic and mimetic. As a child psychologist describes this initial interaction,

> [A] mother greets a newborn in ecstatic cries with falling pitch, and by gentle fondling. . . . Her speech is a kind of singing, with high gliding

gestures of pitch and repetition of regular gentle phrases on a graceful beat, leaving places for the infant to join in with coos, smiles and gestures of the hands and whole body. . . . These exchanges are intricately coordinated with a subdued choreography that brings out matching rhythms and phrasing in mother and infant.[62]

We can't be sure, of course, how mothers in the Pleistocene interacted with their infants, but there is reason to assume that something like this interaction did occur since primate mothers behave in similar ways. Evolution would have encouraged the development in females of skills in vocalization and mimetic expression, prepping them eventually to take on a more public and communal storytelling role.

In the Pleistocene, women had plenty to fear and very strong incentives to convey that fear to their children. Women were especially vulnerable when gathering food, porting water, or scavenging fresh carcasses, particularly if they were also nursing and tending children.[63] Not only would they have had to hold, or keep one eye on, young children (distracting their attention from predators), but they also would fear that a noisy child would attract carnivores always looking for an easy meal. One can imagine the terror of a nursing female at the approach of a pack of sniffing hyenas. As nature writer Paul Shepard observes, women (as well as men) "have a long genetic memory of infants snatched up by hyenas and leopards."[64] It could be said that Paleolithic women were "never free from predatorial anxiety."[65] Women had a strong incentive to acquire and use communication skills to manage this anxiety, as they do today.

Among the Inuit, for example, women are taught by other women from an early age to fear the bear. Many stories relate "how women were attacked, mutilated, and devoured by hungry bears that unexpectedly appeared in camp when the men were away hunting, or which intercepted solitary and defenceless women along the paths."[66] A study of women in an African tribe found that they feel themselves to be far more endangered by predators than men do, and dream more often about these animals than about anything else.[67]

More importantly, mothers as primary caregivers must have been the first in the tribe to teach the young about predators. The first lesson would have come when the infant saw its mother and others react to a threatening predator with alarm calls, shrieks, scampering for protective cover, or merging with others in group defense. But warnings also would have been conveyed to the young through *stories*, told mimetically and eventually orally. The women of the Pleistocene were strongly motivated to express and transmit their fears to those they loved. Even today, the first frightening stories seen or heard by a child almost always come from its mother.

This aspect of storytelling has been explored by Marina Warner in *No Go the Bogeyman*, a work devoted to putting "the ogre back in the mouth, on the tongue, between the jaws of female speakers—and the children to whom they were speaking."[68] As Warner points out, women play a crucial role in socializing children into fear of carnivorous agents of one kind or another. The process begins in the cradle, with the often unnerving traditional lullabies mothers (and other caregivers) sing to infants. Lullabies are not only sleep songs, Warner explains,

> [T]hey include predictions, singing imaginary lives for the infant in the form of blessing; they attempt to warn off dangers . . . and to forestall harm to the child; they explicitly attempt to keep the bogeyman or bogeywoman from the home. . . . But more particularly, the lullaby also invokes figures of death and brings the stalkers and the cradle-snatchers before the infant's eyes. Both kinds of charm over the child's cot are often repeated over and over, sometimes almost tonelessly, a form of incantation. A lullaby is weak domestic magic.[69]

Certain mythic themes, when seen from a female perspective, seem to reflect these archaic historical realities. Women are the ones rescued from mythic monsters because they are essential to the continuation of the tribe; because they have the most intense fear of predators (for good reason); and because they have to rely on physically stronger males to protect and defend them. It makes as much sense to suppose that these rescue myths were created by women to express their social value and their fears as it is to imagine that they were created by men to show off their bravery. Myths about monsters (animals or cannibals) that eat babies seem to express the primal fear of women—losing their offspring to predators. Myths about young women who survive an assault by a predator by stealth or by conquering their fear—such as the Hawaiian myth about Hiilei—almost certainly were created and told *by* women *to* women to manage predator fear.

Although women may have been the first *domestic* storytellers, were they the first *tribal* storytellers? Evidence suggests that they may have been. Research shows that young female primates are more likely to start "innovative behaviors, such as new ways of processing food." For example, female chimps are more likely than males to make new tools and to teach the next generation how to use these tools. Among modern human hunter-gatherer cultures, most tools "*are made and used by women*, not men," for gathering plants, eggs, small insects, and burrowing animals.[70] For most primates, females are also the repositories of group knowledge about home ranges and resources. "Group knowledge and traditions are passed on from mother to offspring, and stability of the group, both in the present and over time, often is accomplished through female associations."[71] While this is not the same as being custodians of tribal myths, it does suggest that in the distant past females may have been powerfully invested in passing on cultural information to others by whatever means were at hand.

It has also been argued that women may have developed cognitive fluidity before men. Women, according to Steven Mithen, were under considerable pressure as child-bearers to exploit whatever information was available "when developing their social relationships with males."

This means that women may have evolved a more finely tuned Theory of Mind Mechanism and may thus have taken "the first step towards cognitive fluidity."[72] In other words, women may have been more imaginative than males and so were better able to create mythic narratives.

And one shouldn't overlook the possibility that women may have played the leading role in the emergence of modern language. The vocalizations and "baby talk" that females shower on infants has often been cited as evidence that females may have played an instrumental role in the evolution of articulate speech.

All and all, women were well positioned to have played a leading role in the emergence of both mimetic and oral storytelling and may have been the first storytellers.

CONCLUSION

Although *Homo erectus* had enough imagination to envision a future tool and the appearance of an absent predator, and to attribute human agency to animals and other objects in the environment, it could not imagine the sorts of "predators" that took shape within the mythic imagination. This imagination emerged from the cognitive functions and devices that evolved in the primate line in response to the threat posed by predators. In other words, the human imagination was shaped by the selection pressure that predators exerted on the human line. It is fitting that the human imagination, when unleashed by the emergence of cognitive fluidity, should transform actual predators into mythic creatures that expressed both the hardwired human fear of "sudden violent death" and the desperate human need to manage that fear.

The creative powers of the human imagination are not limitless but are constrained by the devices and cognitive domains that form the brain/mind. As Scott Atran explains, "[T]he mythic imagination works within cognitive constraints that reflect its rootedness in intuitive knowledge. Mythic beliefs and creations remain integrally bound to factual, commonsense beliefs and inferences. Mythic creatures generally have the sorts of mundane emotions, beliefs, desires, and needs that humans do."[73]

This explains why some mythic confections do not occur. There are no mythic vampires that are always invisible, no ghosts that *cannot* pass through solid objects, no volcanoes that talk, think, or fly. The mythic creature must be strange enough to capture and hold attention but normal enough to keep in play our usual expectations and inference systems. In other words, counter-intuitive or counter-factual mythic creations are optimally counter-intuitive or counter-factual, but they are not so grossly distorted as to be incapable of bearing any meaningful information needed to survive in the real world. However weird they may seem, they remain understandable enough to those who create them to serve as effective vehicles for the transmission of important survival wisdom.

These observations help explain why the animal predator has been mythologized in what I believe to be four fundamental ways—as monster, as god, as benefactor, and as role model. These four categories, which overlap at times, may not embrace every single depiction of a predatory agent in world myth, but they certainly embrace most of them. It's as if these four versions of the mythic predator—a counter-factual creature that exists only within the human mind and in its cultural productions—express and satisfy the range of emotions and imagined relationships that we need to believe exist so that we can deal with our primal fear of dying by carnivore.

Chapter 6

In the Belly of the Beast

The Predator as Mythic Monster

INTRODUCTION

Monsters fill the mythic landscape.

In Hawaiian myth, there is a human with a "shark-mouth" in the middle of his back. In Aboriginal myth, there is a creature with the body of a human, the head of a snake, and the suckers of an octopus. In South American myth, there is the were-jaguar; in Native American myth, there are flying heads, human-devouring eagles, predatory owl-men, water-cannibals, horned snakes, giant turtles, monster bats, and even a human-eating leech as large as a house. In Greek myth, one finds Polyphemus, the one-eyed cannibal giant; the Minotaur, a monstrous human-bull hybrid that consumes sacrificial victims in the "bowels" of the subterranean Labyrinth; and Scylla, the six-headed serpent who wears a belt of dogs' heads ravenously braying for meat.

What drove us to dream up carnivores that were more frightening and "dangerous" than the ones that actually hunted us? What compelled us to add to our fears? What good came from our doing this? And what harm? Let me attempt to answer these questions.

THE MYTHIC MONSTER
AS ANIMAL PREDATOR

Regardless of their different sizes, features, and forms, monsters have one trait in common—they eat humans. Whatever else they may do for us psychologically, monsters express—and *ex-press*—our dread of being torn apart, eviscerated, chewed, swallowed, and then shit out. This shameful fate of those who are eaten is confronted in an African myth in which a giant predatory bird swallows the hero whole day after day and then excretes him.[1] Myth after myth confronts the stark facts of being consumed by a larger creature, obsessively depicting in graphic detail what both *monsters* and *animal predators* naturally do—turn humans into excrement. The stories express "the most basic anxiety of every living being": "being swallowed and eaten."[2] One sees this anxiety throughout world myth.

The Hawaiian shark-man bites and tears his victims limb from limb; the Australian monster sucks its prey into his mouth headfirst, and then dances around "until the prey is well inside his stomach"; the whowie eats "from thirty to sixty people at a meal";[3] and Scylla and Polyphemus gobble up sailors like appetizers. The seven-headed dragon of the Pygmies "eats man's bones."[4] The monsters of the Polynesians come out of their caves "with open mouth and darting tongue" when they smell a human, "the food they craved."[5] The giant Rainbow Snake of Aboriginal myth opens his unhinged jaws and gorges himself on people "as they ran aimlessly from one refuge to another," dragging "his huge length slowly and painfully across the island, his belly weighted down by the people he had swallowed."[6] Another Aboriginal monster eats so many people that he throws them up, exposing "the heads and feet of infants that had been swallowed whole."[7] In another myth, the monster swallows people who lie in its path and then disgorges them in order to have the pleasure of devouring them a second time "at his leisure."[8] In Native American myth, the Windigo, an omnipotent and fierce monster, disembowels

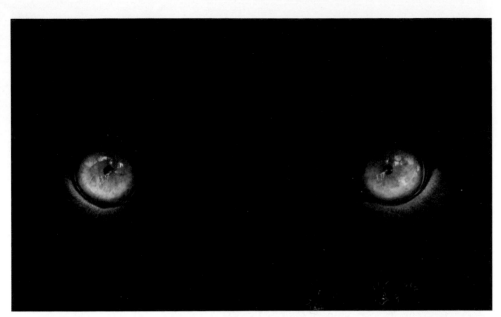

The light-reflective capability of cat eyes makes them appear to emit light supernaturally, the better to detect prey in the dark. Indeed, cats do see better than humans in the dark, and use the cover of darkness to hunt sleeping primates. Eric Gevaert/Shutterstock.com.

In this Maori carving from New Zealand, the predator face is assigned to a mythic raptor, whose wings—also with glaring eye-spots—protrude from the sides of its head. This mythic raptor resembles the mythic monster found in Native American myth, the Flying Head, a rapacious monster made of nothing more than wings and snapping jaws. Tupungato/Shutterstock.com.

Our ancestors understood which features of the predator struck fear in their hearts and they imitated those features in their cultural productions, such as their ceremonial masks. Whatever particular cultural meaning any given mask may have had within a specific tribe, the frightening mask imitating the predator face was fundamentally an attempt to make terror our friend, to harness and command it to do our bidding. Anlogin/Shutterstock.com.

Dressing like and acting like an animal predator or hybrid monster can be found in all cultures. The Chinese celebrate their New Year by dancing the dragon. In other societies papier-mâché monsters are created so that people can gather together to drive them out of town or dismantle them like a piñata. To prepare for battle, warriors dress as predators and dance wildly until they acquire the killing powers of ferocious animals. Performing the predator likely arose from early humanity's fledgling attempts to communicate about, and control their fear of, the carnivores that densely populated the Pleistocene environment. Christopher Testi/Shutterstock.com.

In most cultures heroes, kings, and gods are depicted sitting or standing on the backs of dangerous animals. These images express our longing to control predators in order to control our fear of predators. Elfwilde/Shutterstock.com.

Gargoyles, serpent heads, and dragon forms are often used to scare away evil agents at holy sites, such as at this Thailand temple. These mythic monsters make us feel more confident that the gods are benevolently disposed toward us. Nickolay Stanev/Shutterstock.com.

We are obsessed with dressing up as predators or were-predators of one kind or another, from eagles and jaguars to dragons and zombies. Halloween provides the greatest license to identify with powerful predatory agents. Warriors across the globe have understood the empowering effects of thinking of themselves as animal predators. In Meso-American cultures, warriors often wore head covers that transformed them into a predatory beast able and eager to tear the enemy apart. Del7891/Shutterstock.com.

Fear not only induces us to worship and befriend predators but to imitate and even become them. By dramatically embracing the inner predator and frightening others, people can conquer fear and embrace power. Some go so far as to undergo repeated and extensive surgery to transform themselves into were-predators. Galushko Sergey/Shutterstock.com.

Images can be found throughout the world of animal predators or hybrid monsters swallowing humans or biting into their heads, just as big cats do. Mesoamerican cultures were obsessed with the image of a human head inside the mouth of a jaguar. These images have often been interpreted as depictions of a shaman or god "emerging" from the mouth of the predator, but what is actually seen is a human head inside the carnivore's mouth. In other images, the jaguar is depicted less ambiguously as biting into the neck of the human that it has within its paws. This Asian depiction of a dragon biting into an orb or globe is a powerful envisioning of the archetypal act of carnivores biting into the human head. *PhonProm/Shutterstock.com.*

people with "one swipe of his paw" and devours them "in one gulp."[9] And in African myth, there is a monstrous bird that sweeps down whenever it sees people and "swallows them whole," "all sorts of people, everyone who went by."[10] Myth is a congenial habitat for gigantic creatures—from flying heads to dragons—whose sole purpose is to bite, tear, and swallow any human in their path.[11]

This brief survey hardly captures the depth and intensity of our obsession with such creatures. In some myths, the monster is subjected to a sort of autopsy, which reveals not only the contents of its stomach but also our compulsive need to examine the contents. In one Polynesian myth, the belly of a sea monster is cut open, and "whole bodies of men, women, and children" come tumbling out. "Some other bodies were severed in the middle; some had their heads off; some their arms, some their legs."[12] In another Polynesian myth, a "slayer of monsters" peers down the throat of a sea-serpent to find the remains of his long-lost parents, "who had been swallowed when fishing by this monster of the deep."[13] A Maori myth recounts the autopsy of a monster whose belly was bursting with the "decomposed bodies of their own men, women, and children, along with separated limbs, torsos, and heads."[14] In a myth of the Eyak Indians of the Northern Territories, when the stomach of a giant predatory rat is cut open, the skulls of all the people it had killed and eaten come tumbling out.[15]

In some myths, monster autopsies have happier outcomes. A Polynesian myth explains how a father rescued his daughter from an enfeebled monster. "The legs were kicking, which meant she was still alive. So Iol attacked the ogre while it slept, killing it with powerful spear thrusts and cutting off its hideous head. He then opened the belly and found his poor daughter, somewhat the worse for wear but still alive. He then removed her from the spirit's belly and took her home."[16] In one African myth, a dragon's belly is slit open to release two hapless Pygmies who had been swallowed but were still alive. In an Aboriginal myth, a hero slits open the belly of a crocodile to release two friends "clothed in slime" from head to foot.[17]

Sometimes the belly of the beast is cut open from the *inside* by a brave warrior or a clever Trickster. This theme is widespread in Native American myths. The Nez Perce, for example, relate how Coyote, the most powerful being in the early time, forced himself into the maw of a gigantic monstrous predator, where "he found the emaciated people, their life being slowly drawn out of them, chill and insensible." Together they "cut their way out into the sunlight."[18] In another Native American myth, a heroic fisherman allows himself to be swallowed by a sea monster to save the others already engorged. He and the others hold a war dance inside the "monster's maw," after which he stabs the monster in the heart and then "cuts his way through to the day."[19] The Salish also mythologized their fear and triumph over the all-consuming Terrible Monster. Wandering inside the monster's vast belly, Coyote kills it by slicing through its heart, restoring to life the bones of its victims.[20] In a Zande myth, the Trickster hero, armed with many little knives, contrives to be swallowed by a monster bird. Inside he finds all the bird's victims still alive, and with the knives they cut through the guts of the bird and escape.[21]

This mythic motif is an attempt to *allay* our primal fear of being eaten "alive," an attempt, one might say, to rescue ourselves from the *belly of bestial fear*. As fanciful as these events may appear to us today, they may contain remnants of actual experiences. For instance, sometimes predators simply lose interest in the prey midway through an attack and let it escape, and sometimes they can be intimidated into letting go of the prey. Cape buffalo and apes have been observed rescuing one of their own from the very jaws of death, as in the much-viewed video of buffalo rescuing a calf first from the jaws of lions and then from the jaws of a crocodile! Is it too fanciful to think that over millions of years our ancestors may have managed to literally pull their kith and kin from the clutches of carnivores or maybe to even cut them—still alive—out of the belly of a python? As Anthony Stevens suggests, "[T]he notion of the engulfing belly and digestive tract must come from observations of the giant boa-constrictor ingesting its prey" and sometimes, perhaps, regurgitating it.[22]

Such traumatic near-death experiences may have contributed to the evolution of the role of the shaman, who is thought to gain uncanny power over dangerous animals by virtue of having been attacked and then released by a predator, as in Eskimo myth, in which the shaman is "eaten" and then vomited up by a bear.[23] A person who survives being mauled by a big cat or bear or who is pulled from the gut of a python may be a bit more susceptible to hallucinations or be more inclined to regard himself as more "in touch" with animal powers as a result of this near-death experience.

Every day over the course of several million years, our ancestors saw (and heard) living creatures being torn apart and devoured by hungry animals—with some victims still kicking as they were eviscerated and dismembered. No wonder our brains are wired to make us dread this awful fate, and that the stories we tell ourselves reflect this dread and attempt to *ex-press* it—press it out.

ANIMAL PREDATORS *INTO* MYTHIC MONSTERS

The archetype of the monster is an expression of this primal fear *writ large*, exaggerated and intensified to an outlandish degree. But why does this primal fear take the form of a "monster," that is, a predatory creature that grotesquely mixes animal or human-and-animal physical features? In what way did our experiences as a prey species contribute to the formation of the *mythic* monster?

Let's begin by looking at the most widespread and celebrated of all mythic monsters—the dragon. This creature, in one guise or another, appears in almost every mythology and has been the subject of many books and countless articles. Perhaps the most intriguing of these examinations is *An Instinct for Dragons* by anthropologist David E. Jones. Jones argues that the image of the dragon is composed of the salient body parts of three predator species that hunted and killed our tree-dwelling African primate ancestors for about sixty million years. The three predators are the leopard, the python, and the eagle.[24]

According to Jones (what follows is a condensed summary of a complex argument), ancient primates evolved alarm calls to identify each of the three predators, with each call triggering the defensive response appropriate to the nature of the attack mode of the specific predator. Jones calls this predator-recognition template the "snake/raptor/cat complex." This complex is the source of what Jones refers to as the "brain dragon."[25] The brain dragon emerged when our apelike ancestors left the trees to walk on the ground. Rather suddenly, the relatively small brain of

The archetypal predator is the dragon, a hybrid creature that seems to combine the essential traits of the three dominant predators of the primate line—the cat, the snake, and the raptor. *blizzardwolf/Shutterstock.com.*

Australopithecus had to process a lot of information about many new forms of predators and develop new alarms calls and strategic responses to them. Faced with information overload, the brain of *Australopithecus* resorted to lumping information into manageable and memorable chunks. As a result, the cat, the snake, and the raptor were merged into a hybrid creature that had the salient predatory features of each: the face of a feline, the body of a snake, and the talons of a raptor.[26] This is the hybrid "monster" that came to be known as the "dragon."

Because the image combined features from three dominant predators, it could quickly send the neural message *very dangerous animal.* Indeed, the derivation of the word *monster* seems to acknowledge this ancient function. *Monster* comes from the Latin word *monstrare*, "to show," and *monere*, "to warn." Monsters are warning signs, reminding us of the many threatening creatures lurking in the environment eager to gobble us up.[27]

Jones argues that the image of the dragon—the salient elements of which were already hardwired into the primate brain—became a "pattern" or "template" that could be passed on genetically as well as culturally.[28] He spends a considerable amount of space demonstrating how this process could have worked, but the upshot is that the "brain-dragon" was stored in the human mind for hundreds of thousands of years, where it lay dormant or lurked in the dreams of ancient humans, to be released during times of great communal anxiety. It was only with the development of language and art, Jones argues, that the image of the dragon could be given full expression and a greater semblance of reality.[29] It could be said, then, that the dragon—like other monsters and mythic figures—is a product of the cognitive fluidity that underlies the mythic imagination. The archetype of the dragon gave form to the fears engendered by humanity's developing ability to imagine all kinds of new dangers and threats.

Jones's notion that the dragon is composed of tissue samples taken from real predators could account, as well, for the origin of other mythic monsters. The shape of the snake, for example, could furnish not only the body of the mythic dragon but the neck of the hydra; the beak of the raptor could replace the face of the big cat and also be combined with its paws. For example, the griffin has the body parts of a lion but the face and wings of an eagle. And so on. Whatever the particular form the monster may have taken within a specific geographical area, its essential features would clearly have identified it as a very dangerous creature even to those unfamiliar with local fauna. Monsters were used as a means of imbuing sacred or dangerous geographical areas with taboo and explaining the source and cause of lethal natural disasters, such as typhoons, hurricanes, volcanic eruptions, and so on. But the basic function of the monster was to give fear a face, to graphically capture the dread that is bred into us by millions of years as a prey species that was stalked and sometimes eaten by huge and terrifying carnivores.

NATURAL SOURCES OF MYTHIC MONSTERS

The "monsters" of the mythic imagination also inherited some of their DNA from the very real "monsters" created by Mother Nature herself. Recall the Pleistocene predators described in chapter 2, many with huge jaws, foot-long fangs, and beaks that could split coconuts. In ancient Australia (and perhaps in other areas of the Southeast), there was a flesh-eating lizard measuring up to thirty feet long and weighing two thousand pounds, almost "ten times the weight of its closest relative the 'ora' or Komodo dragon."[30] There were birds too huge to fly, four-legged animals that could walk at times on two legs, and carnivores that possessed both female and male genitals (as does the female hyena). Again, the nineteenth-century writer Charles Gould—a cryptozoologist before the field had a name—understood the natural origin of the first "monsters":

Surely a profound acquaintance with the different branches of natural history should render a man credulous rather than incredulous, for there is hardly conceivable a creature so monstrous that it may not be paralleled by existing ones in every-day life. Are the composite creatures of Chaldaean mythology so very much more wonderful than the marsupial kangaroo, the duck-billed platypus, and the flying lizard of Malaysia which are [that is, exist], or the pterodactylus, rhamphorynchus, and arachaeopteryx which have been.[31]

Until about one hundred thousand years ago—well after the appearance of cognitive fluidity and the human ability to make up stories—our ancestors lived in Africa with a giant ape (*Gigantopithecus blackii*) that stood about ten feet tall and weighed up to one thousand two hundred pounds. The notion of "monster" may also have been shaped by rare instances of what biologists call "hybrid vigor," as when two species interbreed to create an animal far bigger than either the male or the female of the breeding species. Think of the "tigron" and the "liger" (both of which now are bred in captivity). And occasionally a genetic roll of the dice gives rise to natural-born giants. Recently, a tiger (aptly named Hercules) grew to a length of twelve feet and to a weight of one thousand pounds, and a Sumatran python grew to fifty feet and weighed almost nine hundred pounds, provoking local people to worship it as a god. Venerating snakes is hardly a stretch for the human imagination, given that these creatures "monstrously" violate so many categorical boundaries—legless and wingless motion, blinkless eyes, renewable skin, and so on.

The human imagination was also primed to accept the reality of mythic monsters by encounters with the giant "sea serpents" that live in large bodies of water. Such massive creatures must have been especially frightening since they were rarely seen and appeared suddenly, as does the shark in *Jaws*. In 2008, a twenty-five-foot-long squid weighing over a thousand pounds was caught off the coast of New Zealand. A giant pike caught in Siberia had jaws strong enough to snap a small boat in half.[32]

Belief in the actual existence of "monsters" was also supported by cultural memories—passed down in drawings, carvings, and traditional stories—of encounters in the distant past with large carnivores and herbivores. The Cheyenne remember in myth an ancient horselike carnivore with "long-sharp teeth," possibly a cultural memory of "the great sabre-tooth not yet extinct."[33] In New Zealand and Hawaii, there are legends of immense reptiles no longer found in the islands but that once did live in the areas from where the Polynesians migrated a thousand years earlier.[34] Reptiles are practically unknown in the Alaskan fauna, but "the Eskimo nurse cultural memories of a fantastic, much-dreaded reptilian monster . . . and a caterpillar-like human giant."[35] Renowned geoscientist Paul Martin was struck by the fact that southwestern caves contain evidence that "Archaic people venerated animals extinct for thousands of years."[36]

Certain Aztec myths about giants that "pulled down trees as if they had been stalks of lettuces" may have originated in ancestral memories of Columbian mammoths.[37] A mythic monster of the Cheyenne may have been based on "ancestral memories of the giant short-faced bear (*Arctodus simus*), a frightening predator of the Pleistocene-Holocene."[38] Native American myths about the Thunder Bird may be based on "living memories of very large, extinct raptors of the Ice Age," such as condors and teratorns with wingspans of twelve to seventeen feet.[39] In the nineteenth century, monster-lore scholar Charles Gould suggested that some monsters may reflect cultural memories of "a few cretaceous and early tertiary forms" that were thought to have gone extinct but that "struggled on" in isolated and remote areas of the world.[40] This same claim is made today by some cryptozoologists.

Another fertile source of mythic monsters is the *bone yard*. It's long been noted that the fossilized skeletons of long-extinct creatures from the age of dinosaurs contributed to the creation of mythic monsters. It was as far back as 1831 that Gould suggested that belief in monsters arose from the frequent discoveries of the remains of "monstrous amphibians."[41] Gould also pointed out that when the Chinese came across the skeletons of long-extinct dinosaurs, they referred to them as "dragon bones."[42] In the Carpathians, the bones of extinct cave bears also have been interpreted as the remains of dragons.[43] The reptilian or serpentine characteristics given to many mythic monsters may reflect the fact that fossilized skeletons, often reduced to an undulating backbone and neck, look like a snake. In Ovid's *Metamorphoses*, a decomposed human backbone transforms into a snake, a literal and figurative example of the mythologizing process I'm describing.[44]

No one has done more to illuminate the relationship between fossils and mythmaking than Adrienne Mayor, who has documented hundreds of instances during the last two thousand five hundred years when fossil bones provided the scaffolding for elaborate mythmaking, as frightened people sought to give meaning to the startling animal remains they happened across. To cite just one example, the Thunder Bird of Native American mythology may have something to do with discoveries of *Tyrannosaurus rex* skeletons. "Someone who discovered a tyrannosaurid forelimb with its peculiar pair of claws, and perhaps with the elongated, birdlike shoulderblade, might well have identified the fossil as part of the skeleton of some mysterious bird."[45]

The mythologizing process probably did not start with the Greeks and Romans or even with the appearance of the modern brain. *Homo erectus* also must have tried to explain the frightful skulls and bones it came across. These remains must have been particularly terrifying since early humans could not have known that the remains belonged to carnivorous "monsters" long extinct. In fact, the hyper predator detection system of early humans would have prompted them to interpret the bones as the remains of creatures still alive and possibly lurking somewhere in the environment. The tens of millions of bones that accumulated ever since the first skeletal creatures swam in the sea provided our forebears with constant provocations to imagine the existence of monstrous predators.

When our ancient ancestors came across the giant and terrifying skulls of long-vanished dinosaurs, such as this *Tyrannosaurus rex* skull, what did they make of them? Without the concept of "extinction," they must have assumed that these skulls signaled the existence of living versions lurking somewhere in the environment. There can be little doubt that even in the Pleistocene such discoveries must have engendered excited interchanges and storytelling. *psamtik/Shutterstock.com.*

With the emergence of cognitive fluidity, the extraordinary skulls and bones of extinct creatures were easily mythologized into terrifying monsters that "really" existed. How many monsters were created from animal bones is impossible to say, but thanks to Adrienne Mayor and others, we have at least started to count them.

ENVISIONING MONSTERS

Monsters were also created by dreams and reveries.

According to medical anthropologist Alondra Oubre, "proto-humans" of the Early Pleistocene first discovered the emotional and psychological rewards of altering the normal chemistry of the brain. These altered states of consciousness enabled our ancestors to "unlock the doors" to the unconscious and to access its "unlimited reservoir of fantasia, hypnagogic imagery, day-dreaming, and creative ideation."[46] These counter-factual and counter-intuitive images and symbols were fabricated, necessarily, from the bits and pieces of daily life. The memories of these experiences were not stored as accurate snapshots but as somewhat distorted versions of that experience, reshaped, exaggerated, or diminished according to their emotional content. Oubre suggests that early humans engaged in these practices to escape their "anguishing existence in a prey-versus-predator world." Admittedly, it would have been suicidal to "escape" from this world for too long or too often—to lose touch with the real threats that provoked the anxieties in the first place. But periodic escape, during rituals, would have been therapeutic, helping assuage fear and increase confidence.[47]

These fear-management strategies, however, had ironic consequences. Among the salient experiences our ancient ancestors remembered and stored in their unconscious must have been life-threatening encounters with predators. Which means that during altered states, images of predators would have undergone further shaping, twisting, recombination, or hybridization. The upshot is that protohumans were able to conjure up hybrid images of animals well before cognitive fluidity and mythmaking emerged during the Middle Paleolithic. Although protohumans could not spin yarns about monsters, they may have been able to imagine them, and thus unintentionally add to their fears through the same processes they were using to escape their fears.

Obviously we cannot know what protohumans envisioned during consciousness-altering rituals, but we do know that during such states, humans with modern brains envision monsters. In several Native American cultures, visions often entail an encounter with powerful animal spirits. In Pawnee society, the encounter gives the visionary shaman or tribal member the power "to harm or even kill enemies or other Pawnee."[48] Especially potent is the power gained from the snake and the "Water Monster." The Oto tribe of northeast Kansas think that dreaming of rattlesnakes not only forebodes an enemy attack but imbues the dreamer with animal powers that could be either "destructive or creative." Dreaming about the Water Monster could be extremely dangerous "because of the type of power that the dreamer might be given."[49] In short, the dreamer is able to channel the power of monstrous animals.

Altered states of consciousness are crucial to shamanism. As I explained earlier, while in a trancelike state, shamans are thought to make contact with animal monsters and often become one of them. The strange images they see in the mind's eye "are interpreted as culturally meaningful images, perceived as recognizable shapes of people, animals, and monsters." It is during this stage that shamans "may begin to have bodily hallucinations in addition to the visual effects."[50] During such hallucinations, shamans (and others) have imagined themselves werepredators of some kind, possessing incredible power to both protect and kill. In essence, *shamans have envisioned themselves to be monsters.*

OUR "INNER" MONSTER

Mythic monsters are often explained—or explained *away*—as symbols of the "monster within," an embodiment or projection of the greedy, aggressive impulses at the core of what Jung called the Shadow[51] aspects of the "self and the psyche that are disowned and repressed because they are considered to be bad and evil."[52] That Shadow wants to feel "the thrill of fangs and claws, the thrill of copulation without commitment, the dog within going wild after a lifetime on the leash."[53] Monsters allow us to express and confront our dark unconscious, enabling it to materialize—and by so doing, exorcize—hidden and repressed desires and fears.

It can hardly be doubted that monsters "materialize real desires and fears,"[54] but what desires and fears? How did the monster get inside us in the first place?

One answer is to say that the "monster" was always in us, as part of our primate inheritance—the "killer ape" view. This view is based on the behavior of chimpanzees, who have been observed doing gruesome things to other primates and members of their own species. But the behavior of today's chimps may not be an accurate guide to human behavior four million years ago. At that time, the evolutionary lines of humans and chimps had already been separate for at least three million years. Admittedly, the human line had to have enough instinctual aggression to fend off predators. But the early repertoire of display charging, rock hurling, stick swinging, and so on, though aggressive, is hardly on the same plane as the "predatory" behaviors of animal carnivores. Early humans did not possess either the sharp teeth or strong muscles that today's chimps have and that they occasionally use to horrific effect. Although we eventually did kill and eat our own, I'm not convinced that the earliest humans were cannibalistic and murderous thugs.

Not only did our ancient ancestors have neither the physical endowments nor the technological know-how to be much of a danger to other humans (weapons such as clubs were an invention of a more developed brain), they probably had little motive to be so. Faced with so many environmental threats, early humans had to band together in collective group defense rather than kill and eat each other, a task already performed so well by predators. No doubt within the group there was jostling for status and goods, but intra-group and inter-group homicide was probably very rare, or we would not be here to speculate about it. It took a very long time for humans to be transformed—indeed to transform themselves—into the alpha predator of the planet. We were not born "monsters," we became "monsters."

This transformation was accomplished, I suggest, through *mimesis*. We became efficient killers by watching and imitating efficient killers—which is to say that we "performed the predator" in more ways than one. Our ancestors studied predators, learned how to "read their minds" in order to predict their behavior, imitated their hunting behaviors and tactics in ritual and in the hunt, and eventually used the teeth and bones of predators to make weapons. Those who could most successfully imitate the hunting behaviors of predators had a better chance of surviving and passing on their genetic material than those who couldn't. Over a considerable period of time, mimesis managed to transform the *Homo* line into a species able—and sometimes eager—to kill vast numbers of its own kind with such up-close-and-personal weapons as bare hands, stones, knives, scythes, machetes, and garden hoes. If anyone should be called "killer apes," it should be we moderns, not our Pleistocene ancestors.

The irony of this transformation is obvious: the less we needed to fear *animal* predators, the more we needed to fear *human* predators. Each one of us, to some degree, is a turbulent cauldron of hostile and aggressive impulses. We fear and feel guilty about these impulses. The mythic monster probably does function, at times, to ex-press—press out—this fear and guilt about the monster lurking within our psyche. As Charles Dickens, writing of the French Revolution, so brilliantly phrased it, the "monsters imagined since imagination could record itself, are fused in the one realization, Guillotine."[55] A massive, monstrous tooth.

But once again, an irony lurks in this dynamic. It was by imitating and gradually internalizing the tactics and behaviors of predators that we managed to *survive* the Pleistocene. Given this reality, it would be (and it would have been) suicidal for us to "ex-press" all of the monster within, to rid ourselves of the atavistic, primal, bestial power we've inherited or borrowed from predators. At times, to survive, we need to conjure up the monster to combat the monster (as *Alien, The Edge, Beowulf, Predator, While She Was Out*, and so many other survival films dramatize). So it is too simple, and *wrong*, to dismiss the monster as merely a negative projection of the "bad" or "evil" self, as is so often done. We *want and need* to feel there's a monster within us so we can summon its power when necessary. Millions of years as a prey species have taught us that, at times, we must drink the dragon's blood to survive.

OUR *MONSTROUS* IMAGINATION

As should be clear by now, the mythic imagination is cursed by the unsettling irony that it has the power not only to express and vent our primal fear but also to *intensify* and *add* to it. It is because of its power to *imagine* monsters that the mythic imagination *is itself monstrous*.

The mythic imagination is not governed, unfortunately, by some sort of psychic rheostat that shrewdly limits the production of "monsters" to a suitably therapeutic number. Since the mythic imagination has no built-in constraints, it is able to create more and more monsters until it fills the mythic and mental landscapes with them. When the mythic imagination is not held in check by other cultural institutions, it can trigger a runaway feedback cycle: the more monsters, the more fear, the more fear, the more need of monsters to vent that fear. Belief in and fear of monsters can become so intense that they negatively affect the survival of both the individual and the group.

The example of the Inuit is instructive in this regard. The Inuit are an extremely ingenious—indeed creative—people, managing to solve life-threatening problems with minimum technology. But their active imagination has engendered an array of intimidating and dangerous monsters: dwarves and mermaids that entice and then kill people, huge worms that squirm their way toward the villages to crush them, giant predatory birds able to carry off their victims, immense lake fish able to swallow a human with a single bite, ten-legged polar bears, and all manner of malicious ghosts and cannibal sprits that cause illness or death.[56] "There are spirits of snowdrifts, valleys, ice hummocks, rapids, forests; they have jurisdiction over those locales, and many places are named for sprits."[57] In tale after tale, the Inuit, to survive, must battle these strange and dangerous creatures.[58]

The Inuit are so afraid of the very monsters they themselves have conjured into existence that they impose upon themselves rigorous taboos—formal and sacred instructions—designed to keep them from encountering or offending the very monsters they have imagined. As anthropologist Richard Edgerton explains in *Sick Societies*,

> Many [taboos] had no imaginable utility, and on the whole the Inuit felt that their taboos were burdensome and fearsome. Most Inuit groups lived in what Asen Baliciki referred to as "dreadful" fear. To be sure, taboos were not alone in creating fear—evil spirits and all manner of monsters were also a part of the Inuit world. Indeed, when Knud Rasmussen asked a "wise man" among the Iglulik Inuit about their beliefs, this was his answer: "What do we believe? We don't believe, we only fear."[59]

This fear led the Inuit to avoid areas rich in food because monsters were thought to lurk there. "Good hunting and fishing areas could not be visited at night for fear of 'wild babies'—creatures resembling human infants—that were thought to devour people like wolves."[60] European explorers and colonizers took advantage of the situation by hunting and fishing the areas the Inuit were too afraid to enter. There is no avoiding the conclusion that in the case of the Inuit, the mythic imagination— likely excited by the dangers implicit in the extreme conditions of the natural environment—conjured up more monsters than other cultural institutions could contain. The result was a demon-haunted world that exacerbated the natural perils of this inhospitable environment. In this instance, the monster-making imagination was far from therapeutic.

The Inuit are certainly not the only people who have been physically afflicted by their own imaginary monsters. According to two anthropologists who have studied the Navajo, tribal members are plagued by "high anxiety," "worry," and "uneasiness," thanks to the monsters they have invented. The ancient Japanese also lived in a demon-haunted world infested with all kinds of treacherous spirits and monsters.[61] "As in India, these fractious, swarming monsters are . . . in every nook and cranny of the islands, haunting abandoned houses and jumping around rooftops in the cities, flying about, swimming in the oceans, and roaming the countryside looking for victims." By the early nineteenth century, this monster mania became so intense and widespread that it led to panics that threatened the social order. The situation became so extreme that the government actually passed legislation in 1808 forbidding the telling of ghost stories about "flying heads, animal goblins, serpent monsters, fire demons, and suchlike terrors."[62] A similar situation arose in medieval Europe, where the mania for monsters became so socially threatening that European churches were forced to crack down on the exploitation of demonic and grotesque imagery in ecclesiastical art and architecture.[63]

Looking at another example, the monstrous imagination, I believe, drove the Aztecs to cut out the hearts of two hundred thousand human beings every year. These highly intelligent and otherwise civilized people engaged in such gruesome ceremonies because they were terrified of their predator-like gods. These gods, it was thought, would destroy Aztec civilization if they were not regularly fed human flesh. The gods *will* have our blood. Sacrifice was a way to escape from, avoid, alleviate this fear. The psychotic and compulsive nature of this sacrifice reveals just how terrified the Aztecs were of the very gods they themselves created. Ironically, their beliefs and sacrificial practices materially contributed to the destruction they so dreaded. To acquire enough bodies to feed to the predatory jaguar gods and feathered-serpent gods that haunted their imaginations, the Aztecs raided surrounding tribes, sweeping up as many as two hundred and fifty thousand victims a year. When Cortez and his small contingent of soldiers appeared, the ravaged tribes were only too happy to aid him in his conquest of this predatory empire.[64]

Clearly, imagining monsters can be maladaptive as well as therapeutic. It can increase and intensify our anxieties and fear beyond reason, hampering our ability to adjust to and intelligently exploit environmental opportunities. And, by engendering a climate of fear, imagining

The essential features of the predator face are exploited in every culture to intimidate and to communicate power. By imitating the features that inherently trigger our deepest fear, we manage that fear and bend it to enhance our personal and social survival. *markrhiggins/Shutterstock.com.*

monsters can induce us to see monstrous traits in humans who simply are different, foreign, or adversarial. As Marina Warner explains, "[O]ne of the chief moral problems revealed by the fantasies of fear is that they search for a guilty party. Apprehension of dangers—real or imaginary—converts into diagnosis of moral evil."[65] As soon as the guilty party is imagined to be somehow "monstrous," it can be tormented, persecuted, and killed. The scapegoat figure is another device we use to deal with our primal and continuing fear of being attacked and consumed.

But again, this psychic dynamic gives rise to a paradox. If we need to fear our own monster-making imagination, could the production of monsters at times represent an attempt by the imagination *to control itself*? David Gilmore shrewdly observes that the monster symbolizes the hybridizing and boundary-breaking power of the creative imagination.[66] If it does so, then the mythic monster may represent, and be an *expression of*, the *dark side* of that imagination, its disturbing power to torment and grieve us by manufacturing unreal but emotionally powerful agents of fear. It could be said, then, that the monster objectifies (at times) the very "monstrous" imaginative power that created it. The monster would then represent *both* the dark side of the human imagination *and* that imagination attempting to check itself by "ex-pressing" its own frightening power to frighten. Although this attempt sometimes goes too far, as we have just seen, it often appears to work, especially in certain kinds of myths. This interpretation helps explain why mythic monsters—though enormous and incredibly voracious and in every way our superiors—are frequently subdued by clever, often *imaginative* heroes and Tricksters.

Given the dynamics of the human imagination, there can be no end to the production of mythic monsters, but our survival instincts refuse to let these imagined monsters engulf our consciousness. The same imagination that produces monsters also produces the Tricksters and heroes that curtail their power to frighten and harm us.

BATTLING THE MYTHIC MONSTER

One of the central claims of this book—that early humans were hunted by predators—was intuited by mythmakers and can be found in many myths. As one Native American myth puts it, in ancient times "many man-eating giant animals swarmed on the face of the earth hunting people, who were at that time in an uncultured state like babies, weak and not yet the masters of the earth they would later become." It was almost impossible for these people to survive, since "they were too frightened to do much else than cower in their miserable caves." Finally, after eons of this abject subjugation, a local hero rose up to help the people conquer the earth. "With the help of some watchful good spirits, he subdued the swarming man-eaters . . . and drove the monsters underground so that the people could live freely and establish a rightful human hegemony as the gods had intended."[67]

In Zuni myth, primal monsters prey on early humans at each stage of their evolution from lower to higher worlds. Finally, the sun god armed a set of twins with lightning bolts so they could kill the monsters and become known as the "Monster Slayers."[68] Hopi myths recount the distant time when the path of the Hopi was blocked by horrid monsters, giants, and demons, until two young brothers killed them so the Hopi could continue their journey.[69] In a Tagish (Northern Territories) myth, all the first mammals are man-eaters, even Giant Sheep, so Beaver Man kills the eldest, the first, of all the primordial predators but orders the surviving youngsters not to grow any bigger and not to eat human flesh. With the Giant Bear, however, Beaver Man cannot afford such humane scruples. After getting all the Giant Bears in the water, Beaver Man "slits their throats."[70] A similar myth can be found halfway around the world. The !Kung of Southern Africa explain how the Mantis, the first person, had to kill all the "bad ones" that plagued the people—among them giant snakes and eagles and crocodiles.[71]

These myths reflect an uncannily accurate understanding of our prehistoric predicament—that we once were a prey species in danger of being made extinct by a host of dangerous animals. Psychotherapist Anthony Stevens sums it up quite well when he writes that monsters "relate us directly to our primeval origins." "They are hideous manifestations of the archetype of the huge-jawed, slavering, heavily clawed predator, capable of seeking us out wherever we hide. Their natural adversary, and our welcome ally, is the hero."[72]

But there could not have been a "hero" if the relationship between humans and animals had not gone topsy-turvy with the invention of

Although the hero can have a thousand names—in this instance, St. George—his (and sometimes her) role is to kill predators, whether animals or mythic monsters. These creatures came to symbolize different threats depending on the culture, but the image of the hero overcoming a predatory agent recapitulates our primordial struggle with dangerous carnivores and the triumph of our species over them. *c./Shutterstock.com.*

weapons that could kill at a distance—the throwing spear and later the bow and arrow. It is this transformation—which took hundreds of thousands of years to occur—that is symbolized in the figure of the mythic hero. This transformative "event" is captured and celebrated in myth after myth, as in the African myth about the hero Hussein, who rids a village of a "great black serpent" by piercing it with a "spear." "It died quickly."[73] In another African myth, a hero beheads a monstrous snake "with one stroke," and "soon everyone in town knew that the serpent had been killed" and that there was nothing more to fear.[74]

Myths about heroes defeating primordial monsters are less history than therapy, helping us manage our fear. The hero fulfills our longing to escape from our abject vulnerability to dangerous animals. This is why the hero is such a crucial figure in folk tales and myths throughout the world. His triumph is our triumph over the evil predators and deadly powers that might destroy us. "He is our champion, our defender, our liberator and savior."[75] The greater the monster, the greater the sense of relief and triumph when the hero finally kills or controls it. In essence, the monster functions as a scapegoat that carries away not only our fear but also our shame at being so easily transformed into offal. This may explain why, as biologist E. O. Wilson puts it, "we love our monsters."[76] At any rate, we need them.

The transformation of humans from prey to predator was accomplished, I think, through imitation. Evolution selected for early humans who could best read the intentions of predators and imitate their appearance and behavior as part of cultural survival strategies. We became effective predators by literally *imagining* ourselves to be predators: by wearing predator skins, by decorating ourselves with their teeth and claws, and by hunting and killing as they did. These things are also done by mythic heroes, such as Herakles, who covered himself in the skin of a lion.

Again, this change of status is ironic. To kill the beast, the hero has to internalize the beast. To rid the world of monsters, the hero has to act like one. Beowulf, like the monsters he battles, mutilates his vanquished foes, as does the Indian hero Goera, who chops monsters into tiny pieces. The mythic warriors of Polynesia butcher and eat the ogres they kill, and the Nordic hero Sigurd drinks the dragon's blood to acquire its dangerous powers. What these examples suggest is that the mythic hero is often a *frightening* savior, both a benefactor and potential mass murderer, as in the case of Gilgamesh, whose dangerous energies terrify his own people, and Herakles, who not only establishes mastery over a variety of highly dangerous monstrous beasts but kills his tutor and later his wife and children (in a killing frenzy brought on by Hera, it is said). The hero's predator powers, like the shaman's, can be turned against those seeking the protection they can provide. In a Nordic myth, the hero Sigmund kills his friend Sinfiotli because he is overcome by the "wicked wolf's nature" inherent in the wolf skin that he wore. Wolfishly, he "sinks his teeth in Sinfiotli's throat."[77]

The origin of this ambivalent attitude must go back to the time when bipedal primates began to understand that the protective power of the alpha male could be as dangerous as it was reassuring. Who protects us from the protector? Eventually, an answer evolved, and that answer is: *ourselves.* Over time, increasingly more of us internalized predatory powers, as much to defend ourselves as to injure others. Native Americans believe—and rightly so—that anybody can turn into a beast at any time and "then go on a rampage, killing and devouring his fellows." This transformation is triggered, according to legend, when a person somehow compromises "his or her essential humanity, commits a crime against another member of the community, feels cannibalistic urges, or becomes 'too strong' in his or her emotions."[78]

This may explain why myths often insist that monsters and humans are related. In fact, monsters are depicted as giving rise to humans by birth, by totemistic parthenogenesis, by vomiting them up, by spitting them out, or by defecating them.[79] From a historical and evolutionary perspective, this is likely true: predators *did give rise to humans* by providing the selection pressure that turned a timid and relatively pacific bipedal primate into an aggressive and brainy killer. Thanks to our animal progenitors, any one of us has the potential to be a *were-predator* now.

BAFFLING THE MYTHIC MONSTER

Another way to deal with monsters is to *trick* them to death. Almost any creature can be a mythic Trickster—an insect (grasshopper, spider, ant), a prey animal (rabbit, muskrat, mole), or even a small carnivore (lynx, fox, coyote, raven). All that's required is that the creature display some trait or behavior that allows it to trick or confuse a predator (eye spots, crypsis and dynamic camouflage, autotomy, ingenious escape patterns, deftly hidden dens, the ability to misdirect predators by play-acting at being injured). By using these naturally occurring mimetic survival mechanisms, the mythic Trickster honors the life-sustaining cleverness of escape artists wherever they are found in nature.

The mythic Trickster and mythic hero have a lot in common, as when a hero tricks the monster into swallowing him so he can gut it from the inside, or when the Trickster kills the monster through an ingenious trap. For example, the Native American Trickster figure Hare slays monstrous fish and snakes often by using the subterfuge of being swallowed by them to kill them.[80] In Cree myth, the Trickster figure Whiskey-Jack is said to have "killed the harmful animals who ate up all the others" at the beginning of time.[81] In an African myth, Jackal contrives to have the farmer kill a lion that daily demands an ox from the farmer's herd. Jackal, pretending to be God, intimidates the lion into submitting to being hit on the head by the farmer. The farmer swings with all his might and kills the lion.[82] In another African myth, the Trickster rids Ethiopia of a monstrous serpent simply by offering it a goat that he has stuffed with poison.[83]

In most myths, however, the task of the Trickster is not to kill the monster but to baffle it, or escape from it, or render it harmless. In an African myth, a woodcutter seduces a threatening lion into displaying its strength by putting its paw inside a crack in a log. As soon as the paw goes in, the woodsman pulls out the wedge, trapping (but not killing) the lion.[84] In Greek myth, Oedipus defeats the Sphinx, half woman and half winged lion, not by bronze weapons but by his piercing intellect, as does Odysseus when he fools Polyphemus by telling him that his name is "Noman."

In a Navajo story, Turtle keeps from being eaten by Coyote by making the hungry predator think that turtles don't like water. When Coyote drops him into the water, Turtle shouts mockingly (like Odysseus shouts back at the ogre he's just fooled) "Thank you, thank you, dear Coyote, you've brought me home. You've saved my life!"[85] In another myth, Coyote is the Trickster, saving himself from being eaten by Grizzly Bear by *imitating* a buffalo, complete with "bull bellows" and the brandishing of a skeleton buffalo head with huge horns. "The bear trembled. Then Coyote knew that Grizzly Bear was afraid of him."[86] When the Trickster figure Mentis is confronted by the worst of all monsters, Windigo, who "lives on human flesh," Mentis is "numb with fear. He was unable to move. He trembled. His teeth chattered." But then Mentis steadies himself and hatches a plan to "outwit the Windigo." By using Ermine to crawl inside the monster and stop its heart, Mentis is able to boast, "Friends, behold me! It is entirely due to my courage and wisdom that you no longer have to be afraid of the terrible Windigo."[87] Iktomi, the tricky Spider-Man, also uses fear triggers to fend off Man-Eating Monster. Iktomi asks the Monster what he's afraid of (a rattle, a whistle, and a menstruating woman) and then exploits these fear triggers to frighten Man-Eating Monster to death.[88]

The Trickster figure Skunk avoids becoming dinner by helping Coyote hunt and kill Beaver.[89] Rabbit escapes Fox by throwing a big stone down Fox's throat, knocking out all the predator's teeth. As Fox is choking, Rabbit ridicules him. "'You don't have to always believe what people tell you, such as it being unhealthy to eat rabbits without drinking water first,' said Rabbit as he was running away."[90]

It is easy to understand why the Trickster is an archetypal figure in myth and folklore. The Trickster, whatever else he or she might be, is the embodiment of survival intelligence, of lifesaving wit and skills. The Trickster is willing to do or say anything to keep on living. In the mocking Trickster figure we hear the elemental and desperate human cry "I will not be eaten!"[91] In this mythic figure we celebrate the constellation of mental skills and hormonal urges that allow us to *outfox*, when we can't kill, the deadly powers that bedevil us.

One Native American myth captures perfectly the central argument of this section. Wildcat is mean and ferocious, with "big, long, sharp fangs" that he loves to sink into hapless rabbits. One day when he was ravenous he decided to eat Great Rabbit himself. But Great Rabbit's well-developed Theory of Mind Mechanism enabled him, as a member of a prey species, to "sense what others are thinking from a long way off, so he already knew that Wildcat was after him." To combat the strength of Wildcat, Rabbit used "magic"—tricks and delusions—to stay one jump ahead of the increasingly more famished and exhausted Wildcat. The myth depicts the archetypal *chase*, a theme underlying countless stories and myths from Road Runner cartoons to the *Bourne* franchise (with Jason Bourne being a very dangerous Trickster).

What's intriguing about this myth is that Rabbit—obviously a stand-in for humans—resorts to *mimetic illusion* to bamboozle Wildcat (as does Coyote to scare off Great Bear by brandishing buffalo horns and imitating the roar of a buffalo). Rabbit does not just run faster, he outsmarts Wildcat through his command of the powers of the imagination. For instance, Great Rabbit makes the pursuing predator mistake him for an Indian chief and then for a minister presiding over a prayer meeting. During the service, Great Rabbit preaches a long sermon about the wickedness of ferocious wild beasts, which tear victims with sharp fangs and then devour them. "'Such savage fiends will be punished for their sins,' said this preacher over and over."[92]

But Great Rabbit's most successful illusion is that of a battleship armed with muskets and heavy cannon. "Wildcat had never before faced white men's firearms; they were entirely new to him. . . . It didn't matter that the ship, cannon, muskets, cannonballs, bullets, fire, noise, and smoke were merely illusions conjured up by Rabbit. To Wildcat they were real, and he was scared to death. He swam back to shore and ran away. And if he hasn't died, he is running still."[93] Once again, a myth emphasizes the survival value of mimetic performance, especially when under the control of a master Trickster-transformer-illusionist.

By engaging in mimetic performance and magic illusion, the Trickster often functions not just as a storyteller but as a symbol of the transforming and redemptive powers of the human imagination. Like the Shaman, the Trickster uses sleight-of-hand and enactments to sharpen predator-detection skills and to nurture the biology of hope. No wonder, as Joseph Campbell observes, the "curiously fascinating figure of the Trickster appears to have been the chief mythical character of the Paleolithic world of story."[94] But the story, Campbell should have added, was also *being told* by the Trickster.

The deceptions engineered by Tricksters to fool the monster are not just ingenious, they are often funny, as when Great Rabbit inflicts on Wildcat, now starving and thoroughly worn out, a sermon condemning predators, or when a muskrat exploits the echo effect of a cave to terrorize a lion, or when a mole creates a wooden human effigy that breaks the teeth of ravenous predators,[95] or when the Sioux Trickster, Iktomi (the Spider Man) contrives to have his infant son piss while sitting in the lap of the "frightful monster" Siyoko,[96] or when Coyote rams a rock up the anus of Monster Skunk that blocks the monster's farts, causing him to explode.[97] Monsters lose their bite when they are shown as blundering fools and figures to be laughed at. As Marina Warner puts it, "[H]umor relaxes the grip of bogeys, real or fantastic," and "poking fun" can provide as strong a defense against fear as "strong armour."[98]

The Trickster, most of the time, is a clown or comic hero, who

embodies the same life-affirming principles exemplified by the protago-
nists of comedy:

> Thou shalt survive.
> Thou shalt renew oneself.
> Thou shalt overcome obstacles and blocks.
> Thou shalt grasp opportunity.
> Thou shalt assert the drive to life.
> Thou shalt "conspire" with others who love life.
> Thou shalt be only moderately moral.
> Thou shalt look on all Authority with suspicion.
> Thou shalt love thy species.
> Thou shalt be as wise as the Fool.

A world of survival wisdom is bundled up in these ten comic com-
mandments. They reflect the collective experience of a species that once
survived by furtively grabbing meat from the carcasses left by powerful
and dangerous killers. It is no accident that the Trickster is often a thief,
stealing food and other essential items such as weapons from more powerful "authorities" to benefit both himself and others, as the Hawaiian
god Maui did, and as lowly Sergeant Bilko did.

But the mythic Trickster is, like the hero, an ambivalent figure, often
portrayed as living at the margin of society. The fact that the Trickster is
willing to say or do anything to survive makes him or her a potential threat
to social order and social survival. As professor Howard Norman notes,
the Trickster "shakes things up. He can turn the most sacred and long-
established institutions into a scattered jigsaw puzzle in the wink of an
eye."[99] Yes, social rules can become ossified and maladaptive, and sometimes
it takes the Trickster's spirit of infraction to call these rules into question.
But the fact of the matter is that small societies struggling to maintain a
marginal existence in a hostile environment need a lot of social cohesion
and rule stability to survive, and they cannot afford to tolerate a program-

matic violation of their moral order. They must curb hoarding, selfishness, stubbornness, disobedience, blasphemy, backbiting, dishonesty, cowardice, lust, wrath, gluttony, and envy. Unlike established civilizations, they cannot afford wide-scale violations of the moral order.

So the Trickster figure both *celebrates* and *stigmatizes* the comic principle that it's okay to do whatever it takes to survive. Yes, at times, we do need to grasp, cheat, and lie to keep alive. But most of the time these behaviors undermine the trust and self-sacrifice on which both individual and social existence depends. Yes, at times, the Trickster is just the agent needed to defeat and humiliate the monster, but at other times the Trickster himself *becomes* the very *monster* that must be defeated, humiliated, exiled, kicked out, sent on his way.[100] Yet, even when *morally monstrous*, the Trickster directly contributes to the health of society by provoking people to rally against him in self-defense, as they would rally against an animal predator. The Trickster keeps sharp our awareness that we can be preyed upon by all kinds of agents.

By imagining *dark* Tricksters, we are warning ourselves not to embrace *too thoughtlessly or avidly* the cunning amorality of the survival intellect, if we want to survive. This means that, like the monster, the Trickster is something of a scapegoat.

CONCLUSION

For millions of years, our ancestors lived with the visceral fear of being torn apart and eaten by animal predators. This fear, rooted in the survival instincts hardwired into our very being, was passed on through culture and was intensified when humans developed the ability to imagine monsters even more menacing than the ones they had to contend with in real life. These creatures were believed to lurk everywhere in the environment, to have the power to assume strange and frightening forms, and to lust mightily for human flesh.

The human condition became even more frightening as we (gradually) acquired the predator's power to kill. We came to fear each other, and we came to be tormented by aggressive fantasies and by the guilt arising from having them and acting on them. Monsters were the imagination's way of therapeutically externalizing, manipulating, and venting these pent-up fears.

But the imagination was also vulnerable to a perverse feedback cycle—the more fear, the more need of monsters to manage that fear; yet the more monsters, the more fear. If left unchecked by other institutions and psychological processes, as well as by *other ways* of mythologizing predators, this cycle could give rise to social panics, individual paranoia, inter-group conflict, xenophobia, and cultural collapse.

Mythic "heroes" and "Tricksters" represent, in part, an attempt by the imagination to counter its own monster-making powers. "Counter," but not *destroy*. For it is through awesome monsters that we express our guarded indebtedness to animal predators for transforming us from terrified prey to formidable adversary. Yes, the monster *is* in us, but—at times—we gratefully summon it so we may survive.

Another way the imagination countered its own monstrous propensity was to transform predators into *other kinds* of agents rather than dangerous monsters. We will next explore how the human imagination, swinging to the opposite extreme, transformed animal predators into *divinities* or *gods*. As we shall see, this transformation, too, represents our need to manage our primal fear of being eaten alive by imposing and powerful creatures.

Chapter 7

Fear and Trembling in the Pleistocene

The Predator as a God

INTRODUCTION

Fear can have strange effects. It can not only make us run and hide; it can also make us fall to the ground in abject surrender. It can not only evoke aggression; it can also evoke appeasement. It can not only invite the demonizing of predators; it can also invite their deification.

In Hawaiian mythology, "a great bird which lived on human flesh" was not only feared but venerated.[1] Throughout Africa, constrictor snakes are not only "feared and hated" but also "revered" as the most divine of creatures.[2] In Hindu mythology, the god Vishnu takes the form of a lion-headed god-man, and Shiva, the Master of Beasts, is associated with the tiger and the snake. In Mesoamerican mythology, the lord of the jungle—the jaguar—was venerated through blood sacrifice, as was the giant snake and crocodile.[3] In Central Asia and parts of India, the tiger was the object of cult worship requiring human sacrifice.[4] The shark was worshipped as a god throughout Polynesia. The wolf was venerated by the Greeks, Romans, and Japanese.

Nowhere was the worship of predators taken to such extremes as it was in ancient Egypt, where many gods were dangerous carnivores (or dangerous carnivores were gods). Sekhmet—"the powerful one"—was a raging lioness, as was Pakhet—"the rapacious one." In the temple of Amun Ra at Heliopolis, lions were bathed in perfumed water, calmed by incense, and fed choice pieces of meat to the strains of music. Leontopolis was the city of the lion cult, where lions were worshipped as late as 162 BCE.[5] When temple lions died, they were publicly mourned, and the bodies were embalmed and entombed.[6] Also worshipped was the fierce and dangerous Nile crocodile. At the sacred city of Crocodilopolis, crocs were looked after in special temple pools, adorned with pendants and bracelets of gold or precious stones, and embalmed and entombed when they died.[7]

Apparently, the same animals that made us tremble with fear could also make us tremble with fervor. How did the deification of animal predators come about? Why did we come to worship the very animals that ate us?

In short, this process of deification was a rather natural one, activated by the cognitive traits of early humans and some of the characteristic features and actions of large carnivores. It's as if evolution primed us—quite unintentionally, of course—to mythologize predators into gods as well as into demons, with sometimes little to differentiate the two incarnations. As the deification process unfolded over time, predators came to provoke a strange blend of fear, awe, submissiveness, and gratitude—essentially the same complex of emotions associated with the worship of the humanlike deities that emerged much later in human history.

I am not saying that our early ancestors attributed to predators some of the "godly" attributes that they *already assigned to divine agents*. I am saying that animal predators were the *first gods*, eliciting those behaviors that came to be associated with worship or veneration. The mythification of predators into divine agents coevolved with rites intended to control and placate the bloody appetite of these supernatural predatory agents.

The emotional, cognitive, and behavioral sources that went into transforming animal predators into superhuman and supernatural agents can be found in the early Pleistocene. This is why any search for the origins of our relationship with the gods, as Dudley Young understands, "should probably begin there."[8]

FEAR AND THE SACRED

Fear has long been recognized as a powerful motive for worship. The Greeks had two words for fear, *deisdaimonia*, literally, "fear of the gods," and *phrike*, which means hair-raising shudder.[9] Both are deeply implicated in the formation of the sacred.

Religion is best defined, according to anthropologist Robert Lowie, as a mixture of awe and dread.[10] Another student of religion, Rudolf Otto, argued along the same lines, suggesting that worship arises from an encounter with something wholly Other, a *mysterium tremendum*, a shivering mystery that elicits both terror and fascination, fear and attraction. At the same time that this mysterious agent is the object of horror and dread, it also inspires fascination and devotion. Those who tremble before it are not only cowed and cast down but are also impelled to "turn to it, even to make it somehow their own."[11] Biblical scholar Gerardus van der Leeuw observed that "horror and shuddering, sudden fright and the frantic insanity of dread, all receive their form in the daemon; this represents the absolute horribleness of the world, the incalculable force which weaves its web around us and threatens to seize us."[12]

This "daemon" was originally, I believe, the threatening carnivore. It was animal-behavior expert Konrad Lorenz who saw early on the connection between the "holy shiver" of religious awe and the physiological response of an animal when threatened by a predator.[13]

But exactly *how* does fear encourage the deification of predators?

Part of the answer lies in the mixture of powerful emotions triggered by a life-and-death encounter with a predator. A predator attack unleashes not only fear and terror but also a cascade of intoxicating emotions and psychosomatic states best summed up as *survival ecstasy*. The sense of pleasure that floods us during and after a close encounter with a predator is empowering and addictive, inducing in us a longing to seek it out and experience it again and again. To recapture this survival ecstasy, we have gone so far as to replicate aspects of a predator attack during ritual, as when participants wear animal masks and claws to inflict fright and pain during initiation and sacrificial ceremonies. It is not just that the transfiguring emotions evoked during a predator attack came to be associated with the supernatural agents that later came to be called gods. It is that these emotions provided the foundation for the transformation of the animal predator into a supernatural agent called a god. As anthropologist Scott Atran puts it, "[I]t is not an infant-mother, infant-father, or infant-family template per se from which God concepts extend, but a more encompassing evolutionary program for avoiding and tracking predators and prey."[14]

THE PRIMAL INGREDIENTS OF PREDATOR DEIFICATION

As I noted earlier, the predator-detection system evolved to make humans aware of predators and to assume their presence on the slightest pretext. "Predator!" was the default reflex in all ambiguous situations. Thanks to this system, predators were imbued with a salience—with a stature and significance, with a *charisma*—unmatched by any other agent in the environment of early humans. This is not to diminish the emotional significance of infants and mating partners, but there would be no infants and mating partners if each individual human was not intensely tuned into the creatures that could end life with one swipe of a paw or bite of a jaw.

Now, there is something peculiar about this detection system—it cannot be falsified. The mere fact that a predator is not seen is not proof that it isn't there. In fact, it is always strategic to assume that even when a predator cannot be seen, it *is* there, lurking, *invisible*, ready to appear as if by magic. Even today, to tribal peoples it is the extraordinary *stealth* of predators—as seen most spectacularly in leopards, tigers, and constrictors—that renders them *divine*.[15]

Divine, but not always *benign*.

In many myths, stealth—whether that of predatory animals or of predatory people—is associated with evil and devilishness, a result of the gradual demonization of certain predators. In India, even the deer is dreaded as a demon by some tribal people merely because it moves noiselessly and can vanish mysteriously into the forest.[16] Early humans may not have loved the animal gods they felt compelled to worship.

Another way the predator-detection system contributed to the deification of dangerous animals is by cultivating the impression that these animals had the power to fulfill signs, a trait associated with divinities even today. Let's assume that an intuition or an assumption triggered by an ambiguous sign was *confirmed* by the presence of a predator. It may have seemed to our ancestors that the creature was consciously *fulfilling* the sign it had left. In other words, the sign functioned as a sort of promissory note, with the predator fulfilling its promise of being there *by* being there. This conclusion may strike us Westerners as absurd, but as anthropologists have shown, it is a conclusion that comes readily to non-Western people.[17]

Predators possessed other traits that contributed to their deification. Consider, for example, their awesome power to kill. It must have been both terrifying and fascinating to watch a big cat bring down and devour a creature sometimes three times the size and weight of the carnivore killing it. The fury of the attack, the sounds of the kill, the clamor of the animals that were witnessing the assault—such a bloody and violent display of raw carnivore aggression must have seemed thrilling and awesome to our ancestors, as it still does to those of us today who watch these fascinating life-and-death dramas on television. The ferocious hunting power of predators must have struck our early ancestors as superhuman, which, of course, they were.[18] This may help explain why, in Native American mythology, for example, almost any animal that is deemed *powerful*—and this includes almost all carnivores—is deemed a god. In Malay mythology, any *dangerous* animal is customarily credited with having "superhuman powers." The fear and admiration evoked by animal predators played a significant role in their deification and worship.[19]

It's impossible to know how our early predecessors—those before Neanderthals—felt about death, but one thing must have been crystal clear to them. Death—probably more often than not—was "the prerogative of large dangerous animals."[20] It was not just that these animals could kill us; they could tear us apart, reducing our body to blood and bones and scraps of tissue within minutes. No wonder the gaping jaws of devouring beasts still haunt our dreams and cultural images. Such fearsome creatures compelled constant attention, great deference, and whatever form of appeasement our ancestors could devise.

The ferocious killing power of carnivores may have contributed in a more subtle way to their deification. A prey animal in the clutches of a predator often lapses into what is called tonic immobility, or the death trance, a form of shock evolved to spare the animal greater suffering by quieting its futile struggle to tear free of the predator's teeth and claws. The ability of carnivores to induce terror paralysis in their victim could have been viewed by early humans as the power to literally entrance the prey in order to render it a compliant victim in its own death. Of course, strictly speaking, this naturally occurring "entrancing" power could not have been seen as "godlike" by our ancient ancestors, since, at that time, there was no concept of a god. But this ostensible power could have contributed to the brew of behaviors and attributes that eventually led to the creation of the sacred and the deification of the predator.

There is another element in the predator-prey relationship that may have led to the worship of the animal predator—carrion. In most religions, the divine agent is both feared and, paradoxically, thanked as a *gift giver*. This attitude may have its evolutionary origin in our primal experiences with Pleistocene predators, who brought not only death to our early ancestors but also life-sustaining meat. Weaponless, frail, and small, our ancestors first got their meat by scavenging the animal carcasses left by carnivores. To our ancestors, who were inclined by the Agency-Detection Device and the Theory of Mind Mechanism to humanize predators and see them as part of an exchange relationship, this meat was not an accidental by-product of predator activity but a *gift* left on purpose. Even today, hunting-scavenging tribal people around the world venerate predators for the kindly "gifts" they leave at kill sites. So, the same animals that evoked terror also evoked gratitude and would have been seen not only as killers but also as benefactors and providers, as later humanlike gods were seen.

PREDATOR WORSHIP AND THE STOCKHOLM SYNDROME

Our emotions and cognitive biases, as well as the physical attributes of the animals themselves, conspired to imbue predators with supernatural attributes that came to be called divine and worthy of worship and reverence.

Perhaps this long evolutionary process can be seen in a highly compressed form in the phenomenon called the Stockholm syndrome.

This phrase was invented to describe the puzzling relationship that developed between four hostages who worked in a Stockholm bank and their machine-gun wielding captors (August 1973). During the six-day ordeal, the victims had dynamite strapped to their bodies and were repeatedly threatened with death. But every so often, they were given food or granted a small favor by their captors. The hostages were soon racked by two seemingly conflicting emotions—terror and gratitude. They were terrified of the life-and-death power the captors held over them and relieved when the power was used in ways that allayed their terror.

This blend of fear and relief from fear had an astonishing effect on the psyches of the hostages. All four strongly resisted the government's attempts to free them from their captors, and when they were freed, they eagerly defended the two men who had threatened their lives. Even

months afterward, the ex-hostages still had warm feelings for their captors, and one of the women became engaged to one of the assailants.

This strange affiliation provoked social scientists to study the syndrome, and it was found that people who are battered by powerful and
intimidating agents, but who are also dependent upon these agents for
their very lives and who receive favors from these agents, often develop
intense feelings of loyalty and submission to their victimizers. Unques-
tionably, there is an enormous cultural and psychological gulf between
twentieth-century Sweden and the African savanna of the Pleistocene.
Yet, in a way, the general conditions associated with the Stockholm syndrome could be said to have also existed for our ancient ancestors—and
for a lot longer than six days.

Early humans lived in constant fear of predators. With a little luck,
they could escape a specific attack now and again, but they could not
escape from the condition of being always in danger of being killed by
more powerful creatures. Because of this inescapable danger, early
humans had to be constantly aware of predators—always on the alert for
them—and sometimes able to see themselves from the point of view of
the very creatures they feared, the better to assess the threat these creatures posed.

Predators also may have appeared to early humans, at times, as benefactors, not only by leaving meat ("for me!") but also by showing *kindness*
by not attacking when they encountered humans. Our ancient ancestors
came to feel "gratitude" to the very animals they also feared. The conditions were ripe for the experiencing of a *primordial form* of the Stockholm syndrome. This explains why animal deities (as well as more human
ones) often are regarded as both "malevolent" and "benevolent."[21]

This ambivalent attitude was projected by the Aztecs into the capri-
cious god Tezcatlipoca, who could dispense misery and death as well as
wealth, valor, and good fortune. His terrified worshippers prostrated
themselves before him and declared themselves to be his "slaves." Then
as now, the more threatening the power, the more likely it evoked awe,

submission, and the desire to appease it. As anthropologist David Gilmore has noted, the more horrible and carnivorous a monster is, the more likely it will inspire "a measure of awe, even reverence."[22]

Although early humans may have responded to these conditions in very different ways than modern humans do, there must have been a time in the remote past—say, two hundred thousand years ago—when the human mind had evolved far enough for our ancestors to begin to respond to their conditions with more complicated psychological survival strategies than could their primate ancestors. Over time, that mind came to imbue predators with those attributes now associated with what we call the "sacred"—fearsome life-and-death power that could be appeased and solicited (as the occasion required) through such worshipful behaviors as blood sacrifice and prostration. Indeed, it was the vexatious relationship between animal predators and their human prey that *gave rise* to the sense of the "sacred" within the prey.

Of course, the deification of the predator did note erase the fear it evoked, but now that fear could be managed because the animals that provoked it were thought to be under greater human control, first through meat sacrifice, and later through a complex and symbolic system of worship or veneration. It is natural to want to affiliate with a more powerful figure not only to placate that figure but to secure its protection. Gods protect as well as intimidate. It would have been easy for our ancestors to view the godlike animal predator as offering some measure of protection against *other* dangers and threats, including *other predators*. Such "protection" could be detected in the fact that a local predator often does drive off its competitors, an act ripe for interpretation as a sign of "benevolence."

The protective power of the carnivore could be secured in another way: by becoming aligned with it through totemistic ritual that would require wearing the predator's body parts as part of a disguise. In a way, masking and pelt wearing are forms of dynamic camouflage, meant both to protect the wearer and to imbue the wearer with the power of the predator. The totem predator god is the protector of the tribe, the spirit force that can be cajoled, tamed, manipulated, and appeased in order to constrain its impulse to kill us (who are its kin), and so to minimize our fear of being killed by it.

WORSHIPPING THE PREDATOR GOD

Throughout the world, strikingly similar ritualized behaviors are used to demonstrate reverence for the gods. The most important of these are bending and kneeling, bowing the head, closing the eyes, raising or clasping the hands, and singing and dancing. Intriguingly, these behaviors resemble behaviors that primates engage in when they feel physically threatened, as when they are attacked by predators.

Take, for example, the most dramatic sign of worship—physical prostration. As the classical scholar Walter Burkert explains, "[T]o stop aggression, one has to be small and humble, *humilis*, which originally meant 'close to the soil.' To create this impression, one has to bow, to kneel down, to cower to the ground, to crawl—in short, not to puff oneself up." Even in nonhuman primates, the way to avoid damage when charged by a conspecific is "to cower to the ground, touching it with one's head, and above all to avoid staring."[23] As I noted in chapter 3, prostration, as a ploy or as a result of tonic immobility, is at times an effective way to discourage an attack from an animal predator, or to minimize the damage it might inflict.

When predators acquired in the human imagination those characteristics that came to be called "divine," prostration became more than a defensive posture—it became a token of respect and worship. In other words, a biological reaction to a terrifying situation gave rise to a ritual act performed on purpose to appease or solicit the life-and-death powers of the predator god. This act of worship—as well as other behaviors—is rooted in the biological program for dealing with threat and fear.

We find an expression of this relationship in a Yoruba myth about the fearsome leopard god Ajanaku. This predator god demands the most abject submission. In one instance, Giant Rat "prostrated himself before him and stretched out his hand, palm upward."[24] When Ajanaku flashes his eyes of "bright, bright red" at trembling Bush Cow, the cow looks at him and cries, "Horrors! I'm innocent, innocent, Kabieyesi, my Protecting God."[25] It is unlikely that displaying open palms at a charging leopard has ever been an effective deterrent, but it is an effective begging sign for primates when dealing with more powerful group members. Another position of the hands in ancient worship was to hold them in the "stick 'em up!" posture. Not only was this gesture nonthreatening, but it is close to what we automatically do today to fend off a frontal assault.

Another behavior associated with worship is self-defilement. To forestall the negative effects of the "evil eye," Greeks would tear or spit on their own garments. As Walter Burkert notes, the ritual of self-defilement seems to anticipate a dreaded outcome by muting its worst effects through mimetic enactment. People tear at themselves to forestall a more deadly agent tearing at them. "You see," we seem to be saying to angry gods, "I have already done to myself what you were intending to do to me. No need to punish me any further." A second example cited by Burkert reveals, I believe, the predator background to such rituals: "[A] more violent form of self-abasement is self-wounding, which occurs in various cults and has also been observed in other societies."[26] Although Burkert does not speculate about the biological roots of this particular appeasement behavior, it strikes me that it could have arisen in the distant past as an attempt to imitate the wounds inflicted by carnivores. This *ritual mauling* may have been done to show membership in a predator cult, or to demonstrate one's submission to the awesome mutilating power of the sacred animal.

According to Burkert, another way to ward off aggression from powerful agents—whether godly predators or predatory gods—is "to make and keep personal contact; to touch the stronger one if he allows it, to stroke his chin without being bitten, to extend at least an open hand, all of which are signs of dependence."[27] The Fijians take this strategy to a frightening extreme when, twice a year, they ensure safe swimming areas by entering the water to kiss sharks. Similarly, the young Masai male must touch a lion and if possible tug on its tail. These may not strike Westerners as true acts of "reverence" or "worship," but they appear to function this way for the people doing them. These acts also may have had a practical function. Keeping in contact with predators actually may ward off attacks by familiarizing predators to the presence of humans. Although the bears that inhabit Yellowstone Park should always be regarded by visitors as very dangerous animals, many have become so accustomed to the presence of humans that they ignore them as they rummage through garbage cans and campsites.

We also worship the gods by singing and dancing. These acts of veneration may also be biologically linked to the primate/human predator defense system. Primatologist and anthropologist Jane Goodall has observed chimpanzees engaging in "charging displays" when they experience demonstrations of nature's power, such as torrential rain, lightning and thunder, waterfalls, or gale-force winds. These chimpanzee displays are not the same as those elicited by other threats, in that the displays are longer, "rhythmic," and apparently pleasurable, since some chimps repeat them even after a hiatus in the display. Goodall wonders if this "rain dance" could reveal the historical source of the "awe and wonder" that underlie religion.[28]

As anthropologist Stewart Guthrie notes, what Goodall characterizes as "surges of emotion" are really threat displays directed at forces that the chimps see as predators—that is, dangerous and threatening natural agents. "As threats, they stem from a chimpanzee interpretation of storms as living things that, like baboons, leopards, and other chimpanzees, can be frightened away" by frenetic ritual displays of energy and anger.[29] Animal predators, too, must be counted among the "natural phenomenon" that Goodall thought nurtured the emergence of the emotions associated with sacred agents and events.

Alondra Oubre believes that early rituals, by enhancing group solidarity, enabled our ancient ancestors to escape their fear of predators. But these rituals may also have been a very effective survival strategy in another way. The specter of a bunch of shrieking and drumming creatures engaging in strange and irregular body movements may have been quite enough to confuse and intimidate nearby predators, making such rituals effective fear-management strategies. Our ancestors were entirely capable of understanding this. It is plausible to suggest that primordial ritual may have evolved from primate defensive behaviors such as mobbing, and that it could be seen as a sort of "anticipatory" mobbing, one that prepared the group to meet any future threat with greater solidarity.

Although early ritual, as I have described it, would seem to be the opposite of a "worshipful" behavior, it is not. Many forms of conventional religious worship—from rites of purification to sacrificial gift offerings—are designed to *ward off* the danger of divine displeasure, to keep the gods calm and at a safe distance. Warding-off rituals may have originated as practical strategies for managing fear, but they acquired worship connotations as the creatures provoking that fear were imbued by the imagination with increasingly more human attributes and powers. I am not claiming that early ritual deified the predator; only that it provided an established and efficient means of expressing a worshipful attitude once the other forces (described in an earlier section) coalesced to transform animal carnivores into "gods."

There is a Hopi-Tewa myth that imagines this very process. Although the myth is not about predators as I define them, it is about deadly poisonous snakes very much to be feared by humans. According to the myth, a man marries a snake woman from a village where all the inhabitants are snakes. Their child has the power to turn into a snake whenever it wants. Although the myth likely reflects totem relationships within the tribe, its main function seems to be to allay fear by reassuring the Hopi that they are the beloved kin of venomous snakes and can avoid being bitten by them by showing them reverence through the ritual snake dance. As the myth says, "Show respect, and they will not bite. Dance to them to appease them."[30]

To sum up, when predators were imbued by the mythic imagination with superhuman and sometimes supernatural powers, the behaviors appropriate to their worship emerged naturally from the survival strategies and warding-off behaviors evoked by actual animals. In other words, predators evoked in humans the very emotions and behaviors that humans would eventually use to worship them.

THE FLESH OF THE GODS

In *Origins of the Sacred: The Ecstasies of Love and War* (1991), Dudley Young contends that blood sacrifice, found "in every culture known to man," should be seen "as the elementary form of the religious life." To "sacrifice" literally means "to make sacred, and our first way of doing this was to tear living flesh until the blood flowed."[31] Why do humans believe that their gods are best worshiped with offerings of flesh and blood? The answer that makes the most sense is, because the first gods were animal carnivores.

We know that humans have actually sacrificed other humans to appease *animal predators* deemed to be divine. The early Hawaiians deified sharks and sacrificed humans to them. One legend recounts what appears to be a communal rite of self-sacrifice to the shark god Kauhuhu, when "the waters ran red and all were destroyed."[32] A particularly fervent case of shark worship was witnessed by the Portuguese missionary and adventurer Sebastian Manrique in seventeenth-century India. Men and women, while in a state of ecstasy, waded into the sea up to their heads and waited to be seized and devoured by their shark gods. Since the sharks were "accustomed and thus encouraged constantly by tasting human flesh, they had become so bloodthirsty that they rushed up fiercely at a mere shadow."[33]

Most notorious are the sacrificial rites of the great civilizations of Mesoamerica, performed literally as well as symbolically to feed a jaguar god. The butchering of the victims was done on jaguar-headed altars by the "Jaguar priests," who used obsidian blades shaped like jaguar fangs and claws to open the chest and cut out the hearts of their victims. In essence, the sacrificial ritual was consciously designed to imitate the lacerations inflicted by a jaguar, right down to the victims being torn apart. The bodies of the victims may have been thrown to actual jaguars, which were high-ranking deities in the Maya pantheon.[34] As noted mythologist Marcel Detienne asks, "Can one be sure of making a distinction between the sacrificer holding a knife and the wolf with gaping jaws reddened with blood?"[35] As the Roman adage goes, Man is a wolf to man.

In precolonial East Africa, the Baganda people threw parts of the bodies of their enemies to sacred crocodiles, and mediums often gave oracular pronouncements by wagging their heads and opening their jaws as if possessed by a crocodile spirit.[36] As recently as 1885, in Indonesia, the princes of Kupang—as if they were enacting some Greek myth—sacrificed "perfumed and prettily dressed young girls to the crocs."[37] Well into the twentieth century, certain remote tribes in India sacrificed humans to ward off the carnivorous appetites of predator gods, the priests praying that the death of the victim would decrease the appearance of "tigers and snakes." As the priest stabbed the victim, the villagers sang:

> Here we sacrifice the enemy
> Here we sacrifice the "meriah"
> The gods eat-up this sacrifice
> The enemy is thus worshipped
> Let there be no collective loss
> Let no tigers prowl
> The gods need so many bribes
> So many offerings.

The specific deity being sacrificed to was Durga, the goddess who rides on a tiger—and eats like one:

> Durga eats
> Durga eats everything.[38]

As this chant makes clear, deified predators are fed flesh to appease their appetite, thus warding off attack. This is the essence of warding-off rituals: "I give in order that you go away."[39] As one Hawaiian myth succinctly puts it, "Then you will see two dragons with open mouths ready to devour you. Quickly throw food in their mouths and they will become quiet."[40] The constant need to placate, appease, and disarm deified predators explains many of the themes and images found in myths.

Sacrifice may function as a fear-management strategy in another way: by satiating the appetite of the predator. What better way to evoke and defuse the horror of being torn apart by predators than by tearing apart someone else? Spilling the blood of a sacrificial victim makes onlookers feel relieved that they have been spared.[41] In other words, sacrifice evokes in members of the community the same survival ecstasy felt by those who survive an actual attack from an animal predator. For sociologist Barbara Ehrenreich, "rituals of blood sacrifice both celebrate and terrifyingly reenact the human transition from prey to predator."[42] That is, such rituals remind us of the fear and pain we once endured as a prey species, but they also make clear that we have learned to become the predator, a development that both calms and intensifies our fears.

SURVIVAL AND SACRIFICE IN THE PLEISTOCENE

Whatever their ceremonial trappings, these bloody rituals of worship and appeasement are rooted not only in fear management but also in a simple survival strategy older than the Pleistocene. The strategy is "part for whole." Throughout the natural world, animals are willing to give up a part of their body to save their lives. Lizards leave their tails, birds shed their feathers during "terror molt," mammals gnaw off their paws to escape a trap, and so on. Walter Burkert believes that the same "part for whole" principle guided the behavior of hominids and early humans in situations of pursuit or threat.[43]

According to Burkert, the part-for-whole sacrifice is rooted in "biological programs dealing with anxiety and flight that are older than the human species, and these comprise or engender at least the rudiments of the ritual pattern, correlating threat, alarm, pursuit, flight, and the trick of abandoning what can be spared."[44] To save the group, Burkert speculates, our ancient ancestors may have resorted to feeding one of their own—an infant, an old person, a corpse—to menacing predators. "The sacrifice of one for the sake of all, enduring a small, tolerable loss to confirm all life, is a motif dominating both fantastic tales and strange rituals."[45]

Take, for example, a tale told by the Limba of Africa. A group of people needed to cross a river infested with crocodiles. But no one could cross this river, they were told, until the crocodiles were given something to eat. So one of the women took her child and threw him into the water and to his death. "Then the three wives and their man got into the boat and they quickly crossed the river. The crocodiles did not catch them."[46] But it is not just in tales that such cold-blooded sacrifice occurs. During the Assam massacres in India (March 1983), to save himself a father threw his daughter at the raiders chasing him. The reporter who interviewed the man wrote that "there was no guilt or remorse in his voice— just relief that he had survived."[47]

One of the most memorable mythic expressions of part-for-whole sacrifice is the killing and dismemberment of Apsyrtos by his sister Medea, as she and Jason (with whom Medea had fallen in love and was helping on his quest to find the Golden Fleece) are being pursued by Medea's father, Aietes. To delay him, Medea kills her brother, cuts him to pieces, and throws the pieces into the sea, forcing the king to gather them up in respect for his son. As Burkert explains, "[T]he 'part,' in the Argonaut myth, is the small, the feeble, the replaceable member of the community, the younger brother. Any predator has his best chances with young and feeble quarry."[48] The irony, of course, is that Medea must become a predator to escape a predator, a transformation that doubles the protection sought through blood sacrifice since the transformation both assuages and threatens the aggressor.

Heroism may have its biological roots in the compulsion to *sacrifice one's self* to fend off the predator. In desperate situations, a particularly aroused or incensed alpha male may make a heroic but foolhardy charge into the pack of carnivores to intimidate and disperse them. Baboon males, for instance, have been known "literally to sacrifice themselves in defense of the group."[49] Even male zebras and Cape buffalo engage in such sacrificial displays. Perhaps predators could be credited with making us brave as well as fearful.

Sacrifice originated not as an act of worship but as a pragmatic strategy to appease through offerings of blood and meat the appetites of real predators. Sacrifice became an act of worship, properly speaking, only when predators became deified by the human imagination. Needless to say, sacrificial behaviors must have undergone a number of dramatic changes for them to assume the extreme form found in Mesoamerica, where humans were actively butchered by the tens of thousands to appease the imagined appetites of *symbolic* predators. My purpose here, however, is not to trace the evolutionary stages of sacrifice but simply to provide a plausible explanation for why sacrifice came to be closely associated with animal predators, godly predators, and predatory gods.

Once again, we see that practical strategies for dealing with actual animal predators became—with slight alterations—the acts by which these predators were "worshipped," once the mythic imagination imbued them with "godly" as well as "deadly" powers.

PREDATOR CULTS
OF THE PALEOLITHIC

Because the deification process unfolded over hundreds of thousands of years, there is no way to date exactly when humans first came to imagine animal predators as gods. But by the late Paleolithic, if not by the Middle Paleolithic, some predators seem to have been regarded in this very special way.

One of the most formidable of Pleistocene predators was the European cave bear. The bear may have been the first predator worshipped by humans, and well into the twentieth century, this animal was addressed as "O Divine One" by the Ainu, the aborigines of Japan.[50] The creature made quite an impression on our ancestors, given that it was painted fifteen times in the Chauvet Cave (France) alone, sometimes shown rearing up and menacing humans.[51] In the middle of this gallery, a cave bear skull was placed on a rock and surrounded by bones, suggesting to Jean Clottes—France's leading specialist in Paleolithic art—that an "altar" had been created to worship a bear deity.[52] In many other European caves, the skulls and bones of this creature appear to have been arranged "ceremonially." "It seems likely that bears (whose bones have a striking resemblance to human ones) were the object of superstition or veneration, as they were among many recent hunting people of the north."[53] Even where the cave bear was hunted for food, it seems to have been regarded with "religious awe."[54]

It is not hard to understand why Middle- to Upper-Paleolithic humans were impressed by the cave bear and felt compelled to venerate it through art, sculpture, and even sacrificial rites. This animal was immense, ferocious, and probably uncowed by any other predator in the environment, including weapon-bearing humans. When it rose up it was twice the size of a Neanderthal. Vestiges of the Paleolithic veneration of the bear may still lurk in the myths and rituals of North American Indians.

The cave bear was not the only predator given special treatment by Middle- and Upper-Paleolithic people. Lions, hyenas, panthers, and leopards were also painted on cave walls, suggesting that cults formed around great feline predators. Mythologist Joseph Campbell has speculated that these cults may go back "even further in time than the bear cult of Neanderthal."[55] The lion-man from the Hohlenstein Stadel cave—a depiction, perhaps, of a predator god or godly predator—is about thirty-two thousand years old, but *the thinking that gave rise to it* must be even older.

In the eyes of medical anthropologist Alondra Oubre, the archaeological evidence strongly suggests that by the Middle Paleolithic, "Neanderthals possessed some sort of primitive religion."[56] Archaeologist Steven Mithen believes that "religious ideologies as complex as those of modern hunter-gatherers came into existence at the time of the Middle/Upper Paleolithic transition and have remained with us ever since."[57] The evidence that exists at the current time supports the view that predators were the first creatures to be worshipped or venerated as supernatural agents.

FROM PREDATOR GODS TO GODS-R-US

As we've seen, the early human mind was inclined to attribute human traits to predators as part of a sophisticated predator-defense program. This crucial ability to anthropomorphize predators became more pronounced as the human mind became increasingly more creative and imaginative. By giving humanlike mental and emotional traits to predators, our ancestors came to believe that they could "understand" and negotiate with them, since dangerous animals were thought to be constrained by the same rules that governed the interaction of humans. In short, our ancestors thought they had placed terrifying creatures under some measure of control.

Crucial to the gradual transformation of predator gods into *human-like* gods was our growing need to feel emotionally connected to the gods, to love them, and to feel loved *by* them. This need for intense emotional connectedness with the gods was an outgrowth of our developing social intelligence and stronger and broader social ties. Connecting to the powerful forces that seemed to control every aspect of life—the gods are everywhere, for the mythic imagination—became easier as the gods became more "like us." According to anthropologist Barbara King, we long to feel emotional intimacy with the gods:

> For millions of years, human ancestors sought belongingness within their social groups; as they continued to evolve physically, behaviorally, culturally, and spiritually, humans began to seek an emotional connection with God, gods, or spirits. What happened was gradual rather than a spiritual "big bang." The human religious imagination developed in ever widening circles of engagement from immediate social companions, to members of a larger group, then across groups, and eventually, to a wholly other dimension, the realm of sacred beings.[58]

The archaeological record may give us an indication of the emotional needs of early humans. The discoveries at the Qafzeh and Skhul Caves in Israel have pushed back the date of intentional burial to one hundred and twenty thousand years ago. The *sapiens* skeletons found in these caves were stained with red ocher, perhaps to imbue dry bones with the life force of red blood.[59] These burials reveal not only a belief in an afterlife but also an intense emotional bonding with fellow humans that was thought to transcend physical existence.

Because we thrive when together, we have always craved emotional connections with each other and with our gods. As our emotional needs for understanding, connectedness, compassion, acceptance, and love intensified, it became increasingly more difficult to find emotional satisfaction through worship of animal predators. Eventually, the old predator gods were largely supplanted by humanlike supernatural agents, who could *love us* and *be loved by us* as we loved and cared about each other. Humanlike gods were more approachable, more benevolent, more emotionally satisfying than the predator gods that preceded them. As we became more human, so, too, did our gods.

I don't mean to oversimplify this change. It occurred in stages, with intermediate stages represented by hybrid animal-human figures and human deities closely associated with animals (they ride them, they act like them, and so on). Many anthropomorphic gods—even when conceived as being truly altruistic and deeply caring about humans—have features that betray their predator ancestry, such as delighting in blood sacrifice and hunting down and killing anyone who offends them—even if that means all creation. And the change was never complete. As many examples make clear, predator gods continued to be worshipped by humans with perfectly modern minds.

Could it be that these holdovers and disguised predator gods betray our reluctance to relinquish the fantasy of being able to control and exploit the deadly powers of the predator? It is, after all, such gods as Tezcatlipoca, the death-bringing gift giver, who engender the most intense, sometimes fanatical, worship. "We are your slaves," the Aztecs chanted, about the time that Stockholm was founded. If it is comforting to have a god as your friend, it is even more comforting to have a *dangerous god* as your friend (or as your "godfather").

The features of the deified predator were reincarnated with a vengeance in the fanged and taloned *demons* and *devils* also conjured up by the mythic (and monster-making) imagination. The conjuring, of course, is rooted in the evolutionary imperative to look out for predators and other dangerous creatures, an imperative that "breeds ubiquitous cognitions of super demons, demiurges, devils, ghouls, goblins, vampires, and other more or less overtly rapacious agents."[60] This explains why the "worship of serpent deities and would-be destroyers is at least as prevalent as God the Father and mother goddesses."[61] At times there is not much of a distinction between the two poles of worship.

Over hundreds of thousands of years, the motives for worshipping predators became less compelling. Not only did we change emotionally and cognitively, but we also invented weapons and others kinds of defensive strategies (such as cave dwelling, hut making, wall building, and so on) that made us feel safer from, and physically superior to, the animals that once bedeviled us. Predators gradually lost much of the fearsomeness and awesomeness that formed the foundation of their sacralization, or they became the demons and devils that not only hurt us but scare us into the comforting arms of more friendly humanlike gods. But the very real dangers posed by actual predators never vanished, and even today, in remote locales, people still worship carnivores and other deadly powers in an effort to appease their terrifying appetite for human blood.

ALMOST DETECTING THE PREDATOR

There are other writers who believe, as I do, that the sacred was born in the spilling of our blood, but they do not believe, as I do, that the blood was spilled by animal predators.

In *Origins of the Sacred*, English professor Dudley Young remarks that "the further back one goes, the more disturbing, even violent, sacredness becomes."[62] "The ripping of flesh," he writes, "consecrates the ground in the oldest and simplest sense we know." "To sacrifice means literally to make sacred, and our first way of doing this was to tear living flesh until the blood flowed."[63] But for Young, the first sacramental ripping of flesh occurred when a group of protohumans became possessed with what he calls a "mutilating ecstasy" and tore apart the group member—the alpha male—who dared to isolate himself within the middle of the frenzied group.[64] This bloody act gave rise both to guilt and to an astonishing sense of power and bloodlust that has haunted and entranced the human mind ever since.

As riveting as this scenario is, it overlooks the fact that long before early humans could have been galvanized into enacting this strange and traumatic sacrificial rite, they saw their kind (as well as other creatures) torn apart by *animal predators*. It is more reasonable to assume that predators—rather than members of the same kin group—consecrated "the ground in the oldest and simplest sense we know."[65]

Some of the most interesting speculation about the relationship between violence and the sacred has been done by French critic René Girard in a series of books, the most important being *Violence and the Sacred*.[66] Girard argues that the sacred was born from humanity's first efforts to defend itself by curative or preventive measures from its own violence. These efforts involved the invention of the scapegoat, on whom the terrible fury of society could be discharged, and through whose death general emotional calm could be restored. But Girard's scenario, like Young's, ignores the fact that giant animal predators were a greater threat to our ancient ancestors than were other humans. Girard's claim should be reformulated: Religion in its broadest sense resulted from our first efforts to defend ourselves by curative or preventive measures *from the violence of predators*. It was on the killing ground of the savanna that humans felt the first impulses to revere awesome, intimidating, and deadly superhuman agents—and to feed them a scapegoat.

Many decades ago, religious historian Zenaide Ragozin suggested that the impulse to worship arose from the sense of helplessness felt by "man in the most primitive stage of his existence."[67] Among the forces that evoked this sense of helplessness were "the huge and powerful animals ... whose numbers and fierceness threatened him at every turn with destruction, from which his only escape would seem to have been constant cowering and hiding."[68] Sounds like what I've been saying. But not quite. Notice the phrasing "would seem to have been." Humans, according to Ragozin, had another escape route besides cowering and hiding. Here's her astonishing claim: "Small in size, weak in strength, destitute of natural clothing and weapons ... [early man] could kill and tame the huge and powerful animals which had the advantage of him in all these things."[69] Apparently helpless and weaponless primeval humans were somehow able to kill the fierce animals that made them feel helpless in the first place.

Ragozin is mistaken here. She doesn't want to see that the first "gods" that were venerated by humans may have been bone-chewing predators. Quite naturally for the time at which she wrote, Ragozin prefers to think that our ancestors decorously worshipped celestial or climatic forces. But, as two anthropologists trenchantly observe, "we get nowhere when we suppose that, at an early stage in human development, survival came to depend on the propitiation of clouds of imaginary and quite insubstantial spirits."[70] It is much more reasonable to infer that the worship of animals predates the worship of more abstract or distant things. There is no escaping the fact that for several million years the most immediate, dramatic, and constant menace to human survival was posed by animal predators.

The connection between fear, predators, and the sacred fascinated the Indian scholar Balaji Mundkur, who explored the connection in an essay titled "Human Animality, the Mental Imagery of Fear, and Religiosity."[71] Mundkur argues that religious sentiments arose from "vague and instinctively grounded fears and anxieties." To relieve the tensions arising from this mental state, "primeval" humans projected them "onto inanimate and animate objects that commanded attention in one way or another, eventually as numina. In the course of hominid evolution the choice of a particular animal to symbolize deep emotion was bound to be whimsical"—but, as it turns out, not so "whimsical." In the "competition" to be chosen to symbolize deep emotion, it is "formidable species of reptiles, raptorial birds and fierce carnivores [that] hold the edge." "It is the reptile, felids, and raptorial birds which, by dint of numbers and fierceness . . . have excelled as metaphors and shared their power with other species ever since they instilled 'fear and loathing' and 'the instinct of religiosity' in our primeval forebears. The serpent is but one of a very few extraordinarily powerful impellers and symbols of this urge."[72]

Mundkur *almost* detects the predator as the source of the sacred, but not quite. If I understand him correctly, these formidable animals merely function as *repositories* of instinctual anxieties and fears, not as the *source* or *cause* of them. It was not predators as fearsome beasts that instilled "religiosity" into early humans, according to him, but their capacity to function as metaphors and symbols for otherwise "vague" anxieties and fears. "Only a few potentially dangerous species" could be used as symbols to capture the emotions of "stressful experiences, not necessarily involving these species."[73] Mundkur is led to this conclusion because he mistakenly believes that our ancestors actually had little to fear: "[A]nthropods and humans generally evolved under rather low pressure from predators."[74] The phrase "low pressure," while unquantifiable, strikes me as diminishing the level of threat posed by the menagerie of giant carnivores that bedeviled our weaponless ancestors every moment of every day for millions of years. I would characterize the pressure as *intense* and *unnerving*, strong enough, in my estimation, to explain why predators were natural candidates for deification, and why they played a formative role in the creation of the sacred.

"Religion" (to use Mundkur's term) did not begin in the fear of the *supernatural*, but in the fear of the *natural*, which became seen as supernatural—or at least as superhuman—as the human mind developed ever greater powers to think imaginatively and mythically.

CONCLUSION

The *first agents* to acquire godlike attributes and to be worshipped in some rudimentary way were animal predators. Our cognitive biases (the defensive system, the predator detection system, ToMM, anthropomorphism), our emotional need to relieve our primal fear, the salient natural attributes of Pleistocene carnivores—all these conspired to form a complex set of beliefs, feelings, and behaviors now labeled "sacred" or "divine" that imbued animal predators with divine attributes and provided our ancestors with behavior patterns that could be used to worship them. In short, the sense of the sacred arose from humanity's long, traumatic, and complex interaction with predators.

Contributing to the divinization process was the desperate human need to reduce the fear of dangerous animals. A scholar who studies crocodiles says that it's impossible to tell "whether the crocodile was first made sacred out of terror or because the god of such fearful beasts was in need of placation."[76] There is no "or" about it. Early humans searched for any device or technique that made them feel safer, that assuaged their fear of sudden, violent death by predator. Death could come in other ways, of course, but none was quite so shudderingly gruesome as being torn apart and eaten alive. It was this fear that drove the search for such warding-off behaviors as appeasement, sacrifice, supplication, submission and debasement, song and dance, and even praising. Each of these has some connection to the defensive strategies hardwired into the primate and hominid line. Each was seen (and still is) as "effective" in staying the destructive powers of predatory animal gods, in throwing them *off our scent*, so to speak.

Animal predators or predatory creatures/monsters were not the *only* creatures ever worshipped. All kinds of animals—and animal-human hybrids—have been venerated, from elephants to insects. Once the human brain possessed a sufficient level of cognitive fluidity, the mythic imagination went about deifying just about anything—with varying degrees of success and durability. The gods worshipped today are humanlike because gods with human attributes meet more of our emotional and cognitive needs than do animal or insect gods. As Campbell phrases it, the human mind is "the ultimate mythogenetic zone—the creator and destroyer, the slave and yet the master, of all the gods."[75] And the gods we now feel happy with are gods like us.

If "animals made us human,"[77] as Paul Shepard believes, we returned the favor by making them "gods."

Chapter 8

Kindly Killers

The Predator as Kin, Friend, Protector, and Benefactor

INTRODUCTION

We have imagined mythic predators to be not only gods and monsters but also our friends, relatives, guardians, and patrons.

In a Native American myth, the eagle is credited with fashioning "all the sacred survival things."[1] In an African myth, a python is the tribe's great benefactor, credited with giving the first man, who was born blind, the gift of sight, and giving priests of the Python cult knowledge of poisons and their antidotes.[2] In Amazonian myths, the deadly jaguar is the source of life-sustaining technology, giving humans fire, cooking, and the bow and arrow.[3] In an African myth, a hunter who befriends a crocodile is later attacked by the croc and dragged into the water to be eaten. But the hunter appeals to the other crocs swarming in for the scraps. "Is that fair? This crocodile lost his way in the bush. I brought him back to the river. And now he wants to eat me." The moral appeal works, and the hunter is freed.[4] Another African tale tells of a contract struck between a woodcutter and a lion. The lion's paw is stuck in a log, and he asks the man to free him. Free me, the lion promises, and "I swear to you that I shall never devour the sons of women so long as they are brave." But the woodcutter has a lawyerly-like mind and doesn't like the wording of the contract. So the lion rephrases the promise, "I will not touch the sons of

219

women so long as they are alive." At this wording, the woodcutter frees the lion. "From then on the man and the young lion were good friends. When the lion was hungry the woodcutter gave him a sheep."[5]

Why should a prey species imagine that its predators are kindly disposed toward it? Once again, the answer is to be found in the very distant past.

ANTHROPOMORPHISM AND FEAR MANAGEMENT

Our mind is compelled to interpret the world in the only terms it knows—its own. We unconsciously project human traits onto everything in the environment and then comfort ourselves with the "discovery" that the world pulses with human motives and desires. The compulsion to anthropomorphize the environment evolved, some scholars believe, as long ago as the early Pleistocene in response to the threat posed by predators. Early humans who could view predators as having human moods, intentions, and desires had a survival edge since this ability helped them anticipate the behavior of predators, as if they could read their minds.

To a certain extent, anthropomorphism does provide practical survival benefits because animal predators do have moods, intentions, and desires that can be understood in human terms. When a predator gets hungry, it looks for something to eat, as we do. And, like us, predators mate, bear young, take care of their offspring, play, communicate, rest and sleep, socialize, and fight among themselves. It would have been very easy and valuable for early humans to detect human traits in the very animals that hunted and haunted them. And very *comforting*.

Thanks to anthropomorphism, our ancient ancestors inadvertently and unconsciously thought themselves to be in a *social relationship* with dangerous animals, a relationship that essentially entangled predators in the same net of rules, expectations, and emotions that governed and constrained humans. That would mean that predators—despite their supernatural characteristics and blood-curdling aggressiveness—could be talked to, interacted with, managed, bribed, communed with, and subdued. If the deadly powers afflicting us are *like* us, notes Stewart Guthrie, "we can breathe a bit more freely."[6]

There was a grain of truth in the belief that the same rules governing humans could influence animal predators. The displays of threatening behavior humans used to intimidate each other could, at times, intimidate predators as well, a sign that the same interpretative rules governed both prey and predator. And certain forms of appeasement that tied together members of the group—such as meat sharing—could diminish the threat posed by local predators. Regular food offerings can even reduce the predatory instincts of voracious crocodiles,[7] and food sharing transformed (some) wolves into dogs about nine thousand years ago. The assumption—not entirely unwarranted—that predators were constrained by social rules allowed our ancient ancestors to operate more freely—and less furtively and fearfully, since they felt they could understand and cope with predators in human terms. To a limited extent, they could.

The consolation gained from humanizing predators is the theme of many myths. In Hawaiian stories, for example, dangerous carnivores, especially the shark, were depicted as having both an animal body and a human body (not one hybrid form). This duality suggested not only that humans sometimes behaved in carnivorous ways but that carnivores could be subjected to the same powers of appeasement that humans could: "*Makani kau* went down to the sea and called the sharks of *ka moho alii*. They appeared in their human bodies in the valley of *Waiipio*, leaving their shark bodies resting quietly in the sea. They feasted and danced near the ancient temple of *kahuku welo welo*."[8]

In myths around the world, tigers and other dangerous animals such as crocodiles are often thought to live in houses made of human bones, skin, and hair, but they are also constrained by a framework of laws that prevents them from taking the life of any of their human neighbors, unless it has been somehow given to them. There are similar myths about elephants, rhinoceroses, wild hogs, and other animals being constrained by compacts and contracts made with relatively helpless humans.

The anthropomorphization of predators certainly complicated our emotional relationship with dangerous animals. When seen within a human social framework, predators were not always evil, dangerous, or fearsome but, at times, honorable, beneficent, praiseworthy, and friendly. We have mythologized predators in four closely related ways to mitigate our primal fear of them. Admittedly, these four mythic depictions of predators overlap considerably in the sense that a kin member is also likely to be a friend and benefactor. But isolating these mythic archetypes enables us to look more closely at the psychological and historical roots of each.

THE PREDATOR AS KIN

In a myth of the Pomo Indians, a girl marries a rattlesnake (technically not a predator of humans, but still a killer) and has four snake sons. When these children see people from the village, they coil to strike, but their mother says to them, "'No, you mustn't bite your relatives.' And the children would obey her." When the snake-boys find that their mother is a human being, they ask if she is afraid of their father, and she says no. Overhearing this exchange, other rattlesnakes decide to crawl over her body to find out if this is true. The rattlesnake's wife was not afraid, calmly letting the snakes crawl over her.[9]

From a psychoanalytic perspective, the story could be interpreted as being about a bride overcoming her fear of sexuality (the snake as male phallus) and of having to leave her kin when she marries. But this interpretation does not explain the mother's admonition to her children that they mustn't bite their relatives, nor does it explain why, once she has overcome her phallus fears (she had four children by this time), there is any further need to let snakes crawl over her. The story makes more sense if it is viewed as being about not fearing *dangerous animals*. It assuages fear by showing that the rattlesnake, as a humanlike agent, is constrained—at least in the minds of the Pomo—by the social rule that governs *kinship*: blood relations do not kill (or eat) one another. As a contemporary Sioux storyteller explains, "[W]e Sioux think of rattlesnakes as our cousins. They always give warning before they strike, as if they wanted to say: 'uncle, don't step on me; then we'll get along.'"[10]

In a Kayan myth (India), a crocodile visits a chief via a dream and calls upon the chief to become his blood-brother. After the two agents have gone through the ceremony by changing names and so on, the chief considers himself quite safe from all crocodiles.[11] A myth told by the Fang of Gabon and Cameroon recounts how people overcame their terrifying dread of a monstrous crocodile that demanded the tribute of two women each day. When the crocodile is killed by a magic thunderbolt, "all the people ate the flesh of the great beast, and then they mourned him as kinsman. In this way, the spirit of Ombure was checked, for although it wandered the village seeking a human on whom to take revenge, all the humans were now flesh of his flesh and immune from him."[12] The immunity, of course, was not from attacks by real crocodiles but from the unnerving fear that crocodiles evoke. Such stories were prized and retold because they eased the anxiety humans felt as they walked and worked in a very dangerous environment.

The concept that one's tribe is biologically related to a progenitor animal is called *totemism*. All members of the totem are related to every member of the animal species that gave rise to the totem. While totemism serves many functions, it certainly plays a crucial role in enabling vulnerable humans to manage their fear of dangerous animals because the totemistic relationship entails obligations on both sides. Clan members are prohibited from killing or eating their animal "cousins," but, more importantly, the totem animals are prohibited from killing or eating their human "cousins." In fact, totem animals are obliged—at least in the minds of humans—to act as guardians and protectors of their human relatives, warning them about impending dangers, including attacks from other predators.[13]

The Nuer of the Nile Valley assured anthropologist E. E. Evans-Pritchard that he was perfectly safe when he waded into streams that were frequented by crocs because "people whose totem was the crocodile lived nearby."[14] If a crocodile did eat someone in the tribe, it was interpreted as a sign that the tribal member must have had blood from another tribe. The Iatmül tribe respect the croc to the point of carving the prows of their canoes in the likeness of croc heads, thus making the canoe itself a croc, which, when afloat, kindly carries its "children" on its back.[15] In an African myth of the Duala, a "giant crocodile" large enough to eat a village is controlled by being addressed as "uncle."[16] Clearly, totemism is a form of fear management that encourages fretful and anxious humans to imagine a closer and friendlier relationship with dangerous animals than they actually have.

Viewing totemism as a fear-management strategy resolves a paradox that troubled the great French sociologist Émile Durkheim. Durkheim did not think that fear was the motivating force for animal cults because even when predators are the totem figures, they are "the cultist's friends, kindred, or natural protectors. . . . The sentiments at the root of totemism are those of happy confidence rather than of terror and oppression."[17] What Durkheim did not realize is that terror and oppression are compatible with "happy confidence"; in fact, they give rise to it. Thanks to the anthropomorphic imperative, humans were (and are) confident that dangerous animals are constrained by the same social rules that inhibit aggression between family members. If so, then totemism is a form of *mimetic magic*, in that it enables humans to *imagine* that predators have the kindly attributes we *want* them to have for our own peace of mind.

This is illustrated by the Shuar of Amazonia, who handle their fear of predators by singing to them. To the Shuar, all living things, including animals, are "agents" with a *wakan*, or spirit, soul, or mind. The assumption is that although the body of the animal may be dead, its *wakan* can hear. This belief allows the Shaur to think that through their chanting they can force dangerous animals to conform to human will. As one tribal member explains, "[T]hose for whom we sing desire what we desire. They bend themselves in our thoughts because it is our desire that fills them."[18] Through performance, animal predators can be made to want what we want. A comforting thought, at any rate, and in this respect also an effective one.

Admittedly, not all totem figures are predators, a fact that may reflect the historical reality that as humans developed more effective defense technologies, they had less need to manage their fear of predators through totemism. The place of predators as totems was taken over by animals and plants that were hunted or grown for sustenance. But my hunch is that the *first* totems likely were dangerous animals, especially predators. I cannot prove this, of course, but it would make sense to give predators priority since they were the most feared creatures for a couple of million years.

THE PREDATOR AS FRIEND

A few years ago, *Parade* magazine featured an article titled "Danger in Your Neighbor's Backyard,"[19] which discussed Americans who kept dangerous animals—especially *tigers*—as pets, with as many as seven thousand tigers roaming suburban properties nationwide. Some pet owners put their four-hundred-plus-pound carnivores on a leash and parade them in public (occasionally with bloody results).

Humans have a powerful drive to imagine themselves the friends of dangerous animals. An African version of the Androcles and the Lion myth recounts how a hunter named Zwa removed a thorn from the paw of a lioness and then brought food to the lioness and her cubs because she couldn't hunt. "After that, the lioness and Zwa hunted together, as though the lioness and her cubs were his dogs."[20] It is unlikely that anything like this ever occurred. What this story of a domesticated and subservient lion does is allow tribal members to make *terror their friend*. As does the story about the Indian warrior who makes "a pact of friendship and brother-hood between Wanblee Oyate—the eagle nation—and his own people."[21] In a way, storytelling functions as a sort of cage in which we place the agents that most frighten us. This impulse to domesticate in myth what terrifies us in real life must have been quite strong in the past, given all the stories that transform predators into agreeable companions.

For people in Asia and Africa, there is probably no animal more ter-rifying and dangerous than the crocodile, with its huge maw full of sharp teeth, enormous physical strength, explosive energy, and eerie ability to appear and disappear with almost supernatural stealth. Just as willing to chomp on a human as a wildebeest, the crocodile would seem to be the least likely creature on the planet to be viewed as a friend or protector. But this is how millions of people, both past and present, do view it. In areas where humans and crocodiles coexist, crocodile cults are "by far the most common" of all the animal cults.[22]

The Kenyah of Borneo, being reasonable people, are so terrified of the crocodile that they avoid mentioning its name, just as the ancient Greeks avoided mentioning the Furies (or *Erinyes*, the "vengeful ones"). Instead, the crocodile is called (totemistically!) Old Grandfather and is regarded as a more or less friendly relative, even when it eats a member of the family. When this happens, it's time to "blame the victim," who is alleged to have either offended or injured the croc. If this explanation doesn't hold up, the fallback position is to blame the attack on a new croc unfamiliar with the friendship that exists between people and the local crocs.

Why these mental gymnastics? They induce people to feel the "happy confidence" they *need to feel* if they are to go about their daily lives in regions filled with this deadly man-eater. At all costs, they must preserve the consoling illusion that crocs (or other predators) are their friends.

Friends can be made through flattery. The best illustration of this tactic is found in the Hawaiian myth about Hiilei, who must make her way through a dragon-infested jungle. As noted earlier, when she calmly flatters the ugly dragon, it literally falls to pieces. What really shatters, of course, is the grip that fear had over Hiilei. In this myth (and in many others), fear is destroyed by word magic, even when word magic is self-deception (inside, Hiilei really is afraid). The ancient Greeks also engaged in this sort of fear management when they renamed the frightening and vengeful *Erinyes* the *Eumenides*, the "kindly ones," as if they were the friends of humanity instead of its tormentors.

THE PREDATOR AS GUARDIAN AND PROTECTOR

At some point in history, people figured out that the fear evoked by predators could be turned against human enemies and evil spirits. Predators were transformed into protectors and guardians, with this strange role best filled by such dangerous creatures as lions, tigers, dogs, bears, pythons, eagles, and hybrid monsters like dragons and griffins.

It is a giant dog, Cerberus, that guards the entrance to the Greek Underworld, while its two-headed brother (whose tail is a snake) guards the cattle of Geryon. The sacred tomb of Osiris is guarded by dragon-like fire-breathing cobras, "who live on the blood of those whom they slaughter."[23] In a myth of the Duala (Africa), a founder protects his new settlement by placing a crocodile in a nearby river and a "powerful leopard" in the center of the settlement. "These creatures provided magical protection to the compound."[24] In Hawaiian myth, the role of protector is given to bloodthirsty dragons and sharks. A dragon is ordered to go up the mountain at the head of Nuuanu Valley to become "the watchman of that place. She was the first dragon on the islands. She watched with magic power. Later, *Mo o inanea* came with many dragons to watch over the islands."[25] In another myth, King Ka-moho-alii calls upon sharks "to guard travelers on their journey."[26] In a Fang myth (Africa), a great crocodile helps a group of people fleeing "red giants" by letting the people use his body as a bridge across a river and then by drowning the giants when they tried to cross.[27]

Throughout the ancient world, images of powerful and deadly creatures can be found protecting gates, portals, thresholds, tombs, and even warriors from other threatening agents. Athena emblazoned her shield with the terrible countenance of Medusa, with its bulging eyes, writhing hair of snakes, protruding tongue, tusks, and forehead of lion tufts—a bit of evil to protect from evil.[28] Mesoamerican cultures were obsessed with such images, revealing the extraordinarily fearful mindset that underlay their rituals of human sacrifice.

Images of predators are often incorporated into public architecture, as was this Aztec depiction of the feathered serpent god. Such images serve to intimidate those who have no right to be in the vicinity and to remind us that we are the food of the "gods." Suzanne Long/Shutterstock.com.

Anthropomorphism cognitively primed our ancient ancestors to interpret certain predator behaviors as *intentionally* protective, as when predators drove off or killed competitors from their hunting grounds and so inadvertently kept down the number of threatening animals in the vicinity. When wolves howled, or hyenas screamed, or wild dogs growled and barked to scare off approaching interlopers, they were in fact also *warning* humans, almost as if they were members of the group. One reason we domesticated the wolf was to have it alert us to other predators.

Predators and monsters of one kind or another often guard *hidden treasure*. In Norse myth, for example, the beautiful daughter of the giant Suttung is turned into a witch with long teeth and sharp nails to guard the Magic Mead hidden in a cave. In *Beowulf,* a dragon guards a treasure of gold and armor. In the myth of Cadmus and the founding of Thebes, a dragon prevents Cadmus from drawing water from a sacred spring it guards. Perhaps this mythic depiction of predators arose from the fact that dangerous animals impeded early humans from gaining access to such nourishing "treasures" as tasty fruits, nuts, leaves, flowers, and fresh water.[29] Eventually, we figured out that the same predators could be used to frighten away those who wanted to take our treasures. Since myths were carried along trade routes, they were a great way to warn strangers to stay away. "Here be dragons."

Predators also protect by supplying us with powerful "medicines." The Fipa (Africa) have a myth about a gigantic python-like monster called "the destroyer." But its lethal power could be harnessed by shamans through a ritual that lured the monster into an attack that impaled it on stakes without killing it. The shaman would then use the blood of the monster python to make powerful healing medicine.[30] Native Americans used the bones of dinosaurs—correctly interpreted as the remains of ancient monstrous predators—to create powerful protective medicine (as do modern Chinese).[31] To make themselves arrow- and bullet-proof, Native American warriors often rode into battle protected by medicine bundles filled with the bones, teeth, claws, and feathers of predators.[32] In South America, the bones of dinosaurs—called "the bones of fear"—were pulverized and swallowed as an antidote against "fright and panic," a dramatic example of overcoming fear by incorporating the source of fear.

Another protection from fright and panic was found in masks that used the fear triggers associated with predators. It's possible that such hideous masks were thought to scare off actual predators, and maybe they actually did, at times. We know for a fact that in many parts of the world today, jungle workers can deter ambush attacks from predators by wearing a mask of the human face—with exceptionally big eyes—on the back of their heads. But it is more likely that most of the time these masks have been used to drive off the *fear* of predators by pretending that one could evoke and command their spirit through imitation. What is there to fear, villagers may have thought, if our antic, bandy-legged shaman can manage such deadly powers?

Even *scarification*—the purposeful laceration of the body to create visible scars—can be seen as a defensive strategy that uses a *sign* of the predator to ward off the predator. Scarification functions as a sort of *ritual mauling*, leaving scars that look as if they had been *inflicted by an animal*. For example, in Melanesia, the Iatmül believe that during a rite of passage the initiate is swallowed by the primeval crocodile and then regurgitated as an adult man. To symbolize this process, the initiate is cut across his or her torso and shoulders to imitate the teeth marks of the croc. This is a "performance of the predator" that draws real blood.[33] The peoples of the Pacific Northwest also "perform the predator" during their initiation rites. The adult men, dressed in wolf masks, "attack" initiates, driving them into the forest where the initiates are then subjected to the ordeal of ritual scarring, with the scars made to look like the claw marks of a wolf.[34]

What could be the point of this ritual mauling? Scarification may have functioned as a form of imitative picture magic designed to ward

off future attacks, a sort of prayer scratched into the body for all predators to see. It declared to the predator, "I have been mauled and I survived. So don't bother to attack me again."

These rites may have arisen from, as well as imitated, actual predator
attacks. Those who managed to escape the jaws and claws of a carnivore
likely had scars to prove it and may have been considered by others to be
particularly heroic, or lucky, or blessed. Perhaps such a near-death experience functioned as a subjective and personal initiation rite into a new
consciousness free from fear—"I have been eaten and spit out. I need
not fear being eaten again." In this sense, scars could be said to function
as a sort of heraldic device etched into the skin, a magic insignia
designed to ward off not only an actual attack but the *fear* of attack.

THE PREDATOR AS BENEFACTOR

There is a charming ancient Egyptian fable about a sailor who gets ship-
wrecked on a remote island. As he crawls out of the water, he is confronted by a giant and angry snake who demands an explanation about
why the sailor has invaded the island. Hearing the sailor's story, the snake
carries the sailor in its jaws to its dwelling without injuring him. Eventually, "the benevolent snake sped him on his way with a gift of a rich cargo
consisting of myrrh, oil, perfumed unguent, eye paint, giraffe tails, elephant tusks, greyhounds, monkeys and baboons."[35] Though there may
be some opaque cultic significance in this myth, the tale strikes me as a
rather simple expression of our indebtedness to animals for all the gifts
they provide humans.

The greatest gift predators gave us was our humanity. Our emotions,
our brains, our skills—all evolved thanks largely to the survival pressures
imposed by dangerous animals throughout the Pleistocene. Somehow,
mythmakers uncannily intuited the crucial role that Pleistocene predators played in the long evolution of the human species.

Predators are often mythologized as creators and curers. In Melanesia, the most ferocious and frightening carnivore in existence— the crocodile—is depicted in myth as a cultural hero, the creator of all things when its lower jaw fell to earth and the upper jaw became the sky, with the points of its terrible teeth being the stars.[36] I have already mentioned that predator power is often elicited as a medicine to cure disease, but there is a historical grounding for this belief. In the early Paleolithic, the actual instruments used to perform primitive surgeries were often made of *predator teeth and bones,* with the teeth of sharks being particularly valued because they were sharp, strong, serrated, naturally flanged, and came in so many shapes that just the right one could be used as the best lancet.[37] Remarkably, the human debt to predators as curers was acknowledged in Hindu surgical instruments, which were shaped as predators: jackal, lion, hawk, and, of course, the crocodile.[38]

Predators were transformed into benefactors when we imagined them to be reliable enforcers of human law and justice. The crocodile seems to be the creature most widely used to punish wrongdoers. In Egyptian myth, Ammit (sometimes Mem-Mut)—part crocodile and part lion—is fed the hearts of the evil dead. In Madagascar, suspected wrongdoers were made to cross a crocodile-infested river so that the crocs' jaws could judge guilt and innocence. In Australian myths, Old Man Croc is thought to eat only the guilty.[39] In parts of Southeast Asia, the croc is believed to be the reincarnation of a departed ruler who continues to impose authority or punitive power through the predator.[40] In Turkana (Kenya) myth, the crocodile also plays the role of enforcer and benefactor, attacking only those who have done evil. Tribal members feel quite safe wading in crocodile-haunted waters so long as their consciences are clear.

This belief is really a form of imitative magic, since it assumes that human behavior controls crocodile behavior. Like other manifestations of imitative magic, this one enables humans to manage their fears of the croc in order to go about their business; after all, people are almost always sufficiently "innocent" in their own self-justifying eyes to feel unthreatened by the jaws of animal justice.

What happens when a person is killed by a croc? The default interpretation is that the death itself is *proof* that the person had done something evil. This view both preserves the alleged efficacy of the mythic belief and helps people manage their fear of evil in *society*. By definition, the croc has rid the world of a malefactor, and so every time a crocodile kills someone, people feel more secure. There is no way to refute mythic logic.

Predators also function as benefactors when used to take private revenge. The crocodile—thanks to its efficiency as a killer—is the go-to assassin. Tribal folklore of Ghana, for example, depicts shamans and witches as sending crocs on terrible errands of revenge.[41] In an ancient Egyptian myth, a shaman makes a wax crocodile come alive to kill his adulterous wife's lover.[42]

Other predators also perform this function. In classical myth, the role of condign avenger fell to the Furies, dog-like predator birds, and to Nemesis, often depicted as half lion, half eagle. There is a Cheyenne myth about a young girl who sees her father cruelly murder her mother and is so traumatized that she suddenly develops shamanistic powers that allow her to bribe two bears to kill her father. "There's your food; eat him up." And they do.[43] The Iroquois tell a story about the Great Spirit creating the Great Buffalo to punish the foolish young people who forgot moral rules. A race of predatory Great Buffalo make war upon the human species, devouring all but a few, until the Great Spirit kills off the race except for a male and female, who are shut up in a mountain but are ready to be let loose again should humans relapse.[44] The notion that a predator can be made to do our bidding is held deep inside the human brain. The Associated Press carried a story a few years ago about a fellow in Bridgeport, Connecticut, who ordered his nine-foot python to attack two police officers trying to arrest him.[45]

To close this treatment of predators as benefactors, let us consider that many myths credit dangerous animals with giving our species the technologies that allowed us to survive—*fire* and *weapons*. In one myth, a boy stranded in a tree is rescued by a jaguar, who takes him to its lair where the boy sees fire and eats cooked meat for the first time. The boy steals a burning ember from the jaguar and so introduces fire and cooking to humans.[46] In another myth, a boy encounters a jaguar armed with a bow and arrow. The jaguar promises not to eat the boy and adopts him as a son and hunting companion (despite the ferocious objections of the jaguar's wife). Once in the jaguar's house, the boy learns not only how to build a fire and cook meat but, more importantly, how to make a bow and arrow. The first creature the boy kills with his newly acquired technology is his benefactor's wife.[47]

What these myths are encoding is our gratitude to predators for providing us with meat. There is no doubt that our ancient ancestors scavenged meat left on the bones of animals killed by predators. *Homo habilis* was scavenging carcasses two and a half million years ago.[48] Feeling dependent upon and indebted to the very animals that *turned us into meat* no doubt threw our hominid ancestors "into a highly ambivalent relationship with the predator beasts."[49]

To be successful scavengers, early humans had to know a lot about the hunting and feeding behavior of all kinds of carnivores, as well as their telltale signs, sounds, and tracks. Those who didn't master these skills probably didn't last that long. The need to be sharp when scavenging, especially when scavenging the kills of big cats in the open savanna, did a lot to speed up human evolution. It was during the early Pleistocene that our line became noticeably larger, stronger, faster, and smarter—thanks in part to the meat "gifts" provided by predators.[50]

Our primordial dependency on predators for meat has often been mythologized, sometimes with a self-flattering twist. In one Native American (Cheyenne) myth, the first humans could control predators and so taught the "panther, the bear, and similar beasts to catch game for them. They increased in numbers and became tall and strong and active."[51] In some Native American myths, the mountain lion is mythologized as a giver of meat. In a Cheyenne myth, panthers, nursed by a woman, kill deer for the tribe.

Although the Koyukon of northwestern Alaska are successful hunters, they also scavenge wolf kills. Sometimes the carcasses left by wolves are so fresh and untouched that they appear to the Koyukon as having been deliberately left for them to find. To explain this "gift," they imagine the creation of a primordial exchange relationship between them and these very dangerous animal powers. In the Distant Time, a wolf-person (a sort of totemic figure) lived among people and hunted with them. When they parted ways, they agreed that wolves would sometimes make kills for people and sometimes drive game to them. This beneficent behavior was a repayment for favors given when wolves were still human. Since the Koyukon have imagined themselves to be in an exchange relationship with the wolf, they are required to give a gift—usually fat—to the wolf for what they have received from the wolf. The belief that they have a gift-exchange relationship with carnivores helps the Koyukon manage their fears. And, of course, it is possible that by giving wolves food, the Koyukon do in fact have fewer bad encounters with wolves and, so, less to fear.[52]

Predators are often given credit in myths for giving us the greatest gift of all—the ability to get *our own* meat. This gift allowed us to eventually become the most successful predator on the planet. To avoid becoming meat, our ancient ancestors must have been sharp-eyed and fascinated observers of animal hunting behavior. From the hyenas and lions, they learned the logistics of hunting in packs; from the leopard and tiger, the effectiveness of stealth and ambush; from the big snakes, the value of patience and camouflage. (A python can wait in one spot up to four days to make a kill.[53]) They may also have learned from watching predators how to share food even with those who didn't hunt and how to cache food for later consumption.[54] And, as myths insist, we are indebted to predators for our first weapons, as in fact we probably were.

Our ancient ancestors must have used anything at hand—animal jaw-bones, rib cages, horned skulls—to defend themselves from dangerous animals, as well as from dangerous humans. It is no accident that knives and spear tips are designed like predator teeth.

CONCLUSION

Despite the fact that carnivores chilled their blood, our ancestors were grateful to them because they understood, at some level, that these deadly forces not only hunted and killed them but also helped them to become physically agile and mentally clever survivalists. This sense of indebtedness is mythologized in myth after myth. In reality, of course, predators were just being predators, going about their business with no or little regard for the humans around them—until the pangs of hunger dictated otherwise. But this is not how the developing human mind was inclined to interpret things. Meat and bones left by predators at kill sites, their hunting strategies, their warning calls—these and many other things came to be interpreted as intentional acts of kindness.

The driving force behind the anthropomorphism and humanization of predators was the need to manage fear of these creatures. By imaginatively entangling predators within a net of social obligations, our ancestors felt that they had gained some measure of control over them. Though an illusion, this belief was consoling, encouraging, and empowering. Stories and myths not only *recorded* this favorable view of predators, they *legitimized* and *perpetuated* it.

Chapter 9

Model of Menace

The Predator as Exemplar and Object of Envy

INTRODUCTION

We humans not only fear animal predators as monsters, worship them as gods, and welcome them as friends and benefactors; we strive—in extreme cases—to *become* them in order to possess their deadly powers.

In the Maya book *Popol Vuh*, King Gucumatz is considered to be a truly marvelous king because for seven days "he changed himself into a snake and really became a serpent; for seven days he changed himself into an eagle; for seven days he became a jaguar; and his appearance was really that of an eagle and a jaguar."[1] In Hindu myth, Narasimha could change into a man-lion, a terrifying figure with fierce eyes, bristling mane, gaping jaws, "terrible tusks and a tongue sharp as a razor blade which waved like a sword."[2]

By wearing a lion's pelt, the Greek hero Herakles also turns himself into a "man-lion." When King Eurystheus, who sent Herakles on the quest to kill the beast, sees the hero coming toward him, with the animal's immense paws knotted around his neck, the jaws gaping above his head, and the tail swinging behind him, the king is so terrified that he hides inside a cauldron and refuses ever again to lay eyes on this were-lion. When Queen Ino is attacked by a lynx, she is so overcome by bacchic frenzy that she is able to strangle the predator with her bare hands and then flay it with her teeth and nails, donning its pelt à la Herakles. Clothed in the lynx skin, she goes to Mount Parnassus to celebrate her stunning and timely transformation into a were-predator.[3]

As Hans Kruuk understands, "[C]arnivores are wonderful, magnificent and almost unbelievably attractive."[4] But what is the source of this attraction, and what are the consequences of it? The clue to the answer can be found in the observation by Spanish philosopher George Santayana: a lion must be more convinced than a gazelle that God is on his side.[5] Well, so, too, must a human who imagines that he has become the lion. Our "rebellion" against the predator, as Barbara Ehrenreich characterizes it, was really a rebellion against our status as prey, not a totalistic rejection of the predator. Yes, we relentlessly and compulsively hunt and kill predators to exorcise the shame and fear they evoke in us, but we also envy them, identify with them, imitate them, and try—in extreme instances—to actually become them. It is this transformative identification—this metamorphosis—that makes King Gucumatz a truly marvelous king, Herakles a fearsome hero, and humans such a dangerous species. This is another plot line in what Ehrenreich calls the story of our transformation from prey to predator.[6]

LEARNING TO IDENTIFY WITH THE PREDATOR

Early humans probably didn't have the mental abilities to imagine that they could actually become an animal predator, as King Gucumatz and his subjects could. These abilities were engendered over a vast expanse of time by our desperate need to understand and deal with predators.

The dangerous environment of the Pleistocene selected for the ability to predict what predators might do not only on the basis of external cues but also from intuiting what was going on in the predator's mind.[7] To survive, early humans not only had to think *about* predators;

they had to think *like* them, viewing themselves from the perspective of the animals that hunted them. This seeming mind-reading ability provided the foundation for the later phenomenon of mythic identification.

At the root of the mythic notion of transformation is mimesis. The ability to identify with predators was nurtured by mimetic performance, which in turn strengthened the ability to identify. As Dudley Young notes, "[W]e become what we become by doing what we do, and mimesis lies at the heart of this simple mystery."[8] Performing as a predator functioned as a conduit to capturing the fearsome killing powers of the predator. It could be said that although mimesis initially began in defense and defiance, it eventually enabled us to ecstatically identify with the very source of terror. Impersonation led to *im-personation*—the sense that one had actually passed into the body of another creature or absorbed the spirit of the creature into one's own body.

HUNTING AS MIMETIC PERFORMANCE

For a couple of million years, our ancestors watched ferocious carnivores hunt and kill their prey with awesome efficiency. It eventually dawned on our forbears to imitate these accomplished hunters. By the upper Paleolithic, hunters figured out that they could kill game more effectively by exploiting the highly effective camouflaging colors and markings of predator skins. The wearing of these skins induced hunters to imagine that they were tapping into the animal's killing prowess—its strength, speed, and stealth. And, to the extent that the wearing of a predator's hide encouraged them to act like the predator, they *were* acquiring the animal's prowess, but through mimesis, not osmosis. In African rock art, hunters are often depicted as garbed in leopard skins.[9] Even today, tribal hunters go after their prey dressed in carnivore skins to improve their chances of making a kill. Tribes in the Amazon enhance their hunting prowess by wiping on their bodies broth from boiled raptor talons.[10]

As Dudley Young remarks, "[W]e must imagine primitive man . . . admiring the appalling efficiency of a pack of hunting dogs or hyenas as it closes on its prey: ah, to be seized by such power! And then to seize it!"[11] The power was eventually seized through imitation, by enacting over and over again the killing strategies of dangerous, powerful forces.

FROM HUMAN TO PREDATOR: RITUALS OF TRANSFORMATION

Ritual was another way we came to identify and merge with the predator. Rituals often create an altered state of consciousness during which participants envision all kinds of things, including their transformation into dangerous animals. This is particularly true of initiation rites, which frequently involve a simulated attack on initiates by tribal elders disguised as "man-eating creatures, hungry for human flesh."[12]

In Aboriginal myth and ritual, for example, boys are initiated into a new life as an adult warrior by being swallowed by the giant serpent Yurlunggur, which is impersonated by male elders who "swallow" the boys by sweeping them up and carrying them off to the seclusion of the sacred initiation grounds. When the boys return from their initiation, they are regarded as having been "regurgitated" by the snake, as having died and been reborn—in essence as having been spared by the great mythic predator as a sign of their favored status as hunters and of their invulnerability as warriors.[13]

Among the tribes of the Pacific Northwest, elders don wolf masks, abduct the initiates into the forest, subject them to ordeals (including ritual scarring to mimic wounds left by animal claws), and finally introduce the young to the secrets of the wolf cult. Among certain Indian tribes of California, the boys being initiated are threatened with death from attacks by pumas, bears, ravens, rattlesnakes, even tarantulas. In Africa, initiators dress in lion and leopard skins.[14]

The initiation rites of the Orokaiva of New Guinea, studied by anthropologist Maurice Bloch, reveal the deeper purposes of such rites. The Orokaiva rite begins with male elders—who had been hiding in the bush—suddenly attacking the village as if they were animal predators, springing out of the forest wearing terror masks decorated with bird feathers and pigs' tusks. They chase the children and beat them, shouting, "Bite, bite, bite."[15] All involved in this performance take it very seriously, with a child or two occasionally dying from the ordeal.

The purpose of such terrible rites of passage is not to weaken or humiliate youngsters but to enable them to overcome their fear of predators by magically transforming them *into* predators. Orokaiva children, like children everywhere, are keenly aware of their physical vulnerability and are often haunted by terrible dreams about being attacked by "monsters." For children who live in the very midst of dangerous animals, fear must be especially intense and potentially crippling. If those children are to take part in activities essential to the survival of the group, such as food gathering and hunting, they must overcome their fears. This is the first function of these rites. No matter how frightening the "predator attack," it is performed by tribal members known to the children, and the "attack" is rarely fatal, with almost all children *surviving* it.

This "survival" both empowers and transforms the initiates, who return from the ordeal "not as prey but as hunters of pigs, shouting the same formula which had been addressed to them, 'Bite, bite, bite.'"[16] They, too, will eventually dress and act like predators to transform other initiates into "fearless" hunters and killers. To signal the success of the transformation, the first act of the initiated is to brave the dangers of the jungle by going on a pig hunt. After killing a pig, they strut on the platform and distribute real pigs' meat. "The completion of the transformation of prey into hunter is clear for all to see."

But the transformation entails more than becoming fearless killers of pigs. The initiated become fearless killers of *humans*, as well. This aspect of the transformation is symbolized by a decoration called the *Otohu*, which is presented to each participant in the pig hunt. Significantly, the decoration is presented not by the best *hunter* but by the most lethal *warrior*, who recites to the children the names of the men he has killed during his long life. The point is to encourage children to become warrior killers in their turn. "The pig hunt is thus revealed to be the first stage in an ever-amplifying hunt against neighbours and enemies."[17] The ancient Hebrews put it this way: "Behold, the people shall rise up as a great lion, and lift up himself as a young lion: he shall not lie down until he eat of the prey, and drink the blood of the slain."[18]

This "rite of terror"[19] has taught the novices that by identifying with the predator, they acquire its killing power and rid themselves of fear. Eventually it will be their time to dress as predators and transform a new generation of children into fearless killers of animals and humans. Again we see that mimetic performances—enacted stories—function as wellsprings of reality, and that we imitate the animal predator not always to display our triumph over it but sometimes to identify with it and so to acquire its power to kill. As Marina Warner recognizes, the "magic of make-believe"—whether performed through games, stories, or rituals—can make what is imagined seem as actual as "real life."[20]

Warriors and would-be warriors have long known that by identifying with animal predators, they could transcend their fears and imbue themselves with an almost supernatural power to kill their enemies. To encourage their ferocity, the warrior elites of the Aztecs were called Jaguar Knights and Eagle Knights.[21] The initiates into the warrior cults of northern European tribes wore wolf or bear skins as they ran amok biting people. The more they simulated the savagery of these beasts, the more effective and feared they were as warriors. This was known as going "berserk," which literally means "dressing in bear hide."[22] They wore bear or wolf skins in battle not just to heighten their animal ferocity and to terrify their enemies—which it most certainly did!—but to make themselves impervious to pain and danger, and thus to fear. Berserks were not just humans wearing a disguise: they thought they had actually transformed themselves into dangerous animals. As historian Mircea Eliade explains, "To behave like a beast of prey—wolf, bear, leopard—betokens that one has ceased to be a man . . . that one has in some sort become a god. . . . On the level of elemental religious experience, the beast of prey represents a higher mode of existence."[23] A mode of existence where death holds no power.

The case of Adolf Hitler illustrates the enduring allure of this quest to identify with—and sometimes become—the animal predator. Hitler had a powerful psychic need to identify with the wolf, perhaps dating from the time in his childhood when he discovered that his given name derived from the old German word *athal*—meaning "noble wolf." He named his favorite dog Wolf, called the SS his "pack of wolves," and believed that adoring crowds were responding to his own wolfish essence. One day in 1926, as related by Mimi Reiter, a teenaged Austrian girl who was briefly involved with Hitler, she and Hitler went to her mother's grave at his request. As he stared down at her mother's grave, Hitler muttered, "I am not like that yet!" He then gripped his riding whip tightly in his hand and said to Mimi, "I would like you to call me Wolf."[24] Hitler was possessed by the same impulse that possessed the Germanic warriors of the Middle Ages: to have the gleam of the wild beast in his eyes.

Ehrenreich interprets Hitler's words to mean "to be dead is to be vanquished is to be prey. . . . Those who do not wish to be prey must become predators. Conversely, those who are not predators are prey."[25] I agree, but I would rephrase the interpretation just a bit: To become a predator is to transcend one's fear of death by evoking that fear in others.

HUMAN SACRIFICE AS A PREDATOR KILL

Rituals of blood sacrifice, like rituals of initiation, often simulate a predator attack. For example, in modern-day India, the holy men officiating at the sacrifice of animals often leap on the creatures and bite through their necks, sometimes even chewing out their livers, which they then carry around in their mouths.[26]

It was in pre-Columbian Mesoamerica that rituals of blood sacrifice were most contrived to resemble a predator kill. The bloodletting was performed by "Jaguar priests," who sliced open the gut and chest cavity of their victims using obsidian blades shaped like jaguar fangs and claws to inflict wounds resembling those made by a jaguar.[27] When acquiring sacrificial victims, warriors often dressed in the skins of ocelots, jaguars, and other predators.[28] To make it look even more like a predator attack, the *victims* were sometimes dressed in the skins of the *prey* animals that jaguars hunted.

In *The Highest Altar*, Patrick Tierney discusses a peculiar practice, witnessed by Europeans, that involved the laceration of sleeping victims by shamans bent on selecting candidates for sacrifice. The shamans—called "suckers"—would sneak into houses at night when people were sleeping and stealthily cut them with their fingernails to extract blood, which they sucked. The victims would die of fright within a few days. Tierney also reports instances where Inca priests literally clawed to death their sacrificial victims in order to imitate a puma or jaguar. As Tierney notes, to carry out such predator-like sacrifices, the shamans and priests must have made their fingernails "exceedingly long and specially sharpened for this purpose."[29] Curiously, Ino and Shiva also kill and flay their victims with their fingernails.

Why the urge to make blood sacrifice look like a predator attack? Perhaps it was to recapitulate the primordial and typical behavior of the first gods. "We worship your power, we give to you the blood and flesh you want, and we do this as your minions." If so, then sacrifice functioned, like so many other rites, as a fear-management strategy. The priest as predator controlled the attack, which was comfortingly directed at scapegoats outside society. Strangers died so that members of the tribe could live together less fearfully. One can only marvel at the incredible ability of the human imagination to invent ways to deal with the fears and anxieties that the imagination itself helps create.

CONSUMING IDENTITIES

There is no better way to convince oneself that one has become an animal predator than by eating what it eats. To us, the most salient item on a predator's menu is human flesh. Eating human flesh is the most "radical sign of the Beast" we can devise.[30] It signals one's transformation into a shark-man, a wolf-man, a bear-man, and so on. It is a form of communion establishing oneness with the predator. This is the point of a Borneo myth about a hero who descends into a crocodile's lair in pursuit of gold. Although he disguises himself in the skin of a tiger, the croc smells him out as a man. To test his hunch, the croc seizes a human from the riverbank, cuts him up, stews the parts, and then offers it to his visitor. The hero, as would a tiger, gobbles down the meal of human flesh, and so allays the suspicions of the croc. Ah, the croc says, here is a fellow predator indeed! And the hero actually is, but in a different way than the croc thinks. Once the meal is over, the hero spears the croc in the belly and acquires the treasure he was seeking, his reward for playing the predator to the hilt.[31] But the hero was not really "playing" at being a predator; he was one.

As with initiation ceremonies, ceremonial cannibalism often reenacts the essential elements of a predator kill. In the rites of the African leopard men, the sacrifice and cooking of the victim's flesh and blood were done by a priest "completely covered with leopard skins." At times, the victim's tissue was eaten raw, as a predator would eat it.[32] As was done in Aztec sacrificial ritual, the victim is killed to make it look as if a predator had done it, the body is torn apart—or dismembered—and the belly is opened up with a "leopard knife."[33] And, as in Aztec ritual, parts of the body are dedicated to a "predatory monster" to assuage its hunger for blood, an act that further connects the cannibalistic act with the predator theme.[34]

As *animals* grow stronger by eating human flesh, so, too, do *warriors*, not just because flesh provides nourishment but because the act itself is considered empowering, showing that the warrior has acquired the animal predator's vitality and intimidating power to kill. In Mesoamerican ritual and myth, tribes that ate their enemies were especially feared because they were believed to be possessed by a fierce jaguar-spirit that animated them to savagely devour their enemies. During cannibal feasts, tribal people may have imagined that they were actually possessed by the spirit of a predator since it is easier to convince others when one is also convinced. Humans eat other humans to overcome the fear of being eaten. Once transformed into a predator, what is there to fear?

Clearly cannibalism is constrained by a powerful taboo, with many myths broaching the activity cautiously and with a sense of shame. In a Native American myth, cannibalism occurred "long, long ago, when the world was very young,"[35] or in the "early world" when the "ancients" were "stupid" and did not know "which creatures were deer and which were people, and sometimes they ate people by mistake." Though a mere "mistake," the offense provokes the Great Spirit to "kill all the monsters and other evil beings among the ancients."[36]

The establishment of a taboo against cannibalism is often mythologized as a blood fight against the cannibal monster, with the monster often being dismembered and eaten himself. In Hawaiian myth, the shark-man cannibal is cut into small pieces that are burned in a great oven.[37] Another Polynesian myth recounts the story of how Hina enlists the aid of a human chief to finally kill off Hina's mother, a rapacious cannibal who eats the lovers of her daughter. An African myth of the Jukun kingdom explains that in "earliest times" a woman "ate all her young. She swallowed everything she encountered." But one of her children survived the ordeal to become the hero who eventually kills this cannibalistic monster, thrusting a spear into her belly. However, when the body is burned, it turns into a cannibalistic calabash, "large enough to swallow up the women as they came to fetch water at the stream." Eventually the calabash, too, is broken open, but when burned, its ashes touch some people and transform them into witches and sorcerers.[38] The cannibalistic impulse is hard to kill.

Our ambivalent attitude toward cannibalism—as an act that both *empowers* and *pollutes*—is expressed in the Greek myth of Zeus Lykaion, or Zeus the Wolf. According to legend, Lycaon killed his grandson, cut up his body, cooked it in a kettle used for animal sacrifices, and served the cannibalistic dish to Zeus. For this offense, Zeus turned Lycaon into a wolf, an ambiguous punishment indeed, for Lycaon now possessed the vital though fearful wolfish powers attributed to Zeus himself. This legend was ritualistically reenacted every year atop Mount Lykaion at the Pan-Arcadian Festival, though it was done secretly and at night. "Anyone who ate of the human meat was supposedly transformed into a 'wolf' and had to enter a special clan, and they all lived in exile together for nine years. If they didn't eat any more human flesh during these nine years, the 'wolves' were allowed to rejoin normal society."[39]

Who knows how many times our ancient ancestors witnessed the most gruesome transformation of all—one of their own being dismembered and consumed by an animal carnivore, literally being *incorporated* into a predator. No doubt such scenes evoked profound disgust and fear, but they also may have induced in us a disorienting sense of ourselves as highly desirable flesh—with tasty marrow and nourishing salty blood. As we sensed that we were the objects of predator desire, our attitude toward our pursuers—our impulse to evade them and to fear them—must have become strangely conflicted, eventually leading us to make predators the object of *our* desire.

Thanks to our mythic imagination, we could fantasize about being incorporated into the predator without having to pass through its deadly maw. This transformation was accomplished through mimesis, by wearing the predator's skin and imitating the predator's motions, sounds, and eating habits. By eating our own, we consume our fear of being consumed.

EMBRACING THE
INNER ANIMAL PREDATOR

When the newly initiated Orokaiva children return to the tribe shouting, "Bite, bite, bite," no one believes that they have been transformed into *actual* animal predators. But in other traditions, ritual transformation is thought to create a literal human-beast, not a human playacting at being a beast. In psychiatry, this conviction is thought of as the most intense, complete form of possession.[40] And it can have deadly consequences.

Humans have been dressing up and imitating predators—for one purpose or another—since the early Paleolithic, but at no time or place has the mania to identify with the predator been taken to such grisly extremes as in Africa during the last one hundred and fifty years. The world of myth offers nothing as bizarre as what was actually enacted by humans who were convinced that they had acquired the deadly powers of the carnivore.

As long ago as 1607, a visitor to Sierra Leone wrote of fierce man-eating tribes who lived in the interior of the country and dressed as leopards.[41] Yet it took almost three hundred years before colonial authorities had solid evidence of were-predator *secret societies*. By 1891, there were not only leopard-men societies but also lion-men societies, tiger-men societies, and crocodile-men societies (which I lump under the term "predator-men").

The members of these secret societies transformed themselves into their predator of choice by clothing themselves in its skin or painting themselves to look like it.[42] To intensify their identification, they let their nails grow very long[43] and sometimes wore masks resembling the face of the animal. They also imitated the roar of the beast while roaming the jungle at night searching for human victims.[44] They attacked from ambush and at night, jumping on the victim's back and ripping open the throat.[45] To imitate the wounds inflicted by a big cat, the assassins wore specially designed gloves with curved blades as well as sandals carved to leave paw-like tracks.[46] They mutilated the corpse by ripping out its heart, liver, spleen, and kidneys—the very soft-tissue organs favored by animal carnivores. The corpse was then carved up into parts that were distributed to all present.[47] Some victims were almost entirely consumed, save for the skull, teeth, and a few other parts.[48] Attacks like these occurred into the 1940s.

Something like this sort of killing is recorded in the holy book of the Maya, the *Popol Vuh*. It is written that when members of one tribe ambushed a few members of another tribe, the killing was often blamed on animal predators. "And the tribes said, 'The jaguar ate them,' and they spoke thus because like footprints of the jaguar were the tracks which they had left."[49] But in Africa, predator-men were not trying to cover up a simple robbery or assassination by casting suspicion on wild beasts. They were trying to convince themselves—or were already convinced— that they had become predators, by dressing, acting, sounding, and killing like them. They even went so far as to invent "a pantomimic birth act in which the initiates were pulled out from under the tail of a leopard pelt."[50] They killed their victims ferociously to convince themselves that they had indeed undergone the transformation they coveted through this symbolic rebirth as a leopard, or lion, or crocodile. They were not *pretending* to be an animal; they had *become* an animal. During his trial for murder, a predator-man explained that he simply could not avoid doing the killings because at the time he had been a leopard and thus was "overpoweringly blood thirsty."[51] Colonial authorities remarked that predator-men were "completely convinced" that they had been—when killing—an animal carnivore.[52] Pretense and performance certainly played a role in these terrible enactments, but they functioned as devices to work a magical transformation which, in a sense, they did engender.

These killers imagined themselves to be predators—I suggest—in order to escape fear. As anthropologist Birger Lindskog points out in *African Leopard Men*, Africans lived in a "constant state" of fear, haunted and terrified not only by the very real dangerous animals that roamed the forest, jungles, and grasslands of the continent, but by the prevailing and intense belief that witches and evil shamans could make animal carnivores and even humans kill whomever they pleased, and in ghastly ways. This fear was grounded in all-too-real events. Court documents describe how witch doctors would kidnap and drug young men, glove them with lion claws, and then direct them to kill another member of the village, sometimes for a fee, sometimes to settle a personal score. Some witch doctors also "attempted to train real lions and hyenas to be man-eaters," going so far as to file the teeth of predators to make them even sharper.[53]

Even more disturbingly, there were cases of witch doctors actually trying to physically transform children into animal predators using horrific physical coercion. They would keep the children in dark underground lairs to force them to develop a crouching posture; they would break the wrists of the children and tie their hands back against their forearms to simulate the pads of animals; and, they would cut the tendons in the legs of the children to give them an animal gait. Then, at night, they would release these twisted and tormented creatures to "search for random victims."[54] These outrageously grotesque practices added to the many dangers the people had to be afraid of at this time and in this place.

The role fear played in the predator-man phenomenon is made clear by the "borfima," a medicine bundle of kneaded coagulated human blood, flesh, and bone.[55] This powerful medicine, it was thought, made predator-men *safe from animal and human attack*.[56] To keep the immunizing powers of the borfima fresh, the owner had to periodically smear it with blood and tissue taken from victims. This rite was called "'feeding or blooding the borfima,' and it was conceived of as satiating its 'hunger.'"[57] The sacrificer dressed in a leopard skin and used a leopard knife to cut up still-living victims to get the fat and blood needed to feed the fetish.[58] Leopards, too, eat prey that is still alive. In a sense, the borfima was a fetishized predator. The borfima had the power to convince people that they had actually become the predators they were *im-personating*.[59] By absorbing the stunning life energies of the predator, a person who was once fearful now could cause fear in others, transferring his burden to them. In fact, one of the emotional benefits of being a leopard-man was the belief that one could "never be attacked by a leopard."[60] In the language of *Goodfellas*, an initiate into the cult was a "made man."

African predator-men weren't killing for fun or for gain but to create a mythic and safe world for themselves, using as props *real* victims and *real* blood. In the insightful words of Lindskog, predator men were "staging an effective fiction."[61]

So, too, are the contemporary Westerners who undergo extensive surgeries to literally transform themselves—as much as physically possible—into their favorite predator. In 2009, Animal Planet aired a program on what might be called the "were-predator" movement. One man had his teeth filed into fangs and underwent dozens of operations and got numerous tattoos to make himself look like a tiger. He had long feline-like nylon hairs implanted in his striped face, had his lip cleft upward, had his ears cut and shaped like a tiger's, had a tail surgically implanted where the tail should go, and had his eyes colored yellow to imitate a cat's eye. "Mentally," he says, "I do live life as a tiger. I'm not human. I am it." He legally changed his name to Snap E. Tiger. Then there is Monitor Lizard Man, who had his tongue surgically split, his teeth filed, his skin colored green, his body scarred to imitate the markings of the lizard, and a tail attached. Enough people are getting in touch with their Inner Animal that they have created "were-communities" on the Internet and hold annual conventions (where no actual bloodletting has yet been recorded). Their conviction that they have indeed become animals testifies to the transformative—and at times terrifying—powers of mimesis and the mythic imagination.

FEARING THE WERE-PREDATOR

Ironically, our ability to identify with predators as a fear-management strategy also adds to the very fears we are trying to manage through the identification. Transformers and shape changers can be just as dangerous as the predatory animals they imitate and incarnate, and they can evoke just as much terror. Hunters and warriors can go berserk and turn their predator energies against even their own. Sacrificers and cannibals can gather their victims unnervingly close to home. As Tierney writes in *The Highest Altar*, acquiring the spirit of a powerful animal like the wolf or the leopard conferred a "dangerous status on any . . . who possessed it, or [were] possessed by it."[62] Ever since an alpha male lost control, went berserk, and maimed and killed those he should have protected, we have been wary of our predator heritage, and sometimes terrified by it. The mythic imagination has filled the world not only with imaginary terrors but also with *real* terrors that we have *imagined* into existence.

The Garenganze people explained to a frustrated British colonial agent that they did not kill the wild animals that made their lives a living nightmare because the animals really were "men of other tribes" who had been magically turned into lions, panthers, or tigers. To kill these animals would be tantamount to murder and would risk tribal revenge. The elders also explained that this belief prevents cooperation between tribes since it was not possible for two men from different tribes to go out into the country together without one striding ahead of his neighbor, getting out of sight, and returning as a lion or leopard to devour his traveling companion. Such transformations and attacks occur daily, the elders insisted. Not only do the tribes tolerate the wild animals around; they hold them almost "sacred."[63]

Some tribal peoples, quite aware of the danger in these beliefs, attempt to discourage the inclination to identify too closely with animals. Tribal stories often counsel humans to maintain a respectful distance between themselves and their totem animals, for should that distance be violated, horrible things could happen. Other stories express a certain regret that humans ever learned how to imitate predators and acquire their power to kill. In one African myth, all creatures, including humans, originally lived together in fellowship in one camp. Dissension began after Fox persuaded Mongoose to throw a club into Elephant's face. A quarrel ensued, and the animals separated, each going its own way and each killing the others. In a Nuer myth, the Trickster figure Fox gave men the spear and showed them how to kill with it. "It was then that man began to kill, and his first killing seems to have been that of the mother of cow and buffalo, or rather the mother of cattle, for at that time cows and buffaloes were the same. This led to a feud between men and cattle, buffaloes avenging their mother by attacking men in the bush and cows by causing men to quarrel and slay one another."[64]

In another African myth, two hunters lose control of themselves and angrily dash a woman's infant child on the ground. Carried away by bloodlust, they wind up killing each other. "The woman had watched in horror as this bloody scene took place. When the two hunters lay still, she roused herself, maddened by the death of her child, and began to pound their remains with rocks, screaming curses at their still bodies." Moved by her lamentations, the sky god restored everyone to life. "The hunters stared at each other . . . and fearing that they might again become so estranged and lost to decency as to commit such crimes again, they bound themselves with a great oath," that "hunters are brothers and bound to respect each other."[65]

The same theme is addressed in a story by the Khonds (Africa), which has a less happy ending. A tribesman who routinely transforms himself into a tiger to go hunting needs the help of another person to transform him back into a human. The tiger-man teaches the spell to his friend, but his friend dies, so he teaches it to his wife. But when he returns the next day, carrying his kill in his bloody mouth, his wife is so frightened that she screams and runs away. He tries to remind her to pronounce the spell by lunging and roaring, but his antics terrify her even more. He eventually becomes so angry that he kills and eats her. He then realizes that he has eaten the one person alive who knew the spell to turn him back into a human.[66] This story says that men have to be aware of the dangerous predator spirit within them, and women have to be brave enough to exorcise it.

A charming and haunting tale told by the Passamaquoddy (a Native American tribe) also confronts and exorcises the threat posed to the tribe by its own hunters. A father and mother want to marry off their daughter, but she rejects all suitors. In the same village, there lived an old witch—indeed, she was the night predator owl in disguise—who possessed "evil powers." Her nephew, the great horned owl, "ruled the whole tribe of these bad and scheming birds." He wanted the girl, and thanks to a magic potion supplied by his aunt, the owl disguised himself as a young hunter and fulfilled a condition made by the father of the girl.

He then "seized her by the hand and took her with him to his lodge." The next morning, the bride awakens to find that her husband is an owl—that is, a predator. "The girl sat for a long time petrified with fear, because now she knew that the handsome young hunter was the terrible great horned owl himself." When the aunt enters, the girl lets out a piercing scream and flees. After waiting for the villagers "to forget their fear and suspicion," the nephew tries another trick, changing himself once more into a young hunter. He kills a moose and an elk, drags the meat to the village, and announces to the people that he has come as a friend from another camp, that he does indeed "belong" to the tribe because they both speak the same language, and that he wants to live among them. "I am a great hunter and a generous man. I am putting up a lodge, and I have much meat, so I invite everybody to a feast."

At the feast, the girl exposes the fact that the host is really the great horned owl. "With cries of terror, the guests rushed out of the lodge." The aunt aids her nephew in his courtship by creating a magic flute that will charm this clever and suspicious girl. Meanwhile, the girl feels "imprisoned" by her "fear" of the owl-man and decides to take a walk in the woods to overcome the situation. In the woods, the sharp-eyed avian predator sees the girl and begins to play on the flute. "I could never resist the player who make this wonderful music," she thought. "Then the Great Horned Owl swooped softly down upon her, seizing her gently in his huge talons, carrying her off to the village of the owls." They lived happily ever after.

Certainly at one level, the tale intends to allay a young maiden's fear of marrying a man she scarcely knows. But it is also about a woman confronting and overcoming her fear of the killing energies of the male. Or, in the vague words of the story, "Women have to get used to their husbands, no matter who they are."[67] The tale also deals with the burden males bear in being both a gentle intimate lodge companion and a successful killer of both animals and other humans. Males are required, in other words, to be in perfect control of the deadly power of transformation. This tale encapsulates a fear endemic in every society—the fear that males can transform themselves into animal predators and exercise their killing powers at the wrong time, endangering those they live with, love, and should protect.

CONCLUSION

There was a time when members of the *Homo* line were pretty harmless creatures, without weapons, without a big brain, and without much size or strength, thus posing little threat to bigger animals or to others of their kind. Though capable of violence in self- and group-defense (as all primates are), they probably understood that survival depended on cooperation and avoidance, not confrontation.

It was by watching and imitating animal carnivores, and by evolving effective ways to respond to the threat they posed, that we became—as a species—the alpha predator of the planet. This development, however, did not release us—as individuals—from the primal fears that tor-

These two images graphically portray the ambivalent relationship between humans and animal predators. In the figure on the left, the Trojan citizen Laocoön and his sons—all weaponless— are being strangled by sea snakes. While freighted with meaning, this famous sculpture certainly captures the anguish and fear humans must have felt as they battled unsuccessfully with powerful animal predators. *Danilo Ascione/Shuttterstock.com.* In the second image, a figure called "Saint George," but who seems more like Herakles, beats down the monster, an image that celebrates the triumph of the hero—and of humankind—over the animal predator. Take away the weapon, however, and the hero/human is more likely than not to undergo the same fate as Laocoön and his sons. *Tupungato/Shutterstock.com.*

mented our Pleistocene ancestors. When unarmed, each of us is still as physically vulnerable to an animal predator as our ancient ancestors were, though we are not as likely to encounter one.

Myths of a hero overcoming an animal predator not only celebrate the transformation of humankind from prey to predator but also subtly remind us that the transformation is not complete. After all, a hero is exceptionally redoubtable and well armed when he takes on deadly powers. We love such stories not so much because we want to dance with glee on the corpse of the carnivore but because we need to exorcise our lingering fear of dying by carnivore. There is no end to stories about dragon slayers because there is no end to dragons and to the anxiety they symbolize.

So *Homo praeda* ("man the fearful") was not replaced by *Homo necans* ("man the killer") but rather merged with it. This amalgamation was made possible by mimesis and the mythic imagination, which conspired to legitimize the belief that a human can be transformed into an animal predator, and by doing so, escape for a time the terrible burden of being prey by turning others like us into prey. If we took revenge on animal predators by hunting them to near extinction, animal predators also took their revenge on us.

Chapter 10

Scaring Ourselves to Life

Storytelling and mythmaking are rooted in the mental modules and inference systems that evolved within the primate line to deal with the survival threat posed by predators (as well as by less urgent, more occasional dangers such as fire, storms, and floods). These modules and systems provided our ancestors, as they still provide us today, with biases, potentialities, and tendencies to react to threat in ways that had been tested for effectiveness by millions of years of evolution. As I have argued, our ancient ancestors probably did not have pictures of specific predators wired into their brains. What they did have were inherent sensitivities and reaction patterns to certain features, shapes, sounds, motions, and colors that had evolved as characteristics of dangerous creatures (both big and small). Since early humans, as primates, lived in a group, it was crucial that members of the group learned how to communicate about the dangers that threatened their existence. No doubt the earliest forms of communication were vocalizations—alarm and distress calls, shrieks of terror, hooting and howling, whatever—and various kinds of body language, from facial grimaces to jumping up and down and scampering up a tree or into a cave.

Evolution selected for ever more sophisticated forms of communication, not only as a way to keep the group socially cohesive and functioning in times of ease but also to keep it intact when the lions or hyenas came to eat. From this traumatic pressure emerged, first, rudimentary narrative that must have been acted out by creatures who, after all, had no language as we know it and a fairly limited repertoire of behaviors evolutionarily designed to help them survive in a hostile environment. Eventually a more complex form of speech emerged from primitive vocalization, which performed more complex functions than merely soothing or alarming group members. But even this development still would have had to deal with the never-ending threats posed by predators, as well as with other environmental forces. The spoken stories that gradually emerged—accounts of what happened in the past and what could happen in the future—were survival stories whether they were about the location of fruit or the location of predators. But given the nature of the Pleistocene environment, the location of predators would have been an even more pressing topic of communication than the whereabouts of plums. Our early stories likely reflected this existential imperative. More often than not, the most dramatic, the most vivid, the most intense, and the most frequent topic of conversation likely was about the awesome and terrifying animals that made the search for fruit so fraught with fear. Nature and culture working together would have selected for those basic plots that best served the survival needs of our Pleistocene ancestors and of their more recent descendants.

This necessarily hypothetical reconstruction of the distant past goes a long way toward explaining why myths and tales all over the world— and in both Stone Age cultures and thoroughly modernized societies— are filled with all kinds of dangerous animals, whether depicted as monsters, gods, benefactors, or role models. Each incarnation reflects our desperate need to somehow manage our primal fear of being ripped apart and eaten alive by animals.

We can never escape this fear. Our brains are wired to detect threat on the flimsiest pretext, to be afraid even when there's nothing to be afraid of. This sort of fear is a burden and curse at times, giving rise to phobias and conflicts, but we should not too blithely attempt to escape this fear altogether, because it keeps us *alive*. "Fearless" people often wind up with the booby prize of the Darwin Award, annually awarded to people who have died thanks to thoughtless risk taking.

This may help explain why the primordial fear of being stalked or chased by some kind of predator is the stock and trade of popular story-telling even today, stoked again and again by thousands of "predator fictions." Scan the horror, science fiction, thriller, and action sections of any well-stocked video store, and you'll come away convinced that this culture is "virtually" obsessed with watching fictional characters fighting for their lives with rapacious creatures hell-bent on tearing them apart and eating them. By now billions of people have watched at least one of the films in the great "animal predator" franchises: *Jaws* (1975, 1978, 1983, 1987), *Alien* (1979, 1986, 1992, 1997, 2004), and *Jurassic Park* (1993, 1997, 2001), to name the most commercially successful. In these movies, the characters run—or swim—for their lives, and those who don't do it well enough wind up dead. The archetypal carnivore meal is often depicted with such gruesome realism that it's enough to turn the stomach and make the actual predator kills shown on Animal Planet look surgical by comparison.

Hans Kruuk acknowledges that "by merely looking at such predation . . . we satisfy deep urges by proxy."[1] True enough, but what are these urges? How are they satisfied by viewing reenactments of our most primal fear? Why are we driven to watch the chase and the kill (or the escape)?

For one thing, animal predators and "homicidal monsters" "thrill us horribly."[2] The thrill is wired into our predator-defense system. Even a fictionalized threat of being killed by a beast excites our most profound and powerful drives and emotions. And, because the hero usually survives, these reenactments conjure up a bit of that *survival ecstasy* that floods us when we escape a real predator. The appeal of predator fictions is raw and primal, and so very powerful.

These reenactments also *empower*. They allow us to identify with characters who are inspired, as David Quammen puts it, to "transcendent fits of courage," like Ripley in the *Alien* franchise, or the young woman in the Australian movie *Black Water* (2007). We share in the courage and resourcefulness of characters who outsmart or kill the ravaging beast. We all want to be heroes, and always are, in our Walter Mitty moments. Mythic predators can make us feel not only weak but strong.

Fictions can induce us to identify, defensively, not with the victim but with the victimizer. One video game, called *The Altered Beast*, promises to bestow on gamers "the powers of the altered Beast," the power to "transform your being into a part animal, part human creature of formidable force."[3] Then there are those who try to transform themselves into predators through surgery or by wearing threatening masks. One can buy masks called Evil Clown, Venom, Rattler, Unleashed Wickedness, Wolfman, Vampire, Demon, Hellboy, Hellbeast, Autopsy Ghoul, Screaming Corpse, as well as full-body costumes of serial killer Freddy Krueger, and the Alien and Predator monsters from the films named for them. Of course, donning these masks allows us to frighten away fear by identifying with the death-dealing agent that causes fear, to get a hold on our fear by grasping tightly the thing that we fear. But they also can derange us, as Sigurd was deranged by wearing a wolf hide, and as Herakles was by wearing a lion skin.

There's no denying that some people identify with predators less out of fear than out of *bloodlust*. This was brought home to me one night many years ago after watching number two of the *Halloween* franchise in a local theater (1978, 1981, 1982, 1988, 1989, 1995, 1998, 2002, 2007, 2009). The film's bogeyman—Michael Myers—is a speechless serial killer whose face is hidden by a plastic, featureless mask. He is brutally homicidal, cutting throats and pinioning victims to a wall with a carving knife. Ghastly and gruesome stuff, all right, but it did not disturb me as much as the audience did that night. Each time this demon killed someone, the members of the audience erupted in cheers as if at a pep rally. When he sneaks up behind an unsuspecting old woman, a college student behind me coldly yelled, "Kill her!" It was a command—not a joke. When the maniac burns off the face of a nurse with scalding water, many in the audience—including females—applauded and shrieked with excitement like it was a touchdown. When he grabs another woman—almost all the victims are women, as in myths and fairy tales—a fellow yelled out, "Roast her!" And when this butcher enters a hospital's nursery of newborns, another fellow screamed out, "Mangle 'em!" I am not making this up. I was reviewing the movie, so I had a pencil with me and recorded what I heard. These kids—the ones within earshot, at any rate—gleefully identified with the "predator" *because* he spilled blood—frequently, inventively, and gruesomely. One can now purchase a Michael Myers full-body costume.

This audience was made up of the first generation of Americans to have seen on TV or in film about ten thousand homicides by their sixteenth birthday, with almost all of the killings depicted coldheartedly (in some films, the killing is so frequent and massive that it's hard to total up the bodies). Although this episode happened many years ago, displays like it must have occurred countless times across the country by now. One quite like it attracted national attention a few years ago. When some high schools in Chicago screened *Schindler's List* (1993), many of the kids laughed uproariously at the cold-blooded killings, provoking director Steven Spielberg to visit the schools to try to explain how a human being should respond to seeing hapless victims being brutally murdered.

It seems impossible to deny that repeated exposure to *some* predator fictions can induce in *some* people an "affectless state," an inability to feel what another is feeling. This emotional and moral blackout may last no longer than the duration of the story, but it could also lead to a permanent numbing of the moral sense. There have been instances of teenagers who have worn one of the masks I've listed while committing murder, as did African leopard men. Like other things we see, read, and experience, fictions can affect us for both good and ill. As Frank Cawson puts it, "[T]he animal root in our nature has a devastating potential. It is not something that can be played with. Once admitted and invited to take a seat at the table, the animal is like the unwelcomed guest who will not go away and who ends up in possession of the whole house. Jekyll has lost control, his moral centre of gravity has shifted, he has become the victim of a perverse imagination."[4] As we have already seen, ancient mythmakers also understood that the mythic imagination can, at times, be as morally monstrous as any creature it can invent. Then as now, a culture needs to take seriously how it "entertains" itself.

In predator fictions, agents of death can come in all shapes, sizes, and species—from giant worms, rats, and even rabbits (!) to killing slime, crushing monoliths, and reincarnated dinosaurs. Add to this list the monstrous human hybrids that stalk and kill us in film after film—vampires, werewolves, ghouls, ghosts, mutants, evil spirits, zombies, droids, replicants, and so on. Not only can anything be transformed into a "predator" by the mythic imagination but we seem compelled to do so even when belief in such creatures has waned for almost all people in the West. Why this compulsive need to create them? I suggest that many of these mythic creatures function as surrogates or proxies for the agents that nowadays we have real cause to fear. As historian Arnold Toynbee ironically noted, "[T]he human race's prospects of survival were considerably better when we were defenceless against tigers than they are today when we have become defenceless against ourselves."[5]

In the West, where we are more likely to be killed by a car than a carnivore, we no longer need to fear *animal* predators as much as *human* predators—serial killers, child molesters, and feral packs of street marauders. It is a grotesque fact that in a modern civilization a person is more likely to be hunted, killed, dismembered, and even eaten by another member of society than by an animal. These sorts of crimes may not occur all that often, but they occur often enough to require special police units and to have resulted in a truckload of true-crime books and TV crime programs. Perhaps our predator fictions do what a stroll in the African savanna used to do for our ancient ancestors—hone our ability to detect threat and to survive it. As one character from the movie *The Premonition* (1976) puts it, "[A]s a woman I know better than to walk alone at night." This movie functions as many other mass-market fictions function, as a "cultural alarm system" teaching and reminding us about the lethal hazards in our environment and how to detect and deal with them.[6] If only the victims of Ted Bundy, Ivan Milat, or Frederick and Rose West had exercised the same survival wisdom.

What makes our environment particularly hazardous is the difficulty we have in detecting and guarding against its predatory agents. These agents don't usually trigger our alarm system because they don't have long fangs or glare at us with cat eyes. Instead, they seem affable and intelligent, like Ted Bundy or the dorky Hawaiian honeymooners of *A Perfect Getaway* (2009), or the earnest home buyers of *Open House* (2010). They rarely charge at us screaming death threats but creep up on us from ambush, after lowering our guard and putting us at ease, as the Yorkshire Ripper, Jeffrey Dahmer, and killer-clown John Wayne Gacy were so good at doing. We need pretty sharp detection skills to spot predators like these nowadays.

In predator fictions, we are never allowed to feel entirely secure—not even when in a *Panic Room* (2002) or shark-proof cage. Whatever modicum of security we possess in these stories depends almost entirely on our ability to detect danger and to make the right choices in response to it. In *The Edge* (1997) the character played by Anthony Hopkins—an apparently effete and bookish urbanite—has to deal with *two* predators—the first, a Kodiak bear, the second, his *trusted assistant*, who plans to assassinate him for his money and beautiful wife. For sure, the bear is a formidable opponent, but it is easy to recognize. His friend, however, is more dangerous because he has disguised his intent to attack and kill.

This lesson is taught in film after film, as Good Samaritans turn out to be sociopaths, brides turn out to be Black Widows, and grooms, Bluebeards. But it is not just that the characters find it hard to detect the dangers lurking in their environment; it's that they are *reluctant to*, lest they appear as cowardly, unsociable, suspicious, or intolerant. Some of us may be more comfortable with being a "victim" than with exhibiting the tiniest trace of "judgmentalism" or "aggression." This tendency is reflected in the film *Just Cause* (1995), in which a law professor is all too ready to believe, to his peril, in the innocence of his client, who is accused of murder. He, like so many of us, is ashamed to consider himself as either prey or profiler. Perhaps our obsession with predator fictions reflects a creeping awareness, and fear, that we are losing touch with the hard-earned survival skills of our paleo-mammalian brain.

In the cult thriller *Manhunter* (1986), a trusting blind woman is taken to a veterinarian's office by a coworker so she can have the tactile pleasure of petting a tiger that has been tranquilized for surgery. As she lovingly, almost sexually, rubs her face through its fur and her bare arm against its fangs, she has no idea that the coworker who sweetly gave her this ravishing experience is a homicidal maniac who eventually will try to kill her too. Is this strangely poetic scene trying to say that our predator-detection system has been tranquilized by the prevalent social mores of ready trust and acceptance, blinding us to the human predator that might be standing right beside us?

True-crime writer Ann Rule actually experienced this phenomenon, as she acknowledges in her account of her strange relationship with serial killer Ted Bundy, whom she worked with on a crisis hotline during the time he was committing the very murders they were chatting about. In *The Stranger beside Me*, Rule confesses that even as the evidence accumulated, she found it almost impossible to believe that this attractive and intelligent young man was the very serial killer the two of them were analyzing between crisis calls.[7]

What can happen when danger is *not* detected is driven home like a spear thrust in the powerful and unnerving film *Funny Games* (1997). Two predatory sociopaths exploit the generosity, trust, and peaceful nature of good people who think they are safe, having moved from New York to Long Island. Neither the husband nor the wife see soon enough that there's something not quite right about the white-gloved prep-school golf enthusiast who appears at the door politely asking for eggs.

Predator fictions nurture and sharpen survival skills that we still need but seldom use, until, of course, we are suddenly and unexpectedly fighting for our very lives. They serve as alarm calls once removed, showing us how to detect danger and deal with it. As we watch the plot unfold, we look for telltale "signs" that reveal who the killer is before the action makes this clear. We also try to pick out which characters are "marked for mayhem," as the title of an article on real-world victims in *Psychology Today* puts it.[8] Some characters know how to fight for survival, like the young woman in *P2* (2007) who is trapped in an underground parking garage by a deranged killer and his guard dog, or the browbeaten suburban housewife in *While She Was Out* (2008) who suddenly finds herself chased by a pack of teenage sociopaths. But other characters almost invite the attention of the predator, as a thrashing bather invites sharks.

Predator fictions give us a chance to think about what we would do if we suddenly had to fight for our lives. After watching the shattering Australian thriller *Wolf Creek* (2005), we go over in our heads what the victims could have done early on to avoid their horrific fate. The life-and-death struggles depicted in these stories not only tease out fears and desires lurking in the unconscious but also prepare us for real-world encounters with agents—both human and animal (such as pit bulls)—who would do us grave physical harm. Predator fictions function like such folk tales as "Little Red Riding Hood," "Bluebeard," and "Hansel and Gretel"—they sensitize us to subtle signs of danger and encourage us to rehearse ways to counter it, including becoming a predator ourselves (*Death Wish*, 1974, 1982, 1985, 1987, 1994; *The Brave One*, 2007; *While She Was Out*, 2008; and *Hard Candy*, 2005). The Encore Action Channel actually runs a promo for its movies called "Survival Guide," which facetiously identifies the "tools of survival" found in its films.

Even slasher films—"predator porn," as Ehrenreich rightly brands them[9]—wind up offering blood-drenched instructions about what *not to do* in dangerous situations. When being chased, don't go to an elevator, push the button, and wait. Don't use the phone near a bleeding corpse. Don't walk backward into a dark room. Don't pick up hitchhikers or hitchhike. Don't use back roads. Don't get lost in the boondocks. Don't go into the woods (especially in the South), and don't let strangers into your home merely because you saw them standing beside a neighbor.

Predator fictions are "escapist" in the best sense of the word. Only people who assume that they will never be physically endangered are likely to dismiss this ancient function of storytelling as irrelevant or ignoble.

Turning away from storytelling for a moment, let me suggest that our fear of being consumed may contribute to war and genocide. In the wartime propaganda posters reprinted in *Faces of the Enemy: Reflections of the Hostile Imagination* by Sam Keen, the face of the enemy is almost always transformed into the archetypal predator face, with glaring eyes and a gaping maw with sharp fangs.[10] In one poster, a capitalist is ladling gold coins into his enormous mouth, untroubled by the spectral figure labeled "mass starvation" about to be consumed along with the coins. In another, "Militarism" is portrayed as a monstrous ape with staring red eyes and an open mouth with large teeth. Throughout the book, the predator face—dripping with its menace of voracious consumption—is conjured up to create fear and enmity.[11] These propaganda posters should not be dismissed as nothing more than cynical devices for exploiting our primal fear in order to motivate people to fight, kill, and die for a country or cause. They may reveal an underlying *source* of enmity.

Countries, too, can be seen as predators. A country may view a neighbor as wanting to "consume" its resources and culture, especially if the neighbor is dynamic and culturally influential. In the Book of Habakkuk from the Hebrew Bible, the Chaldeans are described as a "dread and terrible" nation as swift as leopards and fierce as "evening wolves."[12] The Other need not be provocatively militaristic, just intrusive and unsettlingly alluring. In fact, in this era of global communication the Other need not even be a "neighbor" to elicit the fear that it is *gnawing at* the life-sustaining cultural values one holds sacred. This fear of being ingested, of being incorporated into the Other, can provoke intense hatred and violence, especially in countries where people already live in fear of animal predators and potentially genocidal next-door neighbors. These conditions prime people to react aggressively to *everyone*.[13] I suggest that at least some bloody conflicts are rooted in the archetypal battle to determine which side does *not* get eaten.

Interdisciplinary scholar Melvin Konner believes that "the situations that most seriously jeopardize human survival and human dignity, past, present, and future, owe much more to irrational fear than to irrational rage."[14] Along the same line, animal-behavior scientist Konrad Lorenz has concluded that "there cannot be the slightest doubt that human militant enthusiasm evolved out of a communal defense response of our prehuman ancestors."[15] If Lorenz is right, then perhaps our great moral struggle is not so much with our innate homicidal impulses—though some people do have them but with the excessive and bloody counter-offensive that springs from our displaced fear of being consumed, a fear that has its roots—like storytelling and mythmaking—in the deep Paleolithic fear of the predator.

In *The Others: How Animals Made Us Human*, Paul Shepard explains the irresistible allure of animals by listing "what they do": "run, leap, crawl, display, call, fly, mate, fight, sing, swim, hide, slither, climb, and die."[16] Notice that the list does not include the word *kill*. *Deadly Powers* has tried to explain why this word must be added to the list. It has not been my aim to either romanticize or demonize animal predators. My aim has been to explain and to describe the role they played in the evolution of storytelling and mythmaking. To do this, animal predators have to be given their due as creatures that hunted, ate, and terrified our species for several million years. And they still do, in both the real world and in the world of story and myth.

NOTES

INTRODUCTION

1. Quoted in Barbara Ehrenreich, *Blood Rites: Origins and History of the Passions of War* (New York: Free Press, 1997), p. 40.

CHAPTER 1: PREDATORS AND MYTH

1. Carl Sagan, *The Dragons of Eden: Speculations on the Evolution of Human Intelligence* (New York: Random House [1977], 1993), p. 104.

2. Barbara Ehrenreich, *Blood Rites: Origins and History of the Passions of War* (New York: Free Press, 1997), p. 56.

3. David Quammen, *Monster of God: The Man-Eating Predator in the Jungles of History and the Mind* (New York: W. W. Norton, 2003), p. 3.

CHAPTER 2: BRINGERS OF DEATH: PREDATORS OF THE PLEISTOCENE AND BEYOND

1. Richard Erdoes and Alfonso Ortiz, eds., *American Indian Myths and Legends* (New York, Pantheon Books, 1984), p. 164.

2. Ibid., p. 227.

3. Ibid., p. 220.

4. Ibid., p. 227.

5. Stephen Belcher, ed., *African Myths of Origin* (New York: Penguin Books), p. 8.

6. Ibid., p. 15.

7. Ibid., p. 81.

8. *Popol Vuh: The Sacred Book of the Ancient Quiche Maya*, transl. Adrian Recinos (Norman, OK: University of Oklahoma Press, 1950), p. 188.

9. Ibid., p. 90, n. 2.

10. Paul Shepard, *The Others: How Animals Made Us Human* (Washington, DC, Island Press, 1996), p. 34.

11. Donna Hart and Robert W. Sussman, *Man the Hunted: Primates, Predators, and Human Evolution* (New York: Westview Press, 2005), p. 74.

12. Hans Kruuk, *Hunter and Hunted: Relationships between Carnivores and People* (Cambridge: Cambridge University Press, 2002), p. 112.

13. Brian Hayden, *Shamans, Sorcerers, and Saints: A Prehistory of Religion* (Washington, DC: Smithsonian Books, 2003), p. 257.

14. Ibid., p. 26.

15. George Constable, *The Emergence of Man: The Neanderthals* (New York: Time-Life Books, 1973), p. 115.

16. Barbara Ehrenreich, *Blood Rites: Origins and History of the Passions of War* (New York: Free Press, 1997), p. 40.

17. Donna Hart, "Humans as Prey," *Chronicle of Higher Education*, April 21, 2006, p. B10.

18. Hart and Sussman, *Man the Hunted*, p. 10.

19. Brian Morris, *The Power of Animals: An Ethnography* (Oxford: Berg, 2000), p. 181.

20. Hart and Sussman, *Man the Hunted*, p. 67.

21. Björn Kurten, *Pleistocene Mammals of Europe* (Chicago: Aldine, 1968), p. 74. See also David Lambert, *Dinosaur Encyclopedia: From Dinosaurs to the Dawn of Man* (New York: DK, 2001), p. 219; Ian M. Lange, *Ice Age Mammals of North America: A Guide to the Big, the Hairy, and the Bizarre* (Missoula, MT: Mountain Press, 2002), p. 106; Miles Barton, Nigel Bean, Stephen Dunleavy et al., *Prehistoric America: A Journey through the Ice Age and Beyond* (New Haven, CT: Yale University Press, 2002), p. 92.

22. Antony J. Sutcliffe, *On the Track of Ice Age Mammals* (Cambridge, MA: Harvard University Press, 1985), p. 180. See also Alan Turner, *The Big Cats and Their Fossil Relatives* (New York: Columbia University Press, 1997), p. 57.

23. Tim Haines, *Walking with Beasts: A Prehistoric Safari* (New York: DK, 2001), p. 188. See also Lange, *Ice Age Mammals of North America*, p. 106.

24. Ibid., p. 77.

25. Hart and Sussman, *Man the Hunted*, p. 68. See also Turner, *The Big Cats*, p. 62.

26. Kurten, *Pleistocene Mammals of Europe*, p. 74.

27. Turner, *The Big Cats*, p. 44, fig. 3-3.

28. Haines, *Walking with Beasts*, p. 168.

29. Hart and Sussman, *Man the Hunted*, p. 63.

30. Kurten, *Pleistocene Mammals of Europe*, p. 87.

31. Hart and Sussman, *Man the Hunted*, p. 80.

32. Kruuk, *Hunter and Hunted*, p. 59.

33. James Clarke, *Man Is the Prey* (New York: Stein and Day, 1969), pp. 148–49.

34. Amanda Barrett and Owen Newman, "Leopards of the Night" (transcript), *NOVA*, PBS, December 1, 1998, http://www.pbs.org/wgbh/nova/transcripts/2519leopards.html, transl. Ulli Beier (accessed March 3, 2011).

35. Kurten, *Pleistocene Mammals of Europe*, p. 85.

36. Lange, *Ice Age Mammals of North America*, p. 109.

37. Kruuk, *Hunter and Hunted*, p. 191.

38. David Quammen, *Monster of God: The Man-Eating Predator in the Jungles of History and the Mind* (New York: W. W. Norton, 2003), p. 405.

39. J. H. Patterson, *Man-Eaters of Tsavo and Other East African Adventures* (London: Macmillan, 1907).

40. Clarke, *Man Is the Prey*, pp. 102–103, 113.

41. Roger D. Abrahams, ed., *African Folktales: Traditional Stories of the Black World* (New York: Pantheon Books, 1983), p. 338.

42. Leo Frobenius and Douglas C. Fox, *African Genesis: Folk Tales and Myths of Africa* (Mineola, NY: Dover [1937], 1999), p. 79.

43. Kruuk, *Hunter and Hunted*, p. 211.

44. Kurten, *Pleistocene Mammals of Europe*, p. 85.

45. Kruuk, *Hunter and Hunted*, p. 211.

46. Ibid.

47. Turner, *The Big Cats and Their Fossil Relatives*, p. 72.

48. Clarke, *Man Is the Prey*, p. 127.

49. Kruuk, *Hunter and Hunted*, p. 211.

50. Clarke, *Man Is the Prey*, p. 127.

51. Ibid., p. 121.

52. Ibid., pp. 128–29.

53. Ibid., p. 136.

54. Sy Montgomery, *Spell of the Tiger: The Man-Eaters of Sundarbans* (New York: Houghton Mifflin, 1995), p. ix.

55. Ibid., p. 176.

56. Ibid., pp. ix–x.

57. Ibid., p. 74.

58. Clarke, *Man Is the Prey*, p. 157.

59. Paul S. Martin, *Quaternary Extinctions: A Prehistoric Revolution* (Tucson: University of Arizona Press, 1984), p. 57.

60. Paul S. Martin and John E. Guilday, "A Bestiary for Pleistocene Biologists," in *Pleistocene Extinctions: The Search for a Cause* (New Haven, CT: Yale University Press, 1967), p. 32.

61. Ibid.

62. Lange, *Ice Age Mammals*, p. 110.

63. *Popol Vuh*, p. 149.

64. Turner, *The Big Cats*, p. 81.

65. Haines, *Walking with Beasts*, p. 193.

66. Kruuk, *Hunter and Hunted*, pp. 16, 50.

67. Laurens Van Der Post, *The Lost World of the Kalahari* (San Diego: Harcourt Brace Jovanovich [1958], 1986), p. 47.

68. Kruuk, *Hunter and Hunted*, p. 11.

69. Kurten, *Pleistocene Mammals of Europe*, p. 99.

70. Björn Kurten, *The Cave Bear Story: Life and Death of a Vanished Animal* (New York: Columbia University Press [1978], 1995), p. 55.

71. Clarke, *Man Is the Prey*, p. 90.

72. Kruuk, *Hunter and Hunted*, p. 11.

73. Hart and Sussman, *Man the Hunted*, pp. 98–103.

74. Kruuk, *Hunter and Hunted*, p. 64.

75. Clarke, *Man Is the Prey*, p. 92.

76. Morris, *The Power of Animals*, p. 180.

77. Clarke, *Man Is the Prey*, pp. 92–93.

78. Kruuk, *Hunter and Hunted*, pp. 69–70. See also Hart and Sussman, *Man the Hunted*, p. 95.

79. Kurten, *Pleistocene Mammals of Europe*, p. 109.

80. Stanley J. Olsen, *Origins of the Domestic Dog: The Fossil Record* (Tucson: University of Arizona Press, 1985), p. 12. See also Martin and Guilday, "A Bestiary for Pleistocene Biologists," pp. 29–30.

81. Clarke, *Man Is the Prey*, pp. 85–86.

82. Marina Warner, *No Go the Bogeyman: Scaring, Lulling, and Making Mock* (New York: Farrar, Straus, and Giroux, 1998), p. 37.

83. Padraic Colum, *Nordic Gods and Heroes* (Mineola, NY: Dover [1920], 1996), p. 175.

84. Anthony Stevens, *Ariadne's Clue: A Guide to the Symbols of Humankind* (Princeton, NJ: Princeton University Press, 1999), p. 353.

85. *Popol Vuh*, p. 91.

86. Kurten, *Pleistocene Mammals of Europe*, p. 109.

87. Hart and Sussman, *Man the Hunted*, p. 103.

88. Björn Kurten and Elaine Anderson, *Pleistocene Mammals of North America* (New York: Columbia University Press, 1980), p. 166.

89. Martin, *Quaternary Extinctions*, p. 55.

90. Clarke, *Man Is the Prey*, pp. 80–81.

91. Hart and Sussman, *Man the Hunted*, p. 104.

92. W. Ramsay Smith, *Myths and Legends of the Australian Aborigines* (Mineola, NY: Dover [1932], 2003), p. 258. See also David Gordon White, *Myths of the Dog-Man* (Chicago: University of Chicago Press, 1991).

93. William D. Westervelt, *Myths and Legends of Hawaii* (Honolulu: Mutual, 1987), p. 203.

94. Martin and Guilday, "A Bestiary for Pleistocene Biologists," p. 31.

95. Martin, *Quaternary Extinctions*, p. 55.

96. Lange, *Ice Age Mammals*, p. 100.

97. Ibid., pp. 101–102.

98. Hart, "Humans as Prey," p. B10.

99. Erdoes and Ortiz, *American Indian Myths and Legends*, p. 172.

100. Ibid., p. 86.

101. Ibid., p. 237.

102. John C. Murphy and Robert W. Henderson, *Tales of Giant Snakes: A Historical Natural History of Anacondas and Pythons* (Malabar, FL: Krieger, 1997), p. 27.

103. Hart and Sussman, *Man the Hunted*, p. 119. See also Murphy and Henderson, *Tales of Giant Snakes*, p. 66.

104. Stevens, *Ariadne's Clue*, p. 341.

105. Hart and Sussman, *Man the Hunted*, p. 121.

106. Ibid., p. 119.

107. Murphy and Henderson, *Tales of Giant Snakes*, p. 81.

108. Hart and Sussman, *Man the Hunted*, p. 117.

109. Stevens, *Ariadne's Clue*, p. 341.

110. Clifford H. Pope, *The Giant Snakes: The Natural History of the Boa Constrictor, the Anaconda, and the Largest Pythons* (New York: Alfred A. Knopf, 1961), pp. 208–209.

111. A. W. Reed, *Aboriginal Myths: Tales of the Dreamtime* (New South Wales, Australia: Reed Books, 1978), p. 81.

112. A. C. Pooley, Tommy C. Hines, and John Shield, "Attacks on Humans," in *Crocodiles and Alligators*, ed. Charles A. Ross (New York: Facts on File, 1989), p. 183. See also Mark C. Ross and David Reesor, *Predator: Life and Death in the African Bush* (New York: Abrams, 2007), p. 193.

113. Ross and Reesor, *Predator*, p. 187.

114. Ralph E. Molnar, *Dragons in the Dust: The Paleobiology of the Giant Monitor Lizard* Megalania (Bloomington: Indiana University Press, 2004), p. 172.

115. Charles Gould, *Mythical Monsters* (New York: Crescent Books [1886], 1986), pp. 34–35.

116. Pooley et al., "Attacks on Humans," in Ross, *Crocodiles and Alligators*, p. 174.

117. C. A. W. Guggisberg, *Crocodiles: Their Natural History, Folklore and Conservation* (Harrisburg, PA: Stackpole, 1972), p. 148.

118. Clarke, *Man Is the Prey*, p. 179.

119. Johannes C. Anderson, *Myths and Legends of the Polynesians* (Mineola, NY: Dover [1928], 1995), pp. 141–42.

120. Montgomery, *Spell of the Tiger*, p. 154.

121. Belcher, *African Myths of Origin*, p. 151.

122. Reed, *Aboriginal Myths*, p. 110.

123. Pooley et al., "Attacks on Humans," in Ross, *Crocodiles and Alligators*, p. 178.

124. Robert B. Edgerton, *Sick Societies: Challenging the Myth of Primitive Harmony* (New York: Free Press, 1992), p. 90.

125. Paul S. Martin, *Twilight of the Mammoths: Ice Age Extinctions and the Rewilding of America* (Berkeley: University of California Press, 2005), pp. 28–29.

126. Ibid. See also Sherman A. Minton Jr. and Madge Rutherford Minton, *Giant Reptiles* (New York: Charles Scribner's Sons, 1973), p. 172.

127. Minton and Minton, *Giant Reptiles*, p. 176. See also Bernard Heuvelmans, *On the Track of Unknown Animals*, trans. Richard Garnett (New York: Hill & Wang, 1959), p. 212.

128. Ibid., p. 179.

129. Ibid., p. 174.

130. Ibid., p. 180. See also Hart and Sussman, *Man the Hunted*, p. 124.

131. Lewis Perdue, "Komodo Dragons," Slatewiper.com, http://www .slatewiper.com/////////komodo.shtml (accessed March 5, 2011).

132. Hart and Sussman, *Man the Hunted*, p. 127.

133. Ibid., pp. 122–24.

134. Nigel Marven and Jasper James, *Chased by Sea Monsters: Prehistoric Predators of the Deep* (New York: DK, 2004), p. 152.

135. Clarke, *Man Is the Prey*, p. 234.

136. William D. Westervelt, *Hawaiian Legends of Ghosts and Ghost Gods* (Honolulu: Mutual [1916], 1999), p. 343–44.

137. Gavin De Becker, *The Gift of Fear* (New York: Dell, 1998), p. 343.

138. Clarke, *Man Is the Prey*, p. 238.

139. James B. Sweeney, *A Pictorial History of Sea Monsters and Other Dangerous Marine Life* (New York: Bonanza Books, 1972), p. 173.

140. Ibid., p. 177.

141. Ibid., p. 180.

142. Ibid., p. 178.

143. Ibid., p. 179.

144. Ibid., p. 170.

145. Michael Benton, *Dinosaur and Other Prehistoric Animal Factfinder* (New York: Kingfisher Books, 1992), p. 229.

146. Adrienne Mayor, *Fossil Legends of the First Americans* (Princeton, NJ: Princeton University Press, 2005), p. 104.

147. Benton, *Dinosaur and Other Prehistoric Animal Factfinder*, p. 229.

148. Mayor, *Fossil Legends of the First Americans*, p. 165.

149. Erdoes and Ortiz, *American Indian Myths and Legends*, p. 227.

150. Gregory S. Paul, *Dinosaurs of the Air: The Evolution and Loss of Flight in Dinosaurs and Birds* (Baltimore, MD: Johns Hopkins University Press, 2002), p. 304.

151. Martin, *Twilight of the Mammoths*, pp. 106–107.

152. Mayor, *Fossil Legends of the First Americans*, p. 104.

153. Carl Zimmer, "Terror, Take Two," *Discover* 18, no. 6 (2007): 74.

154. Hart and Sussman, *Man the Hunted*, p. 147.

155. Leslie Brown, *Eagles of the World* (New York: Universe Books, 1977), p. 34.

156. Hart and Sussman, *Man the Hunted*, p. 6.

157. Justin Kerr and Bruce M. White, *The Olmec World: Ritual and Rulership* (Princeton, NJ: The Art Museum, in association with Harry N. Abrams, 1996), p. 75.

158. Brown, *Eagles of the World*, pp. 60–61.

159. David E. Jones, *An Instinct for Dragons* (New York: Routledge, 2000), p. 82.

160. Brown, *Eagles of the World*, p. 136.

161. Ibid., p. 62.

162. Ibid., p. 114.

163. Hart and Sussman, *Man the Hunted*, p. 136.

164. Ibid., p. 159.

165. Steven Mithen, *The Singing Neanderthals: The Origins of Music, Language, Mind, and Body* (Cambridge, MA: Harvard University Press, 2006), p. 132.

166. Erdoes and Ortiz, *American Indian Myths and Legends*, p. 474.

167. Hartley Burr Alexander, *Native American Mythology* (Mineola, NY: Dover [1916], 2005), p. 139.

168. Ibid., p. 71.

169. Erdoes and Ortiz, *American Indian Myths and Legends*, p. 197.

170. Anderson, *Myths and Legends of the Polynesians*, p. 131.

171. Ibid., p. 128.

172. Abrahams, *African Folktales*, p. 83.

173. Erdoes and Ortiz, *American Indian Myths and Legends*, p. 211.

174. Anderson, *Myths and Legends of the Polynesians*, p. 143.

CHAPTER 3: BE AFRAID, BE VERY AFRAID: FEAR AND SURVIVAL IN THE PLEISTOCENE

1. *Popol Vuh: The Sacred Book of the Ancient Quiche Maya*, transl. Adrian Recinos (Norman: University of Oklahoma Press, 1950), p. 186.

2. Johannes C. Anderson, *Myths and Legends of the Polynesians* (Mineola, NY: Dover [1928], 1995), p. 423.

3. W. Ramsay Smith, *Myths and Legends of the Australian Aborigines* (Mineola, NY: Dover [1932], 2003), p. 149.

4. Scott Atran, *In Gods We Trust: The Evolutionary Landscape of Religion* (New York: Oxford University Press, 2002), p. 285, n. 8.

5. Richard Erdoes and Alfonso Ortiz, eds., *American Indian Myths and Legends* (New York: Pantheon Books, 1984), p. 238.

6. Barbara Ehrenreich, *Blood Rites: Origins and History of the Passions of War* (New York: Free Press, 1997), pp. 46–47.

7. Yi-Fu Tuan, *Landscapes of Fear* (Minneapolis: University of Minnesota Press, 1979), p. 35.

8. Anthony Stevens, *The Two Million-Year-Old Self* (New York: Fromm International [1993], 1997), pp. 75–76.

9. Joseph LeDoux, *The Emotional Brain: The Mysterious Underpinnings of Emotional Life* (New York: Simon & Schuster [1996], 1998), pp. 128, 131.

10. Isaac M. Marks, *Fears, Phobias, and Rituals: Panic, Anxiety, and Their Disorders* (New York: Oxford University Press, 1987), p. 14.

11. Hans Kruuk, *Hunter and Hunted: Relationships between Carnivores and People* (Cambridge: Cambridge University Press, 2002), p. 178.

12. Marks, *Fears, Phobias, and Rituals*, p. 76.

13. Walter Burkert, *Creation of the Sacred: Tracks of Biology in Early Religions* (Cambridge, MA: Harvard University Press [1996], 1998), p. 43.

14. Marks, *Fears, Phobias, and Rituals*, p. 35.

15. David E. Jones, *An Instinct for Dragons* (New York: Routledge, 2000), p. 91.

16. Quoted in David D. Gilmore, *Monsters: Evil Beings, Mythical Beasts, and All Manner of Imaginary Terrors* (Philadelphia: University of Pennsylvania Press, 2003), p. 131.

17. Nancy E. Aiken, *The Biological Origins of Art* (Westport, CT: Praeger, 1998), p. 110.

18. Donna Hart and Robert W. Sussman, *Man the Hunted: Primates, Predators, and Human Evolution* (New York: Westview Press, 2005), p. 3.

19. Ehrenreich, *Blood Rites*, p. 107.

20. Quoted in Gilmore, *Monsters*, p. 131.

21. Smith, *Myths and Legends of the Australian Aborigines*, p. 254.

22. David Quammen, *Monster of God: The Man-Eating Predator in the Jungles of History and the Mind* (New York: W. W. Norton, 2003), p. 316.

23. Ibid., p. 311.

24. Erdoes and Ortiz, *American Indian Myths and Legends*, p. 227.

25. Ibid., p. 211.

26. Burkert, *Creation of the Sacred*, p. 52.

27. Smith, *Myths and Legends of the Australian Aborigines*, p. 334.

28. Ovid, *Metamorphoses*, trans. David Raeburn (New York: Penguin Putnam [8 CE], 2004), p. 605.

29. Pascal Boyer, *Religion Explained: The Evolutionary Origins of Religious Thought* (New York: Basic Books, 2001), p. 225.

30. Quammen, *Monster of God*, p. 308.

31. Aiken, *The Biological Origins of Art*, p. 90.

32. Irenaus Eibl-Eibesfeldt, *Love and Hate: The Natural History of Behavior Patterns*, trans. Geoffrey Strachan (New York: Schocken [1970], 1974), pp. 18–19.

33. Ibid., p. 24.

34. Gilmore, *Monsters*, p. 176.

35. *Popol Vuh*, p. 98.

36. Elizabeth Warner, *Russian Myths* (Austin: University of Texas Press, 2002), p. 76.

37. Anderson, *Myths and Legends of the Polynesians*, p. 427.

38. William D. Westervelt, *Hawaiian Legends of Ghosts and Ghost Gods* (Honolulu: Mutual [1916], 1999), p. 169.

39. Marks, *Fears, Phobias, and Rituals*, p. 35.

40. Jones, *An Instinct for Dragons*, p. 45.

41. Marks, *Fears, Phobias, and Rituals*, p. 40.

42. Ovid, *Metamorphoses*, p. 155.

43. Hart and Sussman, *Man the Hunted*, p. 67.

44. *Popol Vuh*, p. 114.

45. Ovid, *Metamorphoses*, pp. 440–42.

46. Aiken, *The Biological Origins of Art*, p. 133.

47. Stephen Belcher, ed., *African Myths of Origin* (New York: Penguin Books), p. 344.

48. Brian Hayden, *Shamans, Sorcerers, and Saints: A Prehistory of Religion* (Washington, DC: Smithsonian Books, 2003), p. 271.

49. Sy Montgomery, *Spell of the Tiger: The Man-Eaters of Sundarbans* (New York: Houghton Mifflin, 1995), p. 113.

50. Roger D. Abrahams, ed., *African Folktales: Traditional Stories of the Black World* (New York: Pantheon Books, 1983), p. 47.

51. Ehrenreich, *Blood Rites*, p. 107.

52. *Popol Vuh*, p. 90.

53. Adrienne Mayor, *Fossil Legends of the First Americans* (Princeton, NJ: Princeton University Press, 2005), p. 86.

54. Hayden, *Shamans, Sorcerers, and Saints*, pp. 58–59.

55. Mayor, *Fossil Legends of the First Americans*, p. 252.

56. Marks, *Fears, Phobias, and Rituals*, p. 50.

57. Aiken, *The Biological Origins of Art*, p. 125.

58. Smith, *Myths and Legends of the Australian Aborigines*, p. 220.

59. Hart and Sussman, *Man the Hunted*, p. 186.

60. Kruuk, *Hunter and Hunted*, p. 199.

61. Marks, *Fears, Phobias, and Rituals*, p. 50. See also Jones, *An Instinct for Dragons*, p. 80.

62. Jones, *An Instinct for Dragons*, p. 80.

63. Marks, *Fears, Phobias, and Rituals*, p. 50.

64. Mark C. Ross and David Reesor, *Predator: Life and Death in the African Bush* (New York: Abrams, 2007), p. 109.

65. Ibid., p. 166.

66. Dereck Joubert and Beverly Joubert, *Relentless Enemies: Lions and Buffalo* (Washington, DC: National Geographic, 2006), p. 133.

67. Clarke, *Man Is the Prey*, p. 111.

68. Hart and Sussman, *Man the Hunted*, p. 121.

69. Ovid, *Metamorphoses*, p. 440.

70. Kruuk, *Hunter and Hunted*, p. 22.

71. Clarke, *Man Is the Prey*, pp. 90–91.

72. Ross and Reesor, *Predator*, p. 113.

73. Ibid., p. 60.

74. Quoted in Joubert and Joubert, *Relentless Enemies*, p. 51.

75. *Popol Vuh*, p. 193.

76. Burkert, *Creation of the Sacred*, p. 158.

77. Ricard Erdoes and Alfonso Ortiz, *American Indian Trickster Tales* (New York: Penguin [1998], 1999), p. 8.

78. *Popol Vuh*, pp. 186–87.

79. Tuan, *Landscapes of Fear*, p. 15.

80. Anthony Stevens, *Ariadne's Clue: A Guide to the Symbols of Humankind* (Princeton, NJ: Princeton University Press, 1999), p. 194.

81. Steven M. Stanley, *Children of the Ice Age: How a Global Catastrophe Allowed Humans to Evolve* (New York: W. H. Freeman [1996], 1998), pp. 80–81.

82. Tuan, *Landscapes of Fear*, p. 22.

83. Dudley Young, *Origins of the Sacred: The Ecstasies of Love and War* (New York: St. Martin's Press, 1991), pp. 95–96.

84. Ibid., p. 96.

85. Clarke, *Man Is the Prey*, p. 110.

86. Atran, *In Gods We Trust*, p. 56.

87. Tuan, *Landscapes of Fear*, p. 15.

88. Michael James Winkelman, *Shamanism: The Neural Ecology of Consciousness and Healing* (Westport, CT: Bergin & Garvey, 2000), p. 199.

89. Balaji Mundkur, "Human Animality, the Mental Imagery of Fear, and Religiosity," in *What Is an Animal?* ed. Tim Ingold (New York: Routledge [1988], 1994), p. 151.

90. Marks, *Fears, Phobias, and Rituals*, p. 58.

91. Howard Norman, *Northern Tales: Traditional Stories of Eskimo and Indian Peoples* (Lincoln: University of Nebraska Press [1990], 2008), p. 108.

92. Harold Clark Barrett, "Human Cognitive Adaptations to Predators and Prey," unpublished PhD dissertation in anthropology, University of California, Santa Barbara (Ann Arbor, MI: UMI Dissertation Services, 1999), pp. 57, 129–30.

93. Hart and Sussman, *Man the Hunted*, p. 8.

94. Jones, *An Instinct for Dragons*, p. 66.

95. Marks, *Fear, Phobias, and Rituals*, p. 86.

96. Hart and Sussman, *Man the Hunted*, p. 173. See also Todd Tremlin, *Minds and Gods: The Cognitive Foundations of Religion* (New York: Oxford University Press, 2006), p. 30.

97. Ehrenreich, *Blood Rites*, p. 82.

98. Marks, *Fears, Phobias, and Rituals*, p. 45.

99. Ibid., p. 123.

100. Ehrenreich, *Blood Rites*, p. 81.

101. Hart and Sussman, *Man the Hunted*, p. 189.

102. Marks, *Fears, Phobias, and Rituals*, pp. 69–70.

103. Hart and Sussman, *Man the Hunted*, p. 190.

104. Ibid., p. 162.

105. Ehrenreich, *Blood Rites*, p. 94.

106. Alondra Yvette Oubre, *Instinct and Revelation: Reflections on the Origins of Numinous Perception* (Amsterdam, Netherlands: Gordon and Breach, 1997), p. 177.

107. Marina Warner, *No Go the Bogeyman: Scaring, Lulling, and Making Mock* (New York: Farrar, Straus, and Giroux), p. 125.

108. Winkelman, *Shamanism*, p. 84.

109. Marks, *Fears, Phobias, and Rituals*, p. 94.

110. Hayden, *Shamans, Sorcerers, and Saints*, pp. 46–47.

111. Winkelman, *Shamanism*, pp. 199–200.

112. Ehrenreich, *Blood Rites*, p. 95.

113. Eibl-Eibesfeldt, *Love and Hate*, p. 173.

114. Burkert, *Creation of the Sacred*, p. 86.

115. Smith, *Myths and Legends of the Australian Aborigines*, p. 344.

116. Joubert and Joubert, *Relentless Enemies*, p. 138.

117. Hart and Sussman, *Man the Hunted*, p. xviii.

118. Jack London, *Before Adam* (London: Hesperus Press [1906–1907], 2004), p. 3.

119. Ibid., p. 6.

120. LeDoux, *The Emotional Brain*, pp. 132–33.

CHAPTER 4: PERFORMING THE PREDATOR: MIMETIC STORYTELLING IN THE PALEOLITHIC

1. Nancy E. Aiken, *The Biological Origins of Art* (Westport, CT: Praeger, 1998), p. 154.

2. Roger D. Abrahams, ed., *African Folktales: Traditional Stories of the Black World* (New York: Pantheon Books, 1983), p. 184.

3. Merlin Donald, *Origins of the Modern Mind: Three Stages in the Evolution of Culture and Cognition* (Cambridge, MA: Harvard University Press, 1991), chaps. 6 and 7.

4. Ibid., p. 179.

5. Ibid., p. 187.

6. Ibid., pp. 168–69, 177, 186.

7. Ibid., p. 169.

8. Ibid., p. 184.

9. W. Ramsay Smith, *Myths and Legends of the Australian Aborigines* (Mineola, NY: Dover [1932], 2003), pp. 117–18.

10. Richard Erdoes and Alfonso Ortiz, eds., *American Indian Trickster Tales* (New York: Viking, 1998), p. xx.

11. Joseph Campbell, *The Power of Myth* (New York: Random House [1988], 1991), p. 92.

12. Steven Mithen, *The Singing Neanderthals: The Origins of Music, Language, Mind, and Body* (Cambridge, MA: Harvard University Press, 2006), p. 207.

13. Ibid., p. 172.

14. Ibid.

15. Ibid., pp. 157, 172, 223.

16. Ibid., pp. 39–40.

17. Ibid., pp. 15, 72, 23. See also Donald, *Origins of the Modern Mind*, pp. 183–84.

18. Barbara J. King, *Evolving God: A Provocative View of the Origins of Religion* (New York: Doubleday, 2007), p. 92.

19. Donald, *Origins of the Modern Mind*, pp. 178, 184, 187, 197, 200.

20. Ibid., p. 173.

21. Mithen, *The Singing Neanderthals*, p. 218.

22. Michael James Winkelman, *Shamanism: The Neural Ecology of Consciousness and Healing* (Westport, CT: Bergin & Garvey, 2000), p. 100.

23. Howard Norman, *Northern Tales: Traditional Stories of Eskimo and Indian Peoples* (Lincoln: University of Nebraska Press [1990], 2008), p. 211.

24. Donald, *Origins of the Modern Mind*, pp. 169, 171–72, 187.

25. Ibid., p. 169.

26. Charles Gould, *Mythical Monsters* (New York: Crescent Books [1886], 1986), p. 20.

27. Aiken, *The Biological Origins of Art*, p. 112.

28. Donald, *Origins of the Modern Mind*, pp. 41, 169, 187.

29. L. R. Goldman, *Child's Play: Myth, Mimesis and Make-Believe* (Oxford: Berg, 1998), pp. 89, 185.

30. Eva M. Thury and Margaret K. Devinney, *Introduction to Mythology: Contemporary Approaches to Classical and World Myths* (New York: Oxford University Press, 2005), p. 343.

31. Marjorie Shostak, "A !Kung Woman's Memories of Childhood," in *Kalahari Hunter-Gatherers: Studies of the !Kung San and Their Neighbors*, ed. Richard B. Lee and Irven Devore (Cambridge, MA: Harvard University Press, 1976), p. 247.

32. Marina Warner, *No Go the Bogeyman: Scaring, Lulling, and Making Mock* (New York: Farrar, Straus, and Giroux, 1998), p. 14.

33. Ibid., p. 16.

34. Recounted in David D. Gilmore, *Monsters: Evil Beings, Mythical Beasts, and All Manner of Imaginary Terrors* (Philadelphia: University of Pennsylvania Press, 2003), p. 107.

35. Johannes Maringer, *The Gods of Prehistoric Man*, trans. Mary Ilford (New York: Alfred A. Knopf, 1960), p. 143.

36. Warner, *No Go the Bogeyman*, p. 112.

37. William D. Westervelt, *Hawaiian Legends of Ghosts and Ghost Gods* (Honolulu: Mutual [1916], 1999), pp. 168–69.

38. Anthony Stevens, *Ariadne's Clue: A Guide to the Symbols of Humankind* (Princeton, NJ: Princeton University Press, 1999), p. 42.

39. Joseph LeDoux, *The Emotional Brain: The Mysterious Underpinnings of Emotional Life* (New York: Simon & Schuster [1996], 1998), p. 245.

40. Harold Clark Barrett, "Human Cognitive Adaptations to Predators and Prey," unpublished PhD dissertation in anthropology, University of California, Santa Barbara (Ann Arbor, MI: UMI Dissertation Services, 1999), p. 126.

41. Mithen, *The Singing Neanderthals*, p. 317, n. 29.

42. Hans Kruuk, *Hunter and Hunted: Relationships between Carnivores and People* (Cambridge: Cambridge University Press, 2002), pp. 198–99.

43. Winkelman, *Shamanism*, p. 206.

44. Antti Revonsuo, *Inner Presence: Consciousness as a Biological Phenomenon* (Cambridge, MA: MIT Press, 2006), p. 406.

45. Anthony Stevens, *The Two Million-Year-Old Self* (New York: Fromm International [1993], 1997), p. 38.

46. Quoted in John Bierhorst, trans., *History and Mythology of the Aztecs: The Codex Chimalpopoca* (Tucson: University of Arizona Press, 1992), p. 88.

47. Jonathan Winson, *Brain & Psyche: The Biology of the Unconscious* (New York: Random House [1985], 1986), p. 190.

48. Ibid., p. 209.

49. Revonsuo, *Inner Presence*, pp. 419, 423.

50. Ibid., p. 407.

51. Ibid., p. 417.

52. Quoted in Michael Shermer, *How We Believe: The Search for God in an Age of Science* (New York: W. H. Freeman, 2000), p. 43.

53. Sir James George Frazer, *The Golden Bough: A Study in Magic and Religion*, abridged from the 2nd and 3rd eds. (1900, 1906–1915) by Robert Fraser (Oxford: Oxford University Press [1994], 1998), p. 26.

54. Dudley Young, *Origins of the Sacred: The Ecstasies of Love and War* (New York: St. Martin's Press, 1991), p. 186.

55. Quoted by Maringer, *The Gods of Prehistoric Man*, p. 143.

56. Walter Burkert, *Structure and History in Greek Mythology and Ritual* (Berkeley: University of California Press [1979], 1982), p. 90.

57. Maringer, *The Gods of Prehistoric Man*, pp. 144–45.

58. Ibid., pp. 133–34.

59. Stephen Belcher, ed., *African Myths of Origin* (New York: Penguin Books), p. 107.

60. Quoted in Sy Montgomery, *Spell of the Tiger: The Man-Eaters of Sundarbans* (New York: Houghton Mifflin, 1995), p. 168.

61. Belcher, *African Myths of Origin*, p. 242.

62. Joseph Campbell, *The Masks of God: Primitive Mythology*, rev. ed. (New York: Penguin Books [1959], 1987), p. 370.

CHAPTER 5: THE EMERGENCE OF THE MYTHMAKING MIND

1. Paul Shepard, *The Others: How Animals Made Us Human* (Washington, DC, Island Press, 1996), pp. 6–7.

2. Michael James Winkelman, *Shamanism: The Neural Ecology of Consciousness and Healing* (Westport, CT: Bergin & Garvey, 2000), p. 106.

3. Joseph LeDoux, *The Emotional Brain: The Mysterious Underpinnings of Emotional Life* (New York: Simon & Schuster [1996], 1998), p. 18.

4. Todd Tremlin, *Minds and Gods: The Cognitive Foundations of Religion* (New York: Oxford University Press, 2006), p. 80.

5. E. Thomas Lawson, "Introduction," in *Minds and Gods: The Cognitive Foundations of Religion*, by Todd Tremlin (Oxford: Oxford University Press, 2006), p. xiv.

6. Richard Erdoes and Alfonso Ortiz, eds., *American Indian Trickster Tales* (New York: Viking, 1998), p. 117.

7. Ibid., p. 110.

8. Ibid., p. 229.

9. Richard Erdoes and Alfonso Ortiz, eds., *American Indian Myths and Legends* (New York: Pantheon Books, 1984), pp. 347–48.

10. Steven Mithen, *The Prehistory of the Mind: A Search for the Origins of Art, Religion, and Science* (London: Orion Books [1996], 2005), p. 176.

11. Scott Atran, *In Gods We Trust: The Evolutionary Landscape of Religion* (New York: Oxford University Press, 2002), p. 70.

12. Dudley Young, *Origins of the Sacred: The Ecstasies of Love and War* (New York: St. Martin's Press, 1991), p. 116.

13. Quoted in Atran, *In Gods We Trust*, p. 68.

14. Adrienne Mayor, *Fossil Legends of the First Americans* (Princeton, NJ: Princeton University Press, 2005), pp. 326–27.

15. *Popol Vuh: The Sacred Book of the Ancient Quiche Maya*, transl. Adrian Recinos (Norman: University of Oklahoma Press, 1950), p. 92.

16. Quoted in Young, *Origins of the Sacred*, p. 116.

17. Robert B. Edgerton, *Sick Societies: Challenging the Myth of Primitive Harmony* (New York: Free Press, 1992), p. 198.

18. Tremlin, *Minds and Gods*, 75.

19. Joseph Campbell, *The Masks of God: Primitive Mythology*, rev. ed. (New York: Penguin Books [1959], 1987), p. 75.

20. Edgerton, *Sick Societies*, p. 68.

21. Winkelman, *Shamanism*, p. 28.

22. Atran, *In Gods We Trust*, p. 183.

23. Winkelman, *Shamanism*, p. 103.

24. Alondra Yvette Oubre, *Instinct and Revelation: Reflections on the Origins of Numinous Perception* (Amsterdam, Netherlands: Gordon and Breach, 1997), p. 161.

25. Ibid., p. 162.

26. Merlin Donald, *Origins of the Modern Mind: Three Stages in the Evolution of Culture and Cognition* (Cambridge, MA: Harvard University Press, 1991), p. 282.

27. Ibid., p. 115.

28. Ibid., p. 204.

29. Tremlin, *Minds and Gods*, pp. 103–104.

30. Atran, *In Gods We Trust*, p. 108.

31. Donald, *Origins of the Modern Mind*, pp. 256–57.

32. Ibid., p. 215.

33. Ibid., p. 214.

34. Yi-Fu Tuan, *Landscapes of Fear* (Minneapolis: University of Minnesota Press, 1979), p. 6.

35. Ibid., p. 5.

36. Anthony Stevens, *The Two Million-Year-Old Self* (New York: Fromm International [1993], 1997), p. 111.

37. Howard Norman, *Northern Tales: Traditional Stories of Eskimo and Indian Peoples* (Lincoln: University of Nebraska Press [1990], 2008), pp. 205–206.

38. LeDoux, *The Emotional Brain*, p. 134.

39. Atran, *In Gods We Trust*, p. 66.

40. Donna Hart and Robert W. Sussman, *Man the Hunted: Primates, Predators, and Human Evolution* (New York: Westview Press, 2005), p. 77.

41. William D. Westervelt, *Hawaiian Legends of Ghosts and Ghost Gods* (Honolulu: Mutual [1916], 1999), pp. 82–83.

42. Ibid., p. 169.

43. Winkelman, *Shamanism*, p. 82.

44. Ibid., p. 97.

45. Walter Burkert, *Creation of the Sacred: Tracks of Biology in Early Religions* (Cambridge, MA: Harvard University Press [1996], 1998), pp. 68–69.

46. Hartley Burr Alexander, *Native American Mythology* (Mineola, NY: Dover [1916], 2005), p. 5.

47. Norman, *Northern Tales*, p. 176.

48. Peter T. Furst, "Shamanism, Transformation, and Olmec Art," in *The Olmec World: Ritual and Rulership*, ed. Justin Kerr and Bruce White (Princeton, NJ: The Art Museum, Princeton University, and Harry N. Abrams, 1996), p. 72.

49. Winkelman, *Shamanism*, p. 199.

50. Roy Willis, ed., *World Mythology* (New York: Henry Holt [1993], 1996), p. 261.

51. Furst, "Shamanism, Transformation, and Olmec Art," p. 72.

52. Pascal Boyer, *Religion Explained: The Evolutionary Origins of Religious Thought* (New York: Basic Books, 2001), p. 146.

53. Young, *Origins of the Sacred*, p. 166.

54. Ibid.

55. Willis, *World Mythology*, p. 226.

56. Norman, *Northern Tales*, p. 177.

57. Roy Willis, *Man and Beast* (New York: Basic Books, 1974), p. 36.

58. Ibid.

59. Balaji Mundkur, "Human Animality, the Mental Imagery of Fear, and Religiosity," in *What Is an Animal?* ed. Tim Ingold (New York: Routledge [1988], 1994), p. 163.

60. Willis, *World Mythology*, p. 261.

61. Barbara J. King, *Evolving God: A Provocative View of the Origins of Religion* (New York: Doubleday, 2007), p. 81.

62. Quoted in Steven Mithen, *The Singing Neanderthals: The Origins of Music, Language, Mind and Body* (Cambridge, MA: Harvard University Press, 2006), p. 81.

63. Barbara Ehrenreich, *Blood Rites: Origins and History of the Passions of War* (New York: Free Press, 1997), p. 55.

64. Shepard, *The Others*, p. 229.

65. Young, *Origins of the Sacred*, p. 68.

66. Ehrenreich, *Blood Rites*, p. 92.

67. Thomas Gregor, "A Content Analysis of Mehinaku Dreams," *Ethos* 9,

no. 4 (Winter 1981): 384.

68. Marina Warner, *No Go the Bogeyman: Scaring, Lulling, and Making Mock* (New York: Farrar, Straus, and Giroux, 1998), pp. 73–74.

69. Ibid., p. 194.

70. Hart and Sussman, *Man the Hunted*, p. 215.

71. Ibid., pp. 243–44.

72. Mithen, *The Prehistory of Mind*, p. 220.

73. Atran, *In Gods We Trust*, p. 268.

CHAPTER 6: IN THE BELLY OF THE BEAST: THE PREDATOR AS MYTHIC MONSTER

1. Stephen Belcher, ed., *African Myths of Origin* (New York: Penguin Books), p. 426.

2. Walter Burkert, *Structure and History in Greek Mythology and Ritual* (Berkeley: University of California Press [1979], 1982), p. 20.

3. W. Ramsay Smith, *Myths and Legends of the Australian Aborigines* (Mineola, NY: Dover [1932], 2003), p. 148.

4. Roger D. Abrahams, ed., *African Folktales: Traditional Stories of the Black World* (New York: Pantheon Books, 1983), pp. 288–89.

5. Johannes C. Anderson, *Myths and Legends of the Polynesians* (Mineola, NY: Dover [1928], 1995), p. 141.

6. A. W. Reed, *Aboriginal Myths: Tales of the Dreamtime* (New South Wales, Australia: Reed Books, 1978), p. 79.

7. Smith, *Myths and Legends of the Australian Aborigines*, p. 254.

8. Reed, *Aboriginal Myths*, p. 81.

9. David D. Gilmore, *Monsters: Evil Beings, Mythical Beasts, and All Manner of Imaginary Terrors* (Philadelphia: University of Pennsylvania Press, 2003), p. 80.

10. Belcher, *African Myths of Origin*, p. 91.

11. Ibid., p. 111.

12. Anderson, *Myths and Legends of the Polynesians*, pp. 132–43.

13. Ibid., p. 185.

14. Gilmore, *Monsters*, p. 148.

15. Howard Norman, *Northern Tales: Traditional Stories of Eskimo and Indian Peoples* (Lincoln: University of Nebraska Press [1990], 2008), p. 222.

16. Gilmore, *Monsters*, p. 140.

17. Reed, *Aboriginal Myths*, pp. 34–35.

18. Hartley Burr Alexander, *Native American Mythology* (Mineola, NY: Dover [1916], 2005), pp. 205–206.

19. Ibid., p. 45.

20. Richard Erdoes and Alfonso Ortiz, eds., *American Indian Trickster Tales* (New York: Viking), pp. 21–22.

21. Belcher, *African Myths of Origin*, pp. 91–92.

22. Anthony Stevens, *Ariadne's Clue: A Guide to the Symbols of Humankind* (Princeton, NJ: Princeton University Press, 1999), p. 342.

23. Alexander, *Native American Mythology*, p. 5.

24. David E. Jones, *An Instinct for Dragons* (New York: Routledge, 2000), p. 25.

25. Ibid., p. 32.

26. Ibid., p. 62.

27. Marina Warner, *Managing Monsters: Six Myths of Our Time* (New York: Random House, 1994), p. 19.

28. Jones, *An Instinct for Dragons*, p. 59.

29. Ibid., p. 116.

30. Paul S. Martin, *Twilight of the Mammoths: Ice Age Extinctions and the Rewilding of America* (Berkeley: University of California Press, 2005), p. 28.

31. Gould, *Mythical Monsters*, pp. 17–18.

32. Jones, *An Instinct for Dragons*, p. 165.

33. Alexander, *Native American Mythology*, p. 126.

34. Anderson, *Myths and Legends of the Polynesians*, p. 394.

35. Balaji Mundkur, "Human Animality, the Mental Imagery of Fear, and Religiosity," in *What Is an Animal?* ed. Tim Ingold (New York: Routledge [1988], 1994), pp. 171–72.

36. Martin, *Twilight of the Mammoths*, p. 162.

37. Karl Taube, *Aztec and Maya Myths* (Austin: University of Texas Press, 2003), p. 34.

38. Adrienne Mayor, *Fossil Legends of the First Americans* (Princeton, NJ: Princeton University Press, 2005), p. 212.

39. Ibid., pp. 239, 162.

40. Charles Gould, *Mythical Monsters* (New York: Crescent Books [1886], 1986), p. 235.

41. Ibid., p. 164.

42. Ibid., pp. 199, 244.

43. Anthony J. Sutcliffe, *On the Track of Ice Age Mammals* (Cambridge, MA: Harvard University Press, 1985), p. 30.

44. Ovid, *Metamorphoses*, trans. David Raeburn (New York: Penguin Putnam [8 CE], 2004), p. 612.

45. Mayor, *Fossil Legends of the First Americans*, p. 276.

46. Alondra Yvette Oubre, *Instinct and Revelation: Reflections on the Origins of Numinous Perception* (Amsterdam, Netherlands: Gordon and Breach, 1997), p. 182.

47. Ibid., pp. 153–54.

48. Lee Irwin, *The Dream Seekers: Native American Visionary Traditions of the Great Plains* (Norman: University of Oklahoma Press, 1994), p. 38.

49. Ibid., p. 39.

50. James L. Pearson, *Shamanism and the Ancient Mind: A Cognitive Approach to Archaeology* (Walnut Creek, CA: Altamira Press, 2002), p. 88.

51. Frank Cawson, *The Monsters in the Mind: The Face of Evil in Myth, Literature, and Contemporary Life* (Sussex, England: Book Guild, 1995), p. viii.

52. Michael James Winkelman, *Shamanism: The Neural Ecology of Consciousness and Healing* (Westport, CT: Bergin & Garvey, 2000), p. 82.

53. Ibid., p. 6.

54. Warner, *Managing Monsters*, p. 20.

55. Charles Dickens, *A Tale of Two Cities* (New York: Penguin Books [1859], 2003), p. 384.

56. Robert B. Edgerton, *Sick Societies: Challenging the Myth of Primitive Harmony* (New York: Free Press, 1992), p. 60.

57. Norman, *Northern Tales*, p. 205.

58. Ibid.

59. Edgerton, *Sick Societies*, p. 128.

60. Ibid.

61. Gilmore, *Monsters*, p. 136.

62. Ibid., p. 138.

63. Ibid., p. 63.

64. Edgerton, *Sick Societies*, p. 92.

65. Marina Warner, *No Go the Bogeyman: Scaring, Lulling, and Making Mock* (New York: Farrar, Straus, and Giroux, 1978), p. 382.

66. Gilmore, *Monsters*, pp. 20–21, 57, 190–91.

67. Ibid., pp. 92–93.

68. Mayor, *Fossil Legends of the First Americans*, p. 119.

69. Gilmore, *Monsters*, p. 104.

70. Norman, *Northern Tales*, p. 113.

71. Belcher, *African Myths of Origin*, pp. 8–9.

72. Stevens, *Ariadne's Clue*, p. 367.

73. Belcher, *African Myths of Origin*, p. 355.

74. Ibid., p. 367.

75. Stevens, *Ariadne's Clue*, p. 214.

76. Quoted in Gilmore, *Monsters*, p. 115.

77. Padraic Colum, *Nordic Gods and Heroes* (Mineola, NY: Dover [1920], 1996), p. 246.

78. Gilmore, *Monsters*, p. 95.

79. Ibid., p. 149.

80. Alexander, *Native American Mythology*, p. 44.

81. Erdoes and Ortiz, *American Indian Trickster Tales*, p. 196.

82. Leo Frobenius and Douglas C. Fox, *African Genesis: Folk Tales and Myths of Africa* (Mineola, NY: Dover [1937], 1999), p. 90.

83. Belcher, *African Myths of Origin*, p. 137.

84. Frobenius and Fox, *African Genesis*, p. 80.

85. Erdoes and Ortiz, *American Indian Trickster Tales*, p. 49.

86. Ibid., p. 28.

87. Ibid., p. 201.

88. Ibid., p. 101.

89. Ibid., p. 83.

90. Ibid., p. 183.

91. Paul Shepard, *Coming Home to the Pleistocene* (Washington, DC: Island Press, 1998), p. 97.

92. Erdoes and Ortiz, *American Indian Myths and Legends*, p. 349.

93. Ibid., p. 352.

94. Joseph Campbell, *The Masks of God: Primitive Mythology*, rev. ed. (New York: Penguin Books [1959], 1987), p. 273.

95. Abrahams, *African Folktales*, pp. 70–71, 314.

96. Erdoes and Ortiz, *American Indian Trickster Tales*, p. 107.

97. Ibid., p. 85.

98. Warner, *No Go the Bogeyman*, p. 327.

99. Norman, *Northern Tales*, p. 102.

100. L. R. Goldman, *Child's Play: Myth, Mimesis and Make-Believe* (Oxford: Berg, 1998), p. 229. See also ibid.

CHAPTER 7: FEAR AND TREMBLING IN THE PLEISTOCENE: THE PREDATOR AS A GOD

1. William D. Westervelt, *Hawaiian Legends of Ghosts and Ghost Gods* (Honolulu: Mutual [1916], 1999), pp. 68–69.

2. Clifford H. Pope, *The Giant Snakes: The Natural History of the Boa Constrictor, the Anaconda, and the Largest Pythons* (New York: Alfred A. Knopf, 1961) p. 204.

3. G. W. Trompf, "Mythology, Religion, Art, and Literature," in *Crocodiles and Alligators*, ed. Charles Ross (New York: Facts on File, 1989), p. 4.

4. David Quammen, *Monster of God: The Man-Eating Predator in the Jungles of History and the Mind* (New York: W. W. Norton, 2003), p. 357.

5. Paul Shepard, *The Others: How Animals Made Us Human* (Washington, DC, Island Press, 1996), p. 180.

6. Hans Kruuk, *Hunter and Hunted: Relationships between Carnivores and People* (Cambridge: Cambridge University Press, 2002), p. 191.

7. Leonard Ginsburg, "Mummified Egyptian Crocodiles," in Ross, *Crocodiles and Alligators*, p. 158.

8. Dudley Young, *Origins of the Sacred: The Ecstasies of Love and War* (New York: St. Martin's Press, 1991), p. xvi.

9. Walter Burkert, *Creation of the Sacred: Tracks of Biology in Early Religions* (Cambridge, MA: Harvard University Press [1996], 1998), p. 30.

10. Stewart Guthrie, *Faces in the Clouds: A New Theory of Religion* (New York: Oxford University Press [1993], 1995), p. 23.

11. Rudolf Otto, *The Idea of the Holy: An Inquiry into the Non-Rational Factor in the Idea of the Divine and Its Relation to the Rational* (London: Oxford University Press [1923], 1959), p. 31.

12. Quoted in Abraham J. Heschel, *The Prophets* (New York: HarperCollins, [1962], 2001), pp. 311–12.

13. Barbara Ehrenreich, *Blood Rites: Origins and History of the Passions of War* (New York: Free Press, 1997), p. 76.

14. Scott Atran, *In Gods We Trust: The Evolutionary Landscape of Religion* (New York: Oxford University Press, 2002), pp. 77–78.

15. Pascal Boyer, *Religion Explained: The Evolutionary Origins of Religious Thought* (New York: Basic Books, 2001), pp. 147–48.

16. Harold Clark Barrett, "Human Cognitive Adaptations to Predators and Prey," unpublished PhD dissertation in anthropology, University of California, Santa Barbara (Ann Arbor, MI: UMI Dissertation Services, 1999), p. 146.

17. See, for example, Lucien Levy-Bruhl, *Primitive Mentality*, trans. Lilian A. Clare (Boston: Beacon Press [1923], 1966); Claude Levi-Strauss, *The Savage Mind* (Chicago: University of Chicago Press [1962], 1973); E. E. Evans-Pritchard, *Witchcraft, Oracles, and Magic among the Azande*, abridged with an introduction by Eva Gillies (Oxford: Clarendon Press, 1976).

18. Patrick Tierney, *The Highest Altar: The Story of Human Sacrifice* (New York: Viking Penguin, 1989), p. 445.

19. Herbert Schneidau, *Sacred Discontent: The Bible and Western Tradition* (Berkeley: University of California Press [1976], 1977), p. 61.

20. Ibid., p. 81.

21. Atran, *In Gods We Trust*, p. 267.

22. David D. Gilmore, *Monsters: Evil Beings, Mythical Beasts, and All Manner of Imaginary Terrors* (Philadelphia: University of Pennsylvania Press, 2003), p. 72.

23. Burkert, *Creation of the Sacred*, p. 86.

24. Roger D. Abrahams, *African Folktales: Traditional Stories of the Black World* (New York: Pantheon Books, 1983), p. 46.

25. Ibid., p. 51.

26. Burkert, *Creation of the Sacred*, p. 89.

27. Ibid., p. 87.

28. Jane van Lawick-Goodall, "The Chimpanzee," in *The Quest for Man*, ed. Vanne Goodall (New York: Praeger Publishing, 1975), pp. 162–64.

29. Guthrie, *Faces in the Clouds*, p. 202.

30. Richard Erdoes and Alfonso Ortiz, *American Indian Myths and Legends* (New York: Pantheon Books, 1984), p. 456.

31. Young, *Origins of the Sacred*, p. 135.

32. William D. Westervelt, *Myths and Legends of Hawaii* (Honolulu: Mutual, 1987), p. 119.

33. Quoted in Ehrenreich, *Blood Rites*, p. 74.

34. Ehrenreich, *Blood Rites*, p. 75.

35. Quoted in Ehrenreich, *Blood Rites*, p.58.

36. Trompf, "Mythology, Religion, Art, and Literature," in Ross, *Crocodiles and Alligators*, pp. 161–62.

37. Ibid., p. 162.

38. Quoted in Ehrenreich, *Blood Rites*, pp. 68–69.

39. Burkert, *Creation of the Sacred*, p. 152.

40. Westervelt, *Myths and Legends of Hawaii*, p. 188.

41. Ehrenreich, *Blood Rites*, pp. 67–68.

42. Ibid., p. 22.

43. Burkert, *Creation of the Sacred*, p. 41.

44. Ibid., p. 42.

45. Ibid., p. 52.

46. Abrahams, *African Folktales*, p. 125.

47. Quoted in Isaac M. Marks, *Fears, Phobias, and Rituals: Panic, Anxiety, and Their Disorders* (New York: Oxford University Press, 1987), p. 78.

48. Ibid., p. 46.

49. Ehrenreich, *Blood Rites*, p. 54.

50. David E. Jones, *An Instinct for Dragons* (New York: Routledge, 2000),

p. 164. See also Joseph Campbell, *The Masks of God: Primitive Mythology*, rev. ed. (New York: Penguin Books [1959], 1987), p. 336.

51. Paul Bahn, *Journey through the Ice Age* (Berkeley: University of California Press [1988], 1997), p. 152.

52. Ehrenreich, *Blood Rites*, p. 73.

53. Evan Hadingham, *Secrets of the Ice Age: The World of the Cave Artists* (New York: Walker & Company, 1979), p. 55.

54. Johannes Maringer, *The Gods of Prehistoric Man*, trans. Mary Ilford (New York: Alfred A. Knopf, 1960), p. 274.

55. Campbell, *The Masks of God: Primitive Mythology*, pp. 347–48.

56. Alondra Yvette Oubre, *Instinct and Revelation: Reflections on the Origins of Numinous Perception* (Amsterdam, Netherlands: Gordon and Breach, 1997), p. 121.

57. Steven Mithen, *The Prehistory of the Mind: A Search for the Origins of Art, Religion, and Science* (London: Orion Books [1996], 2005), p. 202.

58. Barbara J. King, *Evolving God: A Provocative View of the Origins of Religion* (New York: Doubleday, 2007), p. 178.

59. Ibid., p. 148.

60. Atran, *In Gods We Trust*, p. 77.

61. Ibid., p. 79.

62. Young, *Origins of the Sacred*, p. 310.

63. Ibid., p. 222.

64. Ibid., p. 224.

65. Ibid.

66. René Girard, *Violence and the Sacred*, trans. Patrick Gregory (Baltimore: Johns Hopkins University Press [1972], 1977), p. 17.

67. Zenaide A. Ragozin, *The Story of Chaldea: From the Earliest Times to the Rise of Assyria* (New York: G. P. Putnam's Sons, 1896), p. 150.

68. Ibid.

69. Ibid.

70. Elizabeth Wayland Barber and Paul T. Barber, *When They Severed Earth from Sky: How the Human Mind Shapes Myth* (Princeton, NJ: Princeton University Press, 2004), p. 164.

71. Balaji Mundkur, "Human Animality, the Mental Imagery of Fear, and

Religiosity," in *What Is an Animal?* ed. Tim Ingold (New York: Routledge [1988], 1994).

72. Ibid., pp. 173–74.

73. Ibid., p. 174.

74. Ibid., p. 152.

75. Campbell, *The Masks of God: Primitive Mythology*, p. 472.

76. Trompf, "Mythology, Religion, Art, and Literature," in Ross, *Crocodiles and Alligators*, p. 2.

77. Shepard, *The Others: How Animals Made Us Human.*

CHAPTER 8: KINDLY KILLERS: THE PREDATOR AS KIN, FRIEND, PROTECTOR, AND BENEFACTOR

1. Richard Erdoes and Alfonso Ortiz, *American Indian Myths and Legends* (New York: Pantheon Books, 1984), p. 136.

2. Clifford H. Pope, *The Giant Snakes: The Natural History of the Boa Constrictor, the Anaconda, and the Largest Pythons* (New York: Alfred A Knopf, 1961), pp. 209–19.

3. Roy Willis, ed., *World Mythology* (New York: Henry Holt [1993], 1996), pp. 28, 263.

4. Leo Frobenius and Douglas C. Fox, *African Genesis: Folk Tales and Myths of Africa* (Mineola, NY: Dover [1937], 1999), p. 164.

5. Ibid., pp. 80–81.

6. Stewart Guthrie, *Faces in the Clouds: A New Theory of Religion* (New York: Oxford University Press [1993], 1995), pp. 72–73.

7. C. A. W. Guggisberg, *Crocodiles: Their Natural History, Folklore, and Conservation* (Harrisburg, PA: Stackpole, 1972), pp. 153–60.

8. William D. Westervelt, *Myths and Legends of Hawaii* (Honolulu: Mutual, 1987), p. 108.

9. Erdoes and Ortiz, *American Indian Myths and Legends*, pp. 397–98.

10. Ibid., p. 404.

11. Lynne Kelly, *Crocodile: Evolution's Greatest Survivor* (Crows Nest, New South Wales, Australia: Allen & Unwin, 2006), p. 42.

12. Stephen Belcher, ed., *African Myths of Origin* (New York: Penguin Books), pp. 263–67.

13. Joseph Campbell, *The Masks of God: Primitive Mythology*, rev. ed. (New York: Penguin Books [1959], 1987), p. 295.

14. G. W. Trompf, "Mythology, Religion, Art, and Literature," in *Crocodiles and Alligator*, ed. Charles Ross (New York: Facts on File, 1989), p. 162.

15. Ibid., p. 165.

16. Belcher, *African Myths of Origin*, p. 275.

17. Balaji Mundkur, "Human Animality, the Mental Imagery of Fear, and Religiosity," in *What Is an Animal?* ed. Tim Ingold (New York: Routledge [1988], 1994), pp. 143–44.

18. Harold Clark Barrett, "Human Cognitive Adaptations to Predators and Prey," unpublished PhD dissertation in anthropology, University of California, Santa Barbara (Ann Arbor, MI: UMI Dissertation Services, 1999), p. 147.

19. "Danger in Your Neighbor's Backyard," *Parade*, October 30, 2005, pp. 12–14.

20. Belcher, *African Myths of Origins*, p. 279.

21. Erdoes and Ortiz, *American Indian Myths and Legends*, p. 264.

22. Guggisberg, *Crocodiles*, p. 156.

23. George Hart, *Egyptian Myths* (Austin: University of Texas Press, 2004), p. 54.

24. Belcher, *African Myths of Origins*, p. 269.

25. Westervelt, *Myths and Legends of Hawaii*, p. 161.

26. William D. Westervelt, *Hawaiian Legends of Ghosts and Ghost Gods* (Honolulu: Mutual [1916], 1999), p. 45.

27. Belcher, *African Myths of Origin*, p. 262.

28. Paul Shepard, *The Others: How Animals Made Us Human* (Washington, DC, Island Press, 1996), p. 267.

29. David E. Jones, *An Instinct for Dragons* (New York: Routledge, 2000), pp. 93–94.

30. Roy Willis, *Man and Beast* (New York: Basic Books, 1974), pp. 49–50.

31. Adrienne Mayor, *Fossil Legends of the First Americans* (Princeton, NJ: Princeton University Press, 2005), p. xxxviii.

32. Erdoes and Ortiz, *American Indian Myths and Legends*, p. 245.

33. Trompf, "Mythology, Religion, Art, and Literature," in Ross, *Crocodiles and Alligators*, pp. 164–65.

34. Barbara Ehrenreich, *Blood Rites: Origins and History of the Passions of War* (New York: Free Press, 1997), p. 85.

35. Hart, *Egyptian Myths*, p. 73.

36. Trompf, "Mythology, Religion, Art, and Literature," in Ross, *Crocodiles and Alligators*, p. 164.

37. Richard Rudgley, *The Lost Civilizations of the Stone Age* (New York: Free Press, 1999), pp. 124–29.

38. Guido Majno, *The Healing Hand: Man and Wound in the Ancient World* (Cambridge, MA: Harvard University Press, 1991), p. 274.

39. Trompf, "Mythology, Religion, Art, and Literature," in Ross, *Crocodiles and Alligators*, p. 166.

40. Ibid., p. 162.

41. Ibid.

42. Roy Willis, ed. *World Mythology* (New York: Henry Holt [1993], 1996), p. 54.

43. Erdoes and Ortiz, *American Indian Myths and Legends*, p. 54.

44. Mayor, *Fossil Legends of the First Americans*, p. 54.

45. Associated Press, "Man Orders Python to Attack Police Officers," *Nothing to do with Arbroath* (blog) June 18, 2008, http://arbroath.blogspot.com/2008/06/man-orders-pet-python-to-attack-police.html.

46. Willis, *World Mythology*, p. 28.

47. Ibid., p. 263.

48. Steven Mithen, *The Prehistory of Mind: A Search for the Origins of Art, Religion, and Science* (London: Orion Books [1996], 2005), p. 114.

49. Ehrenreich, *Blood Rites*, p. 70.

50. Ibid., pp. 70–71. See also Donna Hart and Robert W. Sussman, *Man the Hunted: Primates, Predators, and Human Evolution* (New York: Westview Press, 2005), pp. 74–75.

51. Erdoes and Ortiz, *American Indian Myths and Legends*, p. 113.

52. Ehrenreich, *Blood Rites*, p. 72.

53. Hart and Sussman, *Man the Hunted*, p. 117.

54. Hans Kruuk, *Hunter and Hunted: Relationships between Carnivores and People* (Cambridge: Cambridge University Press, 2002), p. 48.

CHAPTER 9: MODEL OF MANACE: THE PREDATOR AS EXEMPLAR AND OBJECT OF ENVY

1. *Popol Vuh: The Sacred Book of the Ancient Quiche Maya*, transl. Adrian Recinos (Norman: University of Oklahoma Press, 1950), pp. 219–20.

2. A. L. Dallapiccola, *Hindu Myths* (Austin: University of Texas Press, 2003), pp. 66–67.

3. Robert Graves, *The Greek Myths*, vol. 1 of 2 (London: Penguin Books [1955], 1960), p. 228.

4. Hans Kruuk, *Hunter and Hunted: Relationships between Carnivores and People* (Cambridge: Cambridge University Press, 2002), p. 2.

5. Ernest Becker, *The Denial of Death* (New York: Free Press, 1973), p. 21.

6. Barbara Ehrenreich, *Blood Rites: Origins and History of the Passions of War* (New York: Free Press, 1997), p. 83.

7. Harold Clark Barrett, "Human Cognitive Adaptations to Predators and Prey," unpublished PhD dissertation in anthropology, University of California, Santa Barbara (Ann Arbor, MI: UMI Dissertation Services, 1999), p. 3.

8. Dudley Young, *Origins of the Sacred: The Ecstasies of Love and War* (New York: St. Martin's Press, 1991), p. 101.

9. Birger Lindskog, *African Leopard Men* (Uppsala, Sweden: Almquist & Wiksell, 1954), p. 83.

10. Penny Olsen, "Raptors in Australian Aboriginal Culture: Neither Sacred nor Mundane," in *Birds of Prey*, ed. Ian Newton (New York: Facts on File, 1999), p. 174.

11. Young, *Origins of the Sacred*, p. 99.

12. Ehrenreich, *Blood Rites*, p. 85.

13. Roy Willis, ed., *World Mythology* (New York: Henry Holt [1993], 1996), p. 281.

14. Ehrenreich, *Blood Rites*, pp. 85–86.

15. Maurice Bloch, *Prey into Hunter: The Politics of Religious Experience* (Cambridge: Cambridge University Press [1992], 1997), p. 9.

16. Ibid., p. 10.

17. Ibid., p. 18.

18. Numbers 23:24 (King James translation).

19. Harvey Whitehouse, "Rites of Terror: Emotion, Metaphor and Memory in Melanesian Initiation Cults," *Journal of the Royal Anthropological Institute* 2, no. 4 (December 1996).

20. Marina Warner, *No Go the Bogeyman: Scaring, Lulling, and Making Mock* (New York: Farrar, Straus, and Giroux, 1998), p. 382.

21. Karl Taube, *Aztec and Maya Myths* (Austin: University of Texas Press, 2003), p. 42.

22. Ehrenreich, *Blood Rites*, p. 11.

23. Ibid., p. 86.

24. Quoted in ibid., p. 212.

25. Ibid.

26. Scott Atran, *In Gods We Trust: The Evolutionary Landscape of Religion* (New York: Oxford University Press, 2002), p. 285, n. 10.

27. Douglas H. Chadwick, "Phantom of the Night," *National Geographic*, May 2001, p. 41.

28. Nigel Davies, *Human Sacrifice in History and Today* (New York: William Morrow, 1981), p. 141.

29. Patrick Tierney, *The Highest Altar: The Story of Human Sacrifice* (New York: Viking Penguin, 1989), p. 445.

30. Marina Warner, *Managing Monsters: Six Myths of Our Time* (New York: Random House, 1994), p. 71.

31. G. W. Trompf, "Mythology, Religion, Art, and Literature," in *Crocodiles and Alligators*, ed. Charles Ross (New York: Facts on File, 1989), p. 63.

32. Lindskog, *African Leopard Men*, p. 30, 39.

33. Ibid., p. 28.

34. Tierney, *The Highest Altar*, p. 133.

35. Richard Erdoes and Alfonso Ortiz, eds., *American Indian Trickster Tales* (New York: Viking), p. 24.

36. Ibid., p. 15.

37. William D. Westervelt, *Myths and Legends of Hawaii* (Honolulu: Mutual, 1987), p. 121.

38. Stephen Belcher, *African Myths of Origin* (New York: Penguin Books), pp. 295–96.

39. Tierney, *Highest Altar*, p. 442.

40. Michael James Winkelman, *Shamanism: The Neural Ecology of Consciousness and Healing* (Westport, CT: Bergin & Garvey, 2000), p. 162.

41. Davies, *Human Sacrifice in History and Today*, p. 135.

42. Lindskog, *African Leopard Men*, p. 21.

43. Ibid., p. 20.

44. Ibid. pp. 138–39.

45. Ibid., p. 78.

46. Ibid., pp. 16–21.

47. Davies, *Human Sacrifice in History and Today*, p. 138.

48. James Clarke, *Man Is the Prey* (New York: Stein and Day, 1969), p. 116.

49. *Popol Vuh*, p. 195.

50. Lindskog, *African Leopard Men*, p. 32.

51. Ibid., p. 178.

52. Ibid., pp. 32, 145.

53. Clarke, *Man Is the Prey*, p. 115.

54. Ibid., p. 116.

55. Lindskog, *African Leopard Men*, pp. 18–19.

56. Ibid., pp. 17, 69.

57. Ibid., p. 26.

58. Ibid., p. 28.

59. Ibid., p. 23.

60. Ibid., p. 70.

61. Ibid., p. 78.

62. Tierney, *The Highest Altar*, p. 443.

63. Arthur C. Lehmann, James Myers, and Pamela A. Moro, *Magic, Witch-*

craft, and Religion: An Anthropological Study of the Supernatural (Boston: McGraw Hill, 2005), pp. 46–47.

64. Roy Willis, *Man and Beast* (New York: Basic Books, 1974), pp. 52–53.

65. Belcher, *African Myths of Origin*, pp. 36–37.

66. Sy Montgomery, *Spell of the Tiger: The Man-Eaters of Sundarbans* (New York: Houghton Mifflin, 1995), pp. 222–23.

67. Erdoes and Ortiz, *American Indian Myths and Legends*, pp. 398–402.

CHAPTER 10: SCARING OURSELVES TO LIFE

1. Hans Kruuk, *Hunter and Hunted: Relationships between Carnivores and People* (Cambridge: Cambridge University Press, 2002), p. 4.

2. David Quammen, *Monster of God: The Man-Eating Predator in the Jungles of History and the Mind* (New York: W. W. Norton, 2003), p. 431.

3. Quoted in Marina Warner, *Managing Monsters: Six Myths of Our Time* (New York: Random House, 1994), p. 58.

4. Frank Cawson, *The Monsters in the Mind: The Face of Evil in Myth, Literature, and Contemporary Life* (Sussex, Great Britain: Book Guild, 1995), p. 79.

5. Quoted in ibid., p. 295.

6. Kruuk, *Hunter and Hunted*, p. 179.

7. Ann Rule, *The Stranger beside Me* (New York: W. W. Norton, 1980). New editions appeared in 1986, 1989, 2000, and 2008. A movie version appeared in 2003, followed by audio book versions and other video forms.

8. "Marked for Mayhem," *Psychology Today*, January/February 2009, pp. 80–83.

9. Barbara Ehrenreich, *Blood Rites: Origins and History of the Passions of War* (New York: Free Press, 1997), p. 295.

10. Sam Keen, *Faces of the Enemy: Reflections of the Hostile Imagination* (New York: Harper & Row [1986], 1988).

11. See Keen, "The Enemy as Beast, Reptile, Insect," in ibid., pp. 113–20.

12. Habakkuk 1:5–11 (King James translation).

13. Kruuk, *Hunter and Hunted*, p. 173.

14. Melvin Konner, *The Tangled Wing: Biological Constraints on the Human Spirit* (New York: Harper & Row [1982], 1983), p. 234.

15. Quoted in Ehrenreich, *Blood Rites*, p. 77.

16. Paul Shepard, *The Others: How Animals Made Us Human* (Washington, DC, Island Press, 1996), p. 10.

Bibliography

Abrahams, Roger D. *African Folktales: Traditional Stories of the Black World*. New York: Pantheon Books, 1983.

Aiken, Nancy E. *The Biological Origins of Art*. Westport, CT: Praeger, 1998.

Alexander, Hartley Burr. *Native American Mythology*. Mineola, NY: Dover [1916], 2005.

Anderson, Johannes C. *Myths and Legends of the Polynesians*. Mineola, NY: Dover [1928], 1995.

Atran, Scott. *In Gods We Trust: The Evolutionary Landscape of Religion*. New York: Oxford University Press, 2002.

Bahn, Paul G. *Journey through the Ice Age*. Berkeley: University of California Press [1988], 1997.

Barber, Elizabeth Wayland, and Paul T. Barber. *When They Severed Earth from Sky: How the Human Mind Shapes Myth*. Princeton, NJ: Princeton University Press, 2004.

Barrett, Harold Clark. "Human Cognitive Adaptations to Predators and Prey." Unpublished PhD Dissertation in Anthropology, University of California, Santa Barbara. Ann Arbor, MI: UMI Dissertation Services, 1999.

Becker, Ernest. *The Denial of Death*. New York: Free Press, 1973.

Belcher, Stephen, ed. *African Myths of Origin*. New York: Penguin Books, 2005.

Benton, Michael. *Dinosaur and Other Prehistoric Animal Factfinder*. New York: Kingfisher Books, 1992.

Bierhorst, John, trans. *History and Mythology of the Aztecs: The Codex Chimalpopoca*. Tucson: University of Arizona Press, 1992.

Bloch, Maurice. *Prey into Hunter: The Politics of Religious Experience.* New York: Cambridge University Press, 1992.

Boyer, Pascal. *Religion Explained: The Evolutionary Origins of Religious Thought.* New York: Basic Books, 2001.

Brodsky, A. T., ed. *Stones, Bones and Skin: Ritual and Shamanic Art.* Toronto: Society for Art Publications, 1977.

Brown, Leslie. *Eagles of the World.* New York: Universe Books, 1977.

Burkert, Walter. *Creation of the Sacred: Tracks of Biology in Early Religions.* Cambridge, MA: Harvard University Press [1996], 1998.

———. *Structure and History in Greek Mythology and Ritual.* Berkeley: University of California Press [1979], 1982.

Campbell, Joseph. *The Masks of God: Primitive Mythology.* Rev. ed. New York: Penguin Books [1959], 1987.

———. *The Power of Myth.* New York: Random House [1988], 1991.

Cawson, Frank. *The Monsters in the Mind: The Face of Evil in Myth, Literature, and Contemporary Life.* Sussex, Great Britain: Book Guild, 1995.

Chadwick, Douglas H. "Phantom of the Night." *National Geographic,* May 2001, pp. 32–51.

Clarke, James. *Man Is the Prey.* New York: Stein and Day, 1969.

Colum, Padraic. *Nordic Gods and Heroes.* Mineola, NY: Dover [1920], 1996.

Constable, George. *The Emergence of Man: The Neanderthals.* New York: Time-Life Books, 1973.

Dallapiccola, A. L. *Hindu Myths.* Austin: University of Texas Press, 2003.

Davies, Nigel. *Human Sacrifice in History and Today.* New York: William Morrow and Company, 1981.

De Becker, Gavin. *The Gift of Fear.* New York: Dell Publishing, 1998.

Dickens, Charles. *A Tale of Two Cities.* Edited by Richard Maxwell. London: Penguin Books [1859], 2000.

Donald, Merlin. *Origins of the Modern Mind: Three Stages in the Evolution of Culture and Cognition.* Cambridge, MA: Harvard University Press, 1991.

Edgerton, Robert B. *Sick Societies: Challenging the Myth of Primitive Harmony.* New York: Free Press, 1992.

Ehrenreich, Barbara. *Blood Rites: Origins and History of the Passions of War.* New York: Henry Holt, 1997.

Eibl-Eibesfeldt, Irenaus. *Love and Hate.* Translated by Geoffrey Strachan. New York: Schocken Books [1970], 1974.

Erdoes, Richard, and Alfonso Ortiz, eds. *American Indian Myths and Legends.* New York, Pantheon Books, 1984.

———, eds. *American Indian Trickster Tales.* New York: Penguin Books, 1998.

Frazer, Sir James George. *The Golden Bough: A Study in Magic and Religion. A New Abridgement from the Second and Third Editions* (1900, 1906–1915). Oxford: Oxford University Press [1994], 1998.

Frobenius, Leo, and Douglas C. Fox. *African Genesis: Folk Tales and Myths of Africa.* Mineola, NY: Dover [1937], 1999.

Furst, Peter T. "Shamanism, Transformation, and Olmec Art." In *The Olmec World: Ritual and Rulership.* Edited by Justin Kerr and Bruce White. Princeton, NJ: The Art Museum and Harry N. Abrams, 1996, pp. 69–81.

Gilmore, David D. *Monsters: Evil Beings, Mythical Beasts, and All Manner of Imaginary Terrors.* Philadelphia: University of Pennsylvania Press, 2003.

Ginsburg, Leonard. "Mummified Egyptian Crocodiles." In *Crocodiles and Alligators.* Edited by Charles Ross. New York: Facts on File, 1989, pp. 158–59.

Girard, Rene. *Violence and the Sacred.* Translated by Patrick Gregory. Baltimore: Johns Hopkins University Press [1972], 1977.

Goldman, L. R. *Child's Play: Myth, Mimesis and Make-Believe.* Oxford: Berg, 1998.

Goodall, Vanne, ed. *The Quest for Man.* New York: Praeger, 1975.

Gould, Charles. *Mythical Monsters.* New York: Crescent Books [1886], 1986.

Graves, Robert. *The Greek Myths.* 2 vols. London: Penguin Books [1955], 1960.

Gregor, Thomas. "A Content Analysis of Mehinaku Dreams." *Ethos* 9, no. 4 (Winter 1981): 353–90.

Guggisberg, C. A. W. *Crocodiles: Their Natural History, Folklore and Conservation.* Harrisburg, PA: Stackpole Books, 1972.

Guthrie, Stewart. *Faces in the Clouds: A New Theory of Religion.* New York: Oxford University Press [1993], 1995.

Hadingham, Evan. *Secrets of the Ice Age: The World of the Cave Artists.* New York: Walker & Company, 1979.

Haines, Tim. *Walking with Beasts: A Prehistoric Safari.* New York: DK, 2001.

Hart, Donna. "Humans as Prey." *The Chronicle of Higher Education* (April 21, 2006): B10–11.

Hart, Donna, and Robert W. Sussman. *Man the Hunted: Primates, Predators, and Human Evolution.* New York: Westview Press, 2005.

Hart, George. *Egyptian Myths.* Austin: University of Texas Press, 2004.

Hayden, Brian. *Shamans, Sorcerers, and Saints: A Prehistory of Religion.* Washington, DC: Smithsonian Books, 2003.

Heschel, Abraham J. *The Prophets.* New York: HarperCollins [1962], 2001.

Heuvelmans, Bernard. *On the Track of Unknown Animals.* Translated by Richard Garnett. New York: Hill & Wang, 1959.

Ingold, Tim, ed. *What Is an Animal?* New York: Routledge [1988], 1994.

Irwin, Lee. *The Dream Seekers: Native American Visionary Traditions of the Great Plains.* Norman: University of Oklahoma Press, 1994.

Jones, David E. *An Instinct for Dragons.* New York: Routledge, 2000.

Joubert, Dereck, and Beverly Joubert. *Relentless Enemies: Lions and Buffalo.* Washington, DC: National Geographic, 2006.

Keen, Sam. *Faces of the Enemy: Reflections of the Hostile Imagination.* New York: Harper & Row [1986], 1988.

Kelly, Lynne. *Crocodile: Evolution's Greatest Survivor.* Crows Nest, New South Wales, Australia: Allen & Unwin, 2006.

Kerr, Justin, and Bruce M. White, eds. *The Olmec World: Ritual and Rulership.* Princeton, NJ: The Art Museum and Harry N. Abrams, 1996.

King, Barbara J. *Evolving God.* New York: Doubleday, 2007.

Konner, Melvin. *The Tangled Wing: Biological Constraints on the Human Spirit.* New York: Harper & Row [1982], 1983.

Kruuk, Hans. *Hunter and Hunted: Relationships between Carnivores and People.* Cambridge: Cambridge University Press, 2002.

Kurten, Björn. *The Cave Bear Story: Life and Death of a Vanished Animal.* New York: Columbia University Press [1978], 1995.

———. *Pleistocene Mammals of Europe.* Chicago: Aldine, 1968.

Kurten, Björn, and Elaine Anderson. *Pleistocene Mammals of North America.* New York: Columbia University Press, 1980.

Lambert, David. *Dinosaur Encyclopedia: From Dinosaurs to the Dawn of Man.* New York: DK, 2001.

Lange, Ian M. *Ice Age Mammals of North America: A Guide to the Big, the Hairy, and the Bizarre.* Missoula, MT: Mountain Press, 2002.

LeDoux, Joseph. *The Emotional Brain: The Mysterious Underpinnings of Emotional Life.* New York: Simon & Schuster [1996], 1998.

Lee, Richard B., and Irven Devore, eds. *Kalahari Hunter-Gatherers: Studies of the !Kung San and Their Neighbors.* Cambridge, MA: Harvard University Press, 1976.

Lehmann, Arthur C., James Myers, and Pamela A. Moro. *Magic, Witchcraft, and Religion: An Anthropological Study of the Supernatural.* 6th ed. Boston: McGraw Hill, 2005.

Lindskog, Birger. *African Leopard Men.* Uppsala, Sweden: Almquist & Wiksell, 1954.

London, Jack. *Before Adam.* London: Hesperus Press [1906–1907], 2004.

Majno, Guido. *The Healing Hand: Man and Wound in the Ancient World.* Cambridge, MA: Harvard University Press, 1991.

Malinowski, Bronislaw. *Magic, Science and Religion.* Garden City, NY: Doubleday Anchor Books [1948], 1954.

Maringer, Johannes. *The Gods of Prehistoric Man.* Translated by Mary Ilford. New York: Alfred A. Knopf, 1960.

Marks, Isaac M. *Fears, Phobias, and Rituals: Panic, Anxiety, and Their Disorders.* New York: Oxford University Press, 1987.

Marshall, Larry G. "The Terror Birds of South America." *Scientific American* 270, no. 2 (February 1994): 90–95.

Martin, Paul S. *Twilight of the Mammoths: Ice Age Extinctions and the Rewilding of America.* Berkeley: University of California Press, 2005.

Martin, Paul S., and H. E. Wright Jr., eds. *Pleistocene Extinctions: The Search for a Cause.* New Haven, CT: Yale University Press, 1967.

Martin, Paul S., and John E. Guilday. "A Bestiary for Pleistocene Biologists." In *Pleistocene Extinctions: The Search for a Cause.* New Haven, CT: Yale University Press, 1967, pp. 1–62.

Martin, Paul S., and Richard G. Klein. *Quaternary Extinctions: A Prehistoric Revolution.* Tucson: University of Arizona Press, 1984.

Marven, Nigel, and Jasper James. *Chased by Sea Monsters: Prehistoric Predators of the Deep.* New York: DK, 2004.

Mayor, Adrienne. *The First Fossil Hunters: Paleontology in Greek and Roman Times*. Princeton, NJ: Princeton University Press, 2000.

———. *Fossil Legends of the First Americans*. Princeton, NJ: Princeton University Press, 2005.

Minton, Sherman A., Jr., and Madge Rutherford Minton. *Giant Reptiles*. New York: Charles Scribner's Sons, 1973.

Mithen, Steven. *The Prehistory of the Mind: A Search for the Origins of Art, Religion, and Science*. London: Orion Books [1996], 2005.

———. *The Singing Neanderthals: The Origins of Music, Language, Mind and Body*. Cambridge, MA: Harvard University Press, 2006.

Molnar, Ralph E. *Dragons in the Dust: The Paleobiology of the Giant Monitor Lizard* Megalania. Bloomington: Indiana University Press, 2004.

Montgomery, Sy. *Spell of the Tiger: The Man-Eaters of Sundarbans*. New York: Houghton Mifflin, 1995.

Morris, Brian. *The Power of Animals: An Ethnography*. Oxford: Berg, 2000.

Mundkur, Balaji. "Human Animality, the Mental Imagery of Fear, and Religiosity." In *What Is an Animal?* Edited by Tim Ingold. New York: Routledge [1988], 1994, pp. 141–84.

Murphy, John C., and Robert W. Henderson. *Tales of Giant Snakes: A Historical Natural History of Anacondas and Pythons*. Malabar, FL: Krieger, 1997.

Newton, Ian, ed. *Birds of Prey*. New York: Facts on File, 1990.

Norman, Howard, ed. *Northern Tales: Traditional Stories of Eskimo and Indian Peoples*. Lincoln: University of Nebraska Press [1990], 2008.

Oakes, Ted. *Land of Lost Monsters: Man against Beast: The Prehistoric Battle for the Planet*. Irvington, NY: Hydra, 2003.

Olsen, Penny. "Raptors in Australian Aboriginal Culture: Neither Sacred nor Mundane." In *Birds of Prey*. Edited by Ian Newton. New York: Facts on File, 1990, pp. 172–74.

Olsen, Stanley J. *Origins of the Domestic Dog: The Fossil Record*. Tucson: University of Arizona Press, 1985.

Otto, Rudolf. *The Idea of the Holy: An Inquiry into the Non-Rational Factor in the Idea of the Divine and Its Relation to the Rational*. Translated by John W. Harvey. London: Oxford University Press [1923], 1959.

Oubre, Alondra Yvette. *Instinct and Revelation: Reflections on the Origins of Numinous Perception*. Amsterdam, Netherlands: Gordon and Breach, 1997.

Ovid. *Metamorphoses*. Translated by David Raeburn. New York: Penguin Putnam [8 CE], 2004.

Paul, Gregory S. *Dinosaurs of the Air: The Evolution and Loss of Flight in Dinosaurs and Birds*. Baltimore, MD: Johns Hopkins University Press, 2002.

Pearson, James L. *Shamanism and the Ancient Mind: A Cognitive Approach to Archaeology*. Walnut Creek, CA: Altamira Press, 2002.

Pooley, A. C., Tommy C. Hines, and John Shield. "Attacks on Humans." In *Crocodiles and Alligators*. Edited by Charles Ross. New York: Facts on File, 1989, pp. 172–87.

Pope, Clifford H. *The Giant Snakes: The Natural History of the Boa Constrictor, the Anaconda, and the Largest Pythons*. New York: Alfred A. Knopf, 1961.

Popol Vuh: The Sacred Book of the Ancient Quiche Maya. Translated by Adrian Recinos. Norman: University of Oklahoma Press, 1950.

Quammen, David. *Monster of God: The Man-Eating Predator in the Jungles of History and the Mind*. New York: W. W. Norton, 2003.

Raffaele, Paul. "Curse of the Devil's Dogs." *Smithsonian*, April 2007, pp. 58–65.

Ragozin, Zenaide A. *The Story of Chaldea: From the Earliest Times to the Rise of Assyria*. New York: G. P. Putnam's Sons, 1896.

Reed, A. W. *Aboriginal Myths: Tales of the Dreamtime*. New South Wales, Australia: Reed Books [1978], 1984.

Revonsuo, Antti. *Inner Presence: Consciousness as a Biological Phenomenon*. Cambridge, MA: MIT Press, 2006.

Ross, Charles A., ed. *Crocodiles and Alligators*. New York: Facts on File, 1989.

Ross, Mark C., and David Reesor. *Predator: Life and Death in the African Bush*. New York: Abrams, 2007.

Rudgley, Richard. *The Lost Civilizations of the Stone Age*. New York: Free Press, 1999.

Sagan, Carl. *The Dragons of Eden: Speculations on the Evolution of Human Intelligence*. New York: Random House [1977], 1993.

Schneidau, Herbert. *Sacred Discontent: The Bible and Western Tradition*. Berkeley: University of California Press [1976], 1977.

Shepard, Paul. *Coming Home to the Pleistocene*. Washington, DC: Island Press, 1998.

———. *The Others: How Animals Made Us Human*. Washington, DC: Island Press, 1996.

Shermer, Michael. *How We Believe: The Search for God in an Age of Science*. New York: W. H. Freeman, 2000.

Shostak, Marjorie. "A !Kung Woman's Memories of Childhood." In *Kalahari Hunter-Gatherers: Studies of the !Kung San and Their Neighbors*. Edited by Richard B. Lee and Irven DeVore. Cambridge, MA: Harvard University Press, 1976, pp. 246–78.

Sluckin, W., ed. *Fear in Animals and Man*. New York: Van Nostrand Reinhold, 1979.

Smith, W. Ramsay. *Myths and Legends of the Australian Aborigines*. Mineola, NY: Dover [1932], 2003.

Stanley, Steven M. *Children of the Ice Age: How a Global Catastrophe Allowed Humans to Evolve*. New York: W. H. Freeman [1996], 1998.

Stevens, Anthony. *Ariadne's Clue: A Guide to the Symbols of Humankind*. Princeton, NJ: Princeton University Press, 1999.

———. *The Two Million-Year-Old Self*. New York: Fromm International [1993], 1997.

Sutcliffe, Antony J. *On the Track of Ice Age Mammals*. Cambridge, MA: Harvard University Press, 1985.

Sweeney, James B. *A Pictorial History of Sea Monsters and Other Dangerous Marine Life*. New York: Bonanza Books, 1972.

Tarboton, Warwick. *African Birds of Prey*. Ithaca, NY: Cornell University Press, 1990.

Taube, Karl. *Aztec & Maya Myths*. Austin: University of Texas Press, 2003.

Thury, Eva M., and Margaret K. Devinney. *Introduction to Mythology: Contemporary Approaches to Classical and World Myths*. New York: Oxford University Press, 2005.

Tierney, Patrick. *The Highest Altar: The Story of Human Sacrifice*. New York: Viking Penguin, 1989.

Toynbee, Arnold. *An Historian's Approach to Religion*. London: Oxford University Press, 1956.

Tremlin, Todd. *Minds and Gods: The Cognitive Foundations of Religion*. New York: Oxford University Press, 2006.

Trompf, G. W. "Mythology, Religion, Art, and Literature." In *Crocodiles and Alligators*. Edited by Charles Ross. New York: Facts on File, 1989, pp. 156–71.

Tuan, Yi-Fu. *Landscapes of Fear*. Minneapolis: University of Minnesota Press, 1979.

Turner, Alan. *The Big Cats and Their Fossil Relatives*. New York: Columbia University Press, 1997.

Van Der Post, Laurens. *The Lost World of the Kalahari*. San Diego: Harcourt Brace Jovanovich [1958], 1986.

van Lawick-Goodall, Jane. "The Chimpanzee." In *The Quest for Man*. Edited by Vanne Goodall. New York: Praeger, 1975, pp. 131–69.

Warner, Elizabeth. *Russian Myths*. Austin: University of Texas Press, 2002.

Warner, Marina. *Managing Monsters: Six Myths of Our Time*. New York: Random House, 1994.

———. *No Go the Bogeyman: Scaring, Lulling, and Making Mock*. New York: Farrar, Straus, and Giroux, 1998.

Westervelt, William D. *Hawaiian Legends of Ghosts and Ghost Gods*. Honolulu: Mutual [1916], 1999.

———. *Myths and Legends of Hawai'i*. Selected and edited by A. Grove Day. Honolulu: Mutual [1987], 2005.

Whitehouse, Harvey. "Rites of Terror: Emotion, Metaphor and Memory in Melanesian Initiation Cults." *Journal of the Royal Anthropological Institute* 2, no. 4 (December 1996): 703–15.

Willis, Roy. *Man and Beast*. New York: Basic Books, 1974.

———, gen. ed. *World Mythology*. New York: Henry Holt [1993], 1996.

Winkelman, Michael James. *Shamanism: The Neural Ecology of Consciousness and Healing*. Westport, CT: Bergin & Garvey, 2000.

Winson, Jonathan. *Brain & Psyche: The Biology of the Unconscious*. New York: Random House [1985], 1986.

Young, Dudley. *Origins of the Sacred: The Ecstasies of Love and War*. New York: St. Martin's Press, 1991.

Zimmer, Carl. "Terror, Take Two." *Discover* 18, no. 6 (June 2007): 68–74.

Index

Page numbers in *italics* refer to illustrations.